American Printmaking Before 1876

Fact, Fiction, and Fantasy

Papers presented at a symposium held at the Library of Congress, June 12 and 13, 1972

LIBRARY OF CONGRESS
WASHINGTON 1975

Library of Congress Cataloging in Publication Data

Main entry under title:

American printmaking before 1876.

Sponsored by the Library of Congress.
1. Prints, American—Congresses. 2. Printmakers—United States—Congresses. 3. United States in art—Congresses. I. United States. Library of Congress.
NE506.A43 769'.973 75–619175
ISBN 0–8444–0168–4

For sale by the Superintendent of Documents
U.S. Government Printing Office, Washington, D.C. 20402
Price $2.15
Stock Number 3014–00002

Preface

The 16th annual Winterthur Conference in March 1970 was entitled "Prints in and of America, to 1850" and recognized the curious fact that, despite the considerable attention paid to American painting, architecture, sculpture, and decorative arts, comparatively little scholarly work had been devoted to early printmaking on this continent. The response to the papers, exhibitions, and informal exchanges at that gathering was so profound that, on the last day, a resolution was offered proposing the continuation of the meetings, at a time and place to be determined.

So it was that a year later, in the spring of 1971, the Colonial Society convened a meeting in Boston, in 1972 the Library of Congress sponsored a symposium in Washington, and in 1973 several Philadelphia institutions arranged a seminar there. This book contains the papers delivered in Washington.

Perhaps the most remarkable thing about this series of scholarly encounters is that there is no ongoing, formal organization that has sponsored or coordinated plans for the meetings. The impetus has come from those who have been present at previous meetings and who were able to offer facilities and to show prints that were in the tradition of the earlier seminars.

If it is appropriate to talk of "traditions" in connection with a group that has no name, no structure, no dues, no bylaws, no membership list, and an existence of less than four years' duration, then two "traditions" can be associated with these seminars. One is that the subject of the meetings shall be an aspect of early American printmaking associated in some way with the concerns of the host institution. The other is that the formal papers shall be published, so the new information and insights can be recorded in some permanent form to inspire future scholarship and reach an audience larger than could be accommodated in the seminar itself.

The Washington meeting took place in June 1972. The papers were read in the Woodrow Wilson Room of the Library of Congress, and pictures from the Prints and Photographs Division collections were on view to complement the papers. The participants had a chance to view the holdings of the Department of Graphic Arts in the National Museum of History and Technology and of the print room of the National Collection of Fine Arts, both in the Smithsonian Institution, during the days of the seminar.

The topic selected was intentionally broad: "American Printmaking before 1876: Fact, Fiction, and Fantasy." The Library's American print collection is vast and encompasses every subject, place, and topic imaginable. Just as the Library's book collections range from poetry to science, so our prints are incredibly diverse. We had long been fascinated by the significance of many of these prints as primary historical documents, as important and revealing in their way as manuscripts, newspaper articles, and books. It is also a fact that prints are not unfailingly reliable and that they require careful scrutiny before their information is yielded up. Just as one cannot comprehend a journal or a diary without knowing how to read the language in which it is written and how to decipher the handwriting of the author, so one has to know how to "read" pictures. Moreover, the scholar must bring to his interpretations of pictures a knowledge of various other subjects; in the papers printed here are explorations into marine history, military engagements, political campaigns, and the establishment of a religious colony.

Several of our authors address themselves to the establishment of the facts behind a hitherto mysterious print. Of equal interest are the fictional and imaginative representations that have been published throughout our history, sometimes purporting to be true when in reality they were not, sometimes adapting an image created for one purpose to a different use, and sometimes purely applying an artist's creativity to the expression of an idea or a concept. These, too, our authors have included in their assessments of our graphic history.

Through studies of this kind, the pictorial past is coming to be more exactly and more deeply understood. The greater number of the prints illustrating these papers are from the collections in the Prints and Photographs Division of the Library of Congress. We are delighted to gain the extra dimension of understanding that these new investigations have given to our holdings, and I feel certain that historians, scholars, curators, and collectors all will find something of value in the proceedings of our seminar.

The symposium itself was made possible through a generous gift to the Library of Congress from Mr. and Mrs. Lionel C. Epstein of Washington, D. C. To them, to my colleagues in the Smithsonian Institution, and to the many Library of Congress staff members who cheerfully assisted in the planning of the seminar and the preparation of this publication, I would like to express our deepest gratitude.

June 1973 EDGAR BREITENBACH, *former Chief Prints & Photographs Division*

Contents

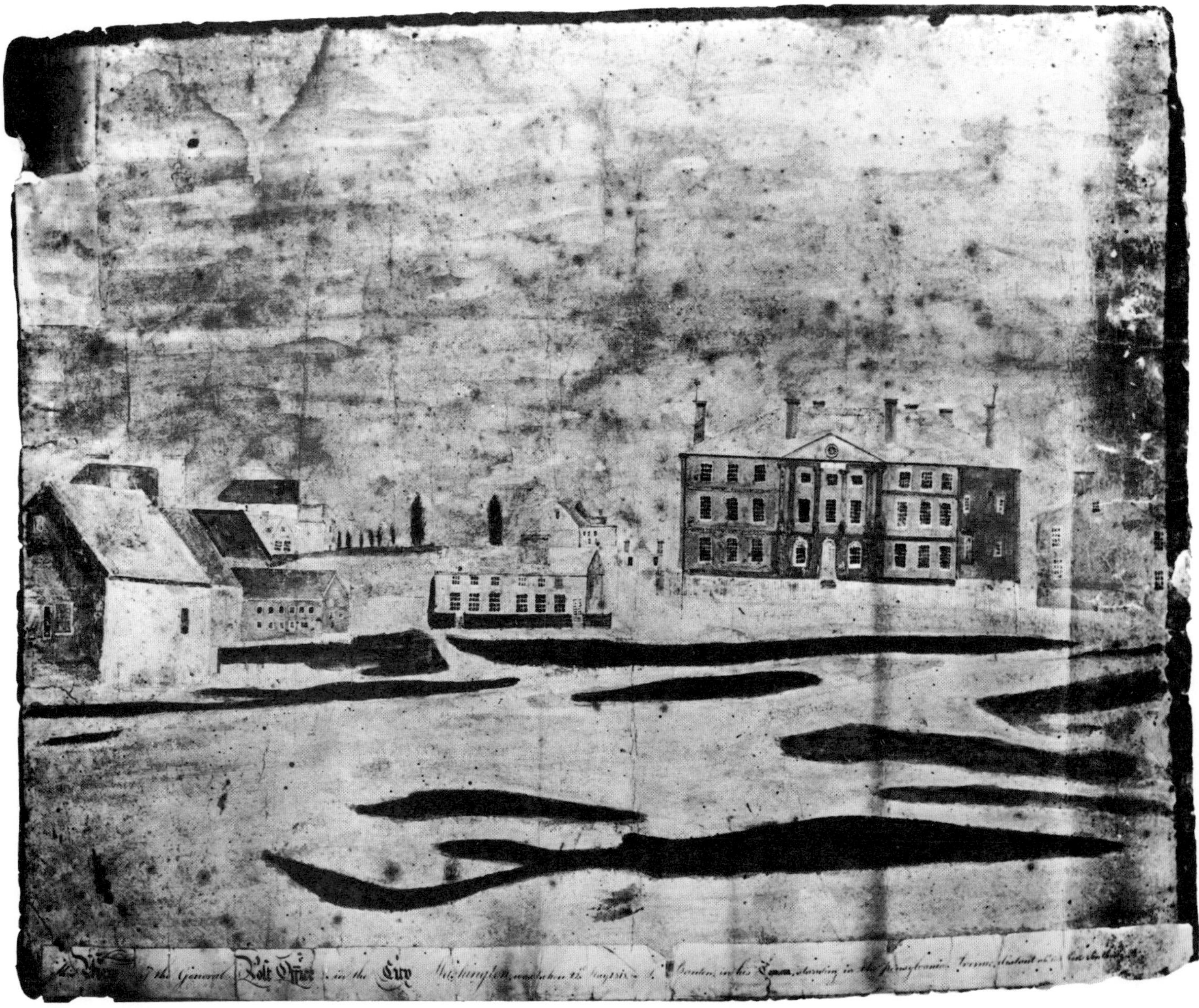

Watercolor drawing of the General Post Office, Washington, D.C., drawn in 1818 by James Banton, using a "camera."

Prints, The Camera, and Historical Accuracy

Josephine Cobb

Until her recent retirement, Josephine Cobb worked at the Photographic Records Branch of the National Archives as a specialist in iconography. She has written articles on early American photographers and American artists before 1880 and is currently active in a number of historical societies in Maine.

Before the discovery of photography, American artists as well as those in Europe and England employed the principle of the camera in art, both for views and portraiture. They commonly made use of the camera obscura, the camera lucida, the physiognotrace, and numerous other contrivances. In so doing, they continued the practice of artists from ancient times. Topographical artists, in particular, relied upon the tools of the engineer and the draftsman. Aided by various mechanical devices, many American artists to whom "a profound rightness" was all important achieved a high degree of accuracy in their delineations. Academic artists as well as the makers of topographical views shared equally in the concern for visual reality characteristic of much of the work produced in the new country.

Writings on art as it developed in America make some mention of the use of mechanical devices by artists, particularly those trained at West Point in sketching for military purposes, but few of these writings provide the names of artists or cite their works. They suggest that all makers of "prospects" or "perspectives" relied upon engineering techniques to obtain the proper balance and correct perspective for their views. Little information is available in general histories of American art on the means whereby American artists achieved their aim for visual accuracy.

Autobiographies, reminiscences, correspondence, wills and estate inventories, catalogs and business records, when published, provide occasional mention of the camera obscura and other tools of the trade used by artists in addition to the palette and the brush. Lithographs and engravings derived from works of art may also note the artists' reliance upon the camera for "authenticity." But the artist's own statement, taken from the title of his work, is by far the best evidence of his use of mechanical devices.

An example is James Banton's watercolor drawing of "Blodgett's Hotel" done in 1818 and titled as follows:

> This View of the General Post Office in the City of Washington was taken 22d May 1818 by J. Banton in his Camera standing in the Pennsylvania Avenue distant about sixty rods southeast.

Little is known of Banton except that he was a profilist, working in New England until at least 1825. This view was made from the site of the National Archives Building, looking to the present National Portrait Gallery. It shows the Post Office as one of the three most important structures in the city at that time, the others being the Capitol and the White House.

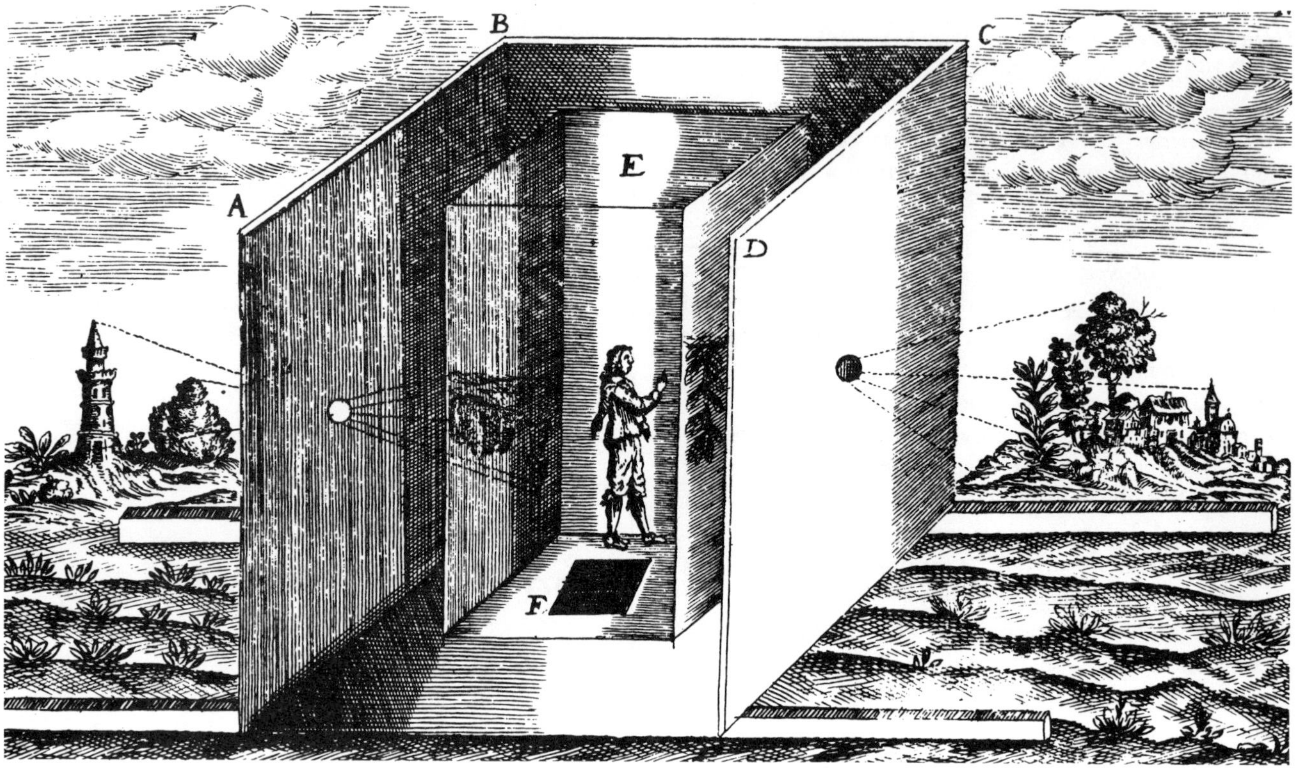

Illustration of an ancient camera obscura in Ars Magna Lucis et Umbrae, *published in Amsterdam in 1671.*

Blodgett's Hotel, housing the Post Office, was built on land acquired from David Burnes in 1792 and was occupied by the U.S. government in 1810. Designed by James Hoban, the hotel which was 120 feet in length and three stories high was erected as part of a lottery scheme. The cornerstone was laid on July 4, 1793, with appropriate Masonic ceremonies. Although the building was never used as a hotel, it housed many government offices and provided lodging for visiting foreign dignitaries. Here in 1800 the first theatrical production in the city was staged. After 1810 the vast storage area on the ground floor was filled with the accumulated models and inventions of the Patent Office, and here also the "ancient records" of the State, War, and Navy Departments were housed for safekeeping. The new Post Office Department and the city Post Office also were located in this building. When the British burned the city in the summer of 1814, Blodgett's Hotel was left undamaged. It then became the meeting place of the 13th Congress. Here the books and papers acquired from Thomas Jefferson to replace those lost in the burning of the Library of Congress were described and cataloged. It was a tragic loss to history when, in 1836, fire destroyed the building and all its contents.[1]

The camera obscura, so frequently used by American artists, was first noted in literature in the 11th century. The *Encyclopaedia Britannica* for 1970 defines it as "any box or chamber within which an image of the external scene is formed by means of a small aperture or lens." The image is projected onto a sheet of drawing paper and the artist traces it in outline; or the artist may paint his picture directly on the canvas. The principle was well understood by ancient scholars, and the camera was used by early artists and astronomers. Architects used it to study classical ruins. By the 1600's a lens and a concave mirror had become parts of the camera, and by the 1700's, the original room or chamber had been reduced in size to a large box.

An illustration of the ancient camera obscura is in the book *Ars Magna Lucis et Umbrae,* published in Amsterdam in 1671. To illustrate its operation, the artist is shown within the room, having entered through a trapdoor in the floor. He is shown standing and tracing the image that he sees on a sheet of ground glass in front of him. Outside on the ground is the rack by which the chamber could be moved from place to place.[2]

The size and style of the ancient camera had changed still further by the 19th century. It was not only much smaller, but it was also more ornate and somewhat more complicated to operate. Academic artists usually purchased their cameras from optical firms in London, but many Americans built their own and patented their improved models.

In 1862 George F. Kolb of Philadelphia patented his camera obscura [3] and described it for the *Scientific American* of June 6, 1863, as a device giving opportunity to "would-be artists of no inherent talents to become faithful limners of the material matters of common life." This model, the inventor said, "proffered a very valuable aid to artistic culture of the hand and eye." In an illustration, the artist's hand may be seen, thrust through the curtained opening of the box to reveal the image, in this case the City Hall of New York City, on the table in front of him "in all its natural colors and in the true light and shade belonging to it."

Well-known artists who used the camera obscura include Benjamin West, who said that he made acquaintance with it as a child. Confined for a time by illness to a darkened room, he amused himself by making drawings of the outdoors as scenes were projected on the wall through openings in the latticed blinds.[4] By the time he was 14, he had built a camera of his own. James Peale, in helping his brother Charles Willson Peale in the Peale Museum, used the camera obscura regularly to copy silhouette likenesses and finished them as enlarged watercolor portraits to bring in additional income.[5] The itinerant, Rufus Porter, working in Alexandria, Va., in 1820, invented a camera obscura to be used in conjunction with a prism. The use of this instrument enabled him to make likenesses, he said, at the rate of one every 15 minutes. In later years, Porter traveled throughout the New England States, making scenic wall murals, which have been the subject of special study in recent times.[6]

The painter of scenes of American history, Tompkins Harrison Matteson, having little formal training in art but considerable native talent, learned from others while still a boy in upper New York State. At one time he followed an itinerant limner until he copied his instrument and learned to improve upon his art. About 1850 Matteson completed his painting called *The First Prayer in Congress,* which was bought by the American Art-Union of that year.[7] Engraved by H. S. Sadd, the scene depicts more than a score of statesmen kneeling in prayer in the meeting place at Carpenter's Hall in Philadelphia in 1790. The precise architectural detail shown in this painting, perhaps obtained through the use of mechanical instruments, served to document the recent reconstruction of the interior of Carpenter's Hall, but the composition of the assemblage has proved less reliable. The artist included certain notable statesmen such as Patrick Henry who did not serve at any time in the U.S. Congress.

Evidence of the use of the camera obscura by John Hesselius is available in the published inventory of his estate. Filed by his executrix early in 1779, among records of Anne Arundel County, Md., the inventory shows that this early American limner possessed the following items of practical utility for his art: a camera obscura, a prism, a case of platting instruments, a gauging rod, a two-foot rule, a candle screen, and a spyglass.[8]

The camera lucida, though not properly a camera, was another device used by artists for making views and taking likenesses. It was invented by William Hyde Wollaston in London in 1807 and consisted of a four-sided prism, having two to four lenses to provide for long or short sight. For portraiture, the lucida was mounted on a stand attached to a table by a clamp, close to the person whose likeness was to be taken. The artist traced the out-

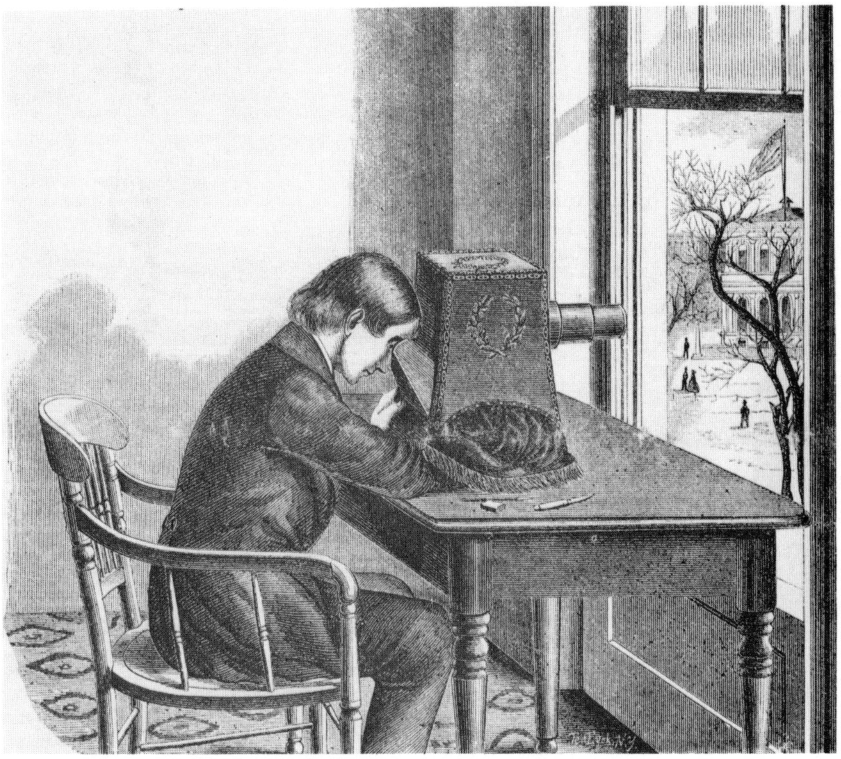

Sketch of the camera obscura patented by George Kolb in 1863.

line of the sitter on paper as it appeared on the table.[9] Considerable skill was required to use this device successfully, especially for the making of outdoor scenes. It differed from the camera obscura in that it was to be used in the light rather than in a dark room or box. Reductions and enlargements could be made with it, but it was helpful principally in obtaining accuracy of perspective and proportion.

The story of the camera lucida was well told by two colorful travelers who visited this country on a 14-month tour in 1827-28. Capt. Basil Hall of the Royal Navy and his wife told of the Captain's success with the camera lucida in his *Forty Etchings* [10] and in her correspondence, published in *The Aristocratic Journey.* Commenting on the use of the instrument, Captain Hall wrote that a portable table and a camp stool, both of which fold up like sticks, are advantageous for the traveler. "With his Sketch Book in one pocket, the Camera Lucida in the other, and the sticks above mentioned in his hand, the amateur may rove where he pleases, possessed of a magical secret for recording the features of Nature . . . exempted from the triple misery of Perspective, Proportion, and Form. . . ." [11]

Some of Captain Hall's original drawings of Niagara Falls done with the camera lucida are in the J. Stuart Fleming Collection at Niagara Falls, N.Y.[12] An additional bit of information about the good Captain was recently noted in the magazine *Antiques* for May 1972, in which the discovery of a likeness of him was reported and

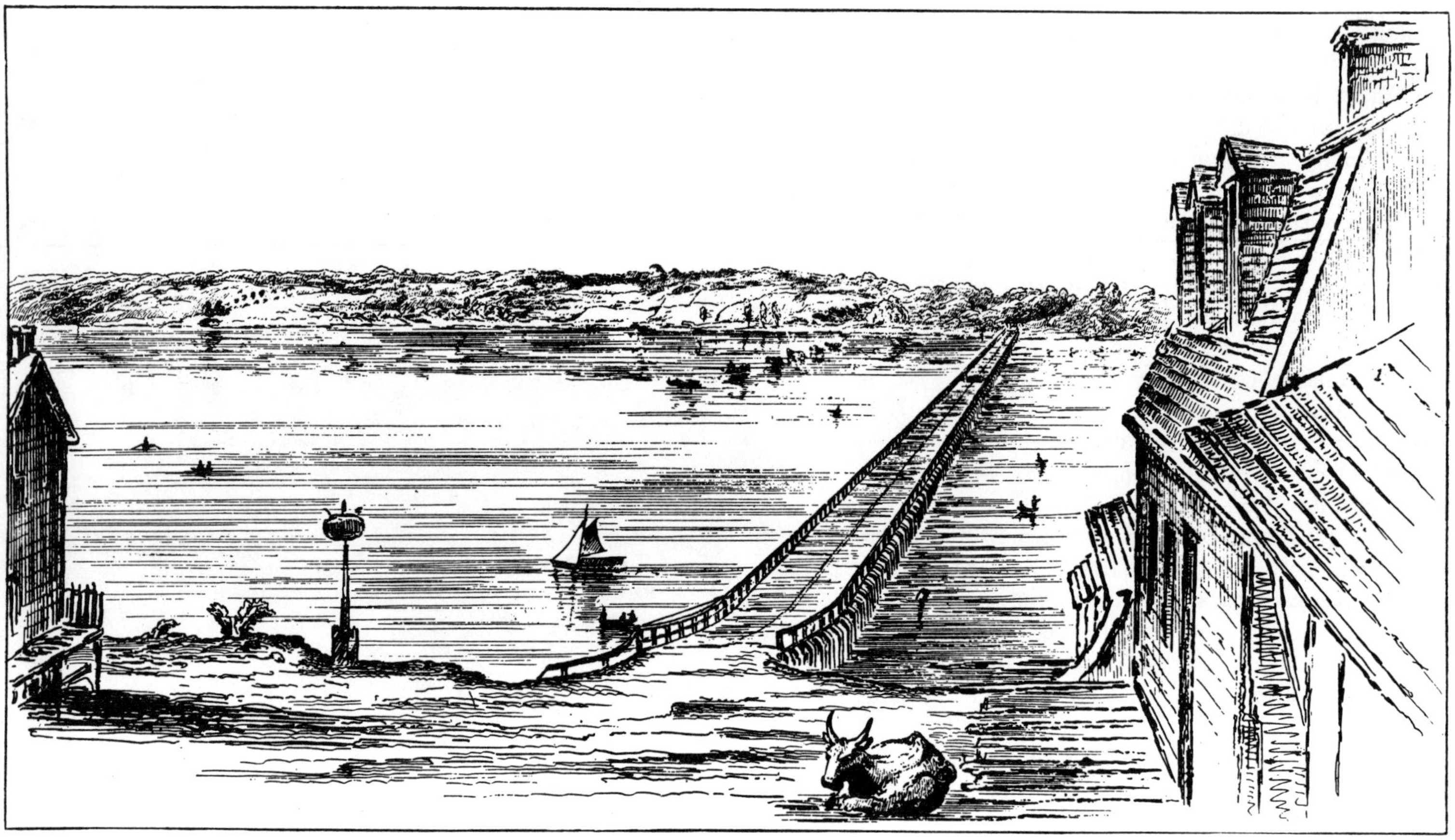

illustrated. His picture was retrieved during excavations now in progress at the site of Fort Stanwix near Rome, N. Y. The broken shards of a piece of Staffordshire china, when pieced together, revealed the smiling face of Captain Hall in the bottom of a big, blue chamber pot!

The use of the camera lucida by the federal government in its varied activities was routinely reported in official records for more than a century, but the significance of the instrument to art history remains to be fully understood. A particular instance may be found in the report on the Northeast Boundary Survey, made in March 1842 to the Hon. Daniel Webster, secretary of state, by Prof. James Renwick of Columbia University, the father of the well-known architect of the same name. Professor Renwick forwarded to the State Department as a part of his report a portfolio of drawings made by his assistants on the survey. Many of them had been made with the camera lucida; one was of supreme importance to the findings of the survey. It showed "the view from Park's hill" on the line between Maine and Canada.[13] Of this view, Professor Renwick said:

> . . . lest any doubt be entertained of its accuracy, it is proper to state that the unassisted vision was not relied upon but that the outlines were carefully delineated by means of the camera lucida.[14]

The original watercolor drawing, together with others made on the survey, are among records of the State Department on deposit in the National Archives. Some of them are signed by the artist, James William Glass, Jr., formerly an engineer with the United States Survey. This young man's work in America ceased with his removal to London in 1847, where he became proficient in painting historical scenes of British military leaders.[15]

From the records, it is clear that Professor Renwick had intended for the commission to include illustrations made from the artists' drawings in the published *Report on the Northeast Boundary Survey.* But no illustrations appeared in the publication except for one map, essential to the delineation of the commission's findings. Omission of the drawings may have been due to the current investigation by Congress of the printing operations of the government, which, until 1861 when the Government Printing Office was established, were carried on by various commercial printers who obtained contracts on bids from the government.[16] Not only the printing but also the making of illustrations by commercial firms such as Hoen, Ackerman, Weber and Co., Sinclair, Sarony, and others were accomplished in this manner. Understandably, these firms could not provide the excellent hand-produced lithography for the large printings of the government that they made for such privately financed works as the Thomas McKenney and James Hall portfolios of portraits of the American Indians for their *History of the Indian Tribes of North America, 1836-1844.*[17] One notable exception to the generally inferior lithographs and engravings in government publications will be found in the 12-volume *Reports of Explorations and Surveys to Ascertain the Most Practicable and Economic Route for a Railroad from the*

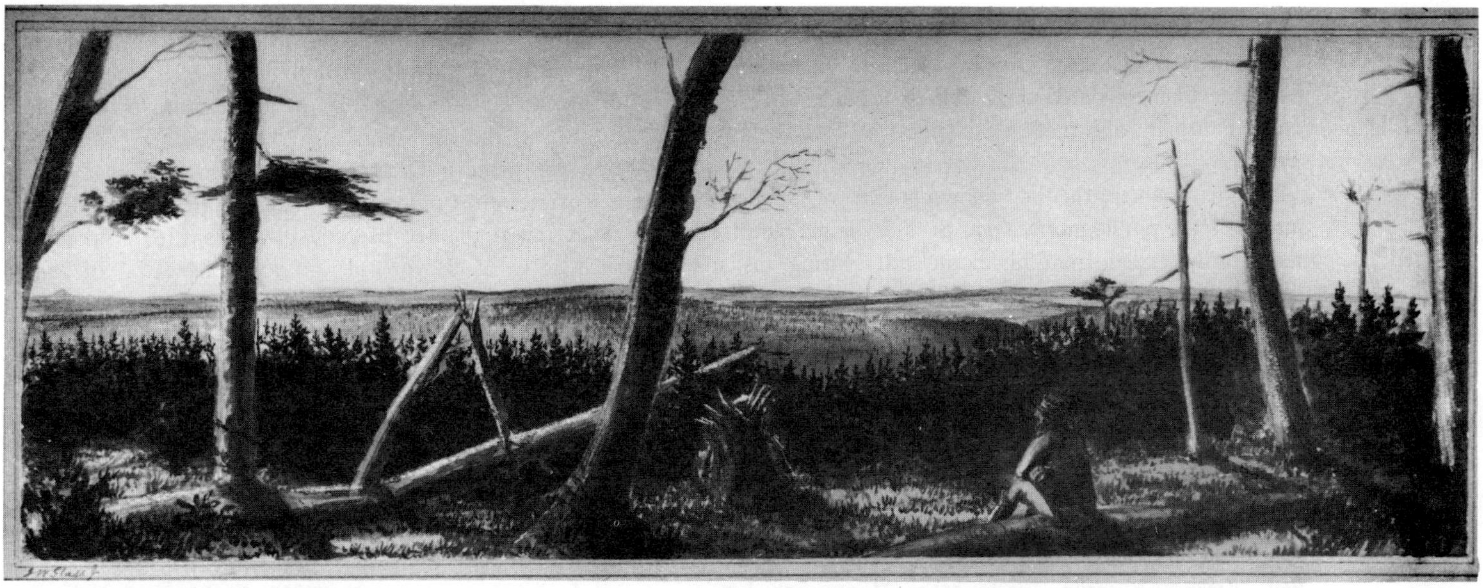

Left: "The Bridge Across Lake Cayuga," drawn with the camera lucida by Capt. Basil Hall during a tour of the United States in 1827-28.

Above: Camera lucida drawing done for the Northeast Boundary Survey and signed by the artist James William Glass, Jr. From the National Archives.

Below: Profile of Joel Barlow from a physiognotrace by Gilles-Louis Chrétien.

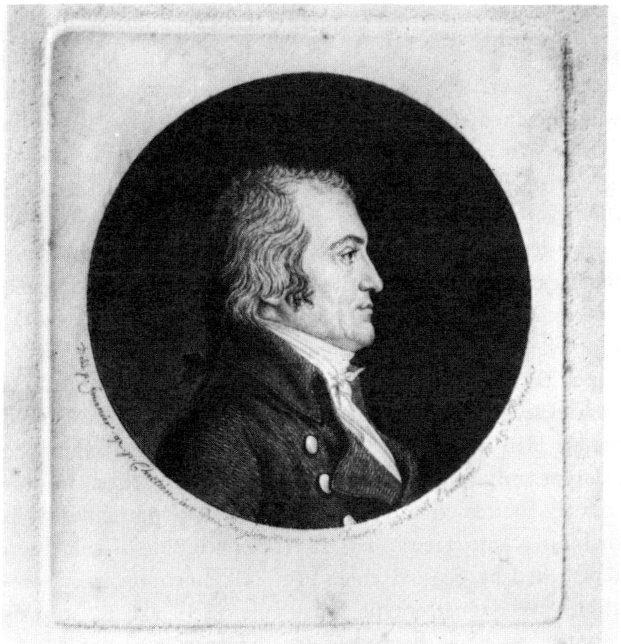

Mississippi River to the Pacific Ocean, 1855-61. The artistic quality of the 13 steel engravings of landscape views done by Frederic Von Egloffstein and engraved by Samuel Seibert in volume 11 is cited by Robert Taft as extraordinarily fine. Taft's work in correlating the varied printings of this sizable government publication is particularly helpful to the student of today.[18]

Mechanical instruments were also used in making the intimate representations of such American statesmen as George Washington. Hundreds of limners and profilists were engaged in producing silhouettes, crayon, pastel, and other likenesses, large and small, creating those examples of primitive art now so greatly treasured by the individuals and museums who own them. Instruments used in making them included the physiognotrace and others of which little is known.

The oval pastel portrait of George Washington now at Mount Vernon was done in 1796 by James Sharples from the life, while the President was still in Philadelphia. It is of great inconographic significance because of the way in which it was made and the remarks of George Washington Parke Custis concerning it. In his *Recollections and Private Memoirs of Washington* published in 1860, Mr. Custis refers to "The profile likeness in crayon by Sharples in 1797 [1796], an admirable likeness, the profile taken by an instrument and critically correct." This likeness, which remained in the family until it was purchased by the Mount Vernon Ladies' Association in 1954 from the heirs of Mary Custis Lee, a granddaughter of Mr. Custis, was often copied by the Sharples, both James and his wife Ellen who operated their business from a "caravan" in Philadelphia. The most logical means of making copies would have been by the physiognotrace, but there is no evidence to show that this is the instrument used by the Sharples for this work.[19]

The invention of the physiognotrace is credited to a Frenchman, Gilles-Louis Chrétien, in 1786. The machine was used to make an exact tracing in outline of the life-sized profile of the sitter. The sitter's features, hair, and clothing were drawn in by hand, often by an accomplished artist. The finished portrait was next reduced in size by means of the pantograph and was transferred directly to a small round copperplate. Prints no larger than 2″ x 2¾″ were then made from the plate. For $12 the sitter received from Chrétien the large original portrait, the small copperplate and 12 prints struck from it.[20] Much of Chrétien's art work was done for him by Quenedy, including the excellent likeness of Thomas Jefferson made in 1789,[21] or by Fournier, who made the likeness of Joel Barlow in France in 1804.[22]

In this country, the best-known maker of profiles by means of the physiognotrace was St. Mémin, a Frenchman, temporarily exiled from his homeland. During his stay in this country in the early 1800's, he made more than 800 likenesses of prominent Americans in New York City, Philadelphia, Boston, Baltimore, Charleston, Richmond, and Washington, D.C. Examples of his work, assembled by our first American archivist Peter Force, are in the Library of Congress, and other collections are in the Corcoran Gallery of Art and the Maryland Historical Society. St. Mémin's contribution to our knowledge of the appearance of hundreds of our early statesmen, including Paul Revere, Bushrod Washington, Meriwether Lewis, James Madison, and Aaron Burr, is perhaps not fully realized even today. In 1860 Jeremiah Gurney photographed all of the St. Mémin likenesses then known to exist. The miniature photographs, 12 to a page, were pasted into each of the volumes of a limited edition of pictures published by Elias Dexter. They are listed and described in *The Crayon* for May and October 1860.[23]

Not all work of this type was produced by professional artists. Rembrandt Peale recalled that the physiognotrace was an attractive feature of his father's museum but that its operation was assigned to Moses [Williams], a slave belonging to Charles Willson Peale. Moses became so skillful that Peale gave him his freedom, and he soon earned enough money to buy a two-story brick house and settle down with a wife. Rembrandt Peale recalled also that Moses cut four profiles at once, reserving to himself the blocks which he called, appropriately, his "blockheads." Peale further recalled that Moses had amassed at least two barrels full of blocks, among which might be found the likenesses of many a friend or relative and sometimes a distinguished personage.

Other devices similar to the physiognotrace invented by Chrétien were in use in this country. The U.S. government had granted two patents to Americans for similar machines, one in 1803 and another in 1805. In Philadelphia, Joseph Sansom [24] designed a machine principally for the making of silhouettes or shadow likenesses and called it his "physionomical sketch machine". In correspondence, Thomas Jefferson often mentioned such devices as these and was particularly concerned with "the polygraph" by which, he said "oil paintings could be copied so exactly as cannot without difficulty and close attention be distinguished from their archetype." [25]

The records of the Patent Office in the National Archives contain much for the serious student of early methods of creating an image, whether of a person or a place. Summary statements of patents are available in the annual reports of the Patent Office, together with line drawings of devices, but the primary records sometimes provide additional information of great significance. The divergent opinions of the patent examiners are often present in the correspondence accompanying the application for patents. Designs for art items are available in a separate series called the Patent Design Series and sometimes reveal the record copy of a projected work of art such as C. Y. Hayne's design for a bas-relief of Henry Clay in 1850 or designs for bust statuary of Abraham Lincoln, Daniel Webster, Stephen H. Douglas, and many others. Accompanying the application for registration of a design, the correspondence of artists may be found, directed often to Titian Ramsay Peale 2d, who served as patent examiner in the areas of ornamentation and photography from 1849 to 1873.[26] Peale had an active interest in photography himself, which may have unduly influenced his judgments. There were controversies over his denial of a patent to L. L. Hill for his color daguerreotypes and his granting of a patent to James A. Cutting, severely restricting the production of ambrotypes. Persons seeking relief in such instances turned to the Congress and filed petitions with the Committee on Patents there. The petitions and accompanying papers of this committee, now on deposit in the National Archives, are another rich source for information on the means whereby artists and photographers accomplished their works and achieved their ends.[27]

In the early 1800's Samuel F. B. Morse, then a student at Yale, tried without success to hold the image seen in the camera obscura. Numbers of others in this country and abroad were experimenting along the same line. Their well-documented efforts are covered in Richard Rudisill's *Mirror Image* (1971). Although some success was achieved, the discovery of a satisfactory means to hold the image over a period of time did not come until 1839. Surprisingly, two different methods were announced in that year, one in France by Daguerre and one in England by Fox-Talbot. The French daguerreotype was immediately adopted in the United States. The English calotype, a paper process, was restricted by the inventor to holders of licenses and thus was not commonly used in the United States. Had it not been for these restrictive patents, the calotype might have served the needs of artists in this country better than the daguerreotype, particularly in making scenic views. By 1851 both methods had been superseded by Scott-Archer's wet collodion process. Thereafter, the daguerreotype was little used except in this country, where it flourished for a few more years.[28]

The effect of the daguerreotype upon art was immediate, reducing to almost nothing the demands for portraiture in oils or miniatures. Although the daguerreotype satisfied the demand for true representations, it was a medium severely limited by the nature of the process. Images registered by means of the daguerreotype camera on the silvered copper plate were unique specimens to be treasured and viewed only by their owners; they could not be duplicated in the manner of the physiognotrace. For the ensuing decade and longer, there was no practical means of making photographs by the negative-positive process of true photography, except by the English method of paper photography. By 1855 the weekly illustrated newspapers occasionally made wood engravings "after" daguerreotypes of famous personages. Steel engravings had been made even earlier, noted particularly in the fine work done for the *Democratic Review* in the 1840's, showing the likenesses of outstanding personages "from daguerreotypes." There were numerous "galleries of the illustrious" which flourished for short periods, beginning with Plumbe's lithographs of 1846, derived from daguerreotypes, and including Brady's National Portrait Gallery of 1850.[29] But scenes made from daguerreotypes, even those showing national shrines or public buildings, appeared only rarely in books or magazines and not at all in newspapers in the 1840's.

A valiant attempt was made in the 1840's by Thomas Doney, a mezzotint engraver, to produce an enormous steel plate for his picture *Henry Clay addressing the Senate in 1842*.[30] For this work, he obtained more than 100 daguerreotypes of Congressmen and other notables from Anthony and other operators in New York City and Washington, D.C. He devoted more than four years to engraving likenesses from these daguerreotypes for his masterpiece. His was a singular but isolated accomplishment in which all the persons were accurately represented. But the same Thomas Doney, to whom accuracy was all important in the 1840's, produced a most inaccurate representation of a historic scene some 20 years later when he engraved his *News of the Emancipation*. For this picture Doney had altered an English engraving entitled *Arrival of the Post in an English Country Village*, from a painting by D'Uglino Latilla of London. Leaving the figures of the villagers unaltered, Doney changed only the mail sack to read "U.S. Mail" and the document to represent the President's Emancipation Proclamation of 1863.[31] In this deception, economics was doubtless a factor as it was in those instances in which the head of Abraham Lincoln was substituted in existing engravings

"Henry Clay Addressing the Senate in 1842," engraved by Thomas Doney from daguerreotype likenesses.

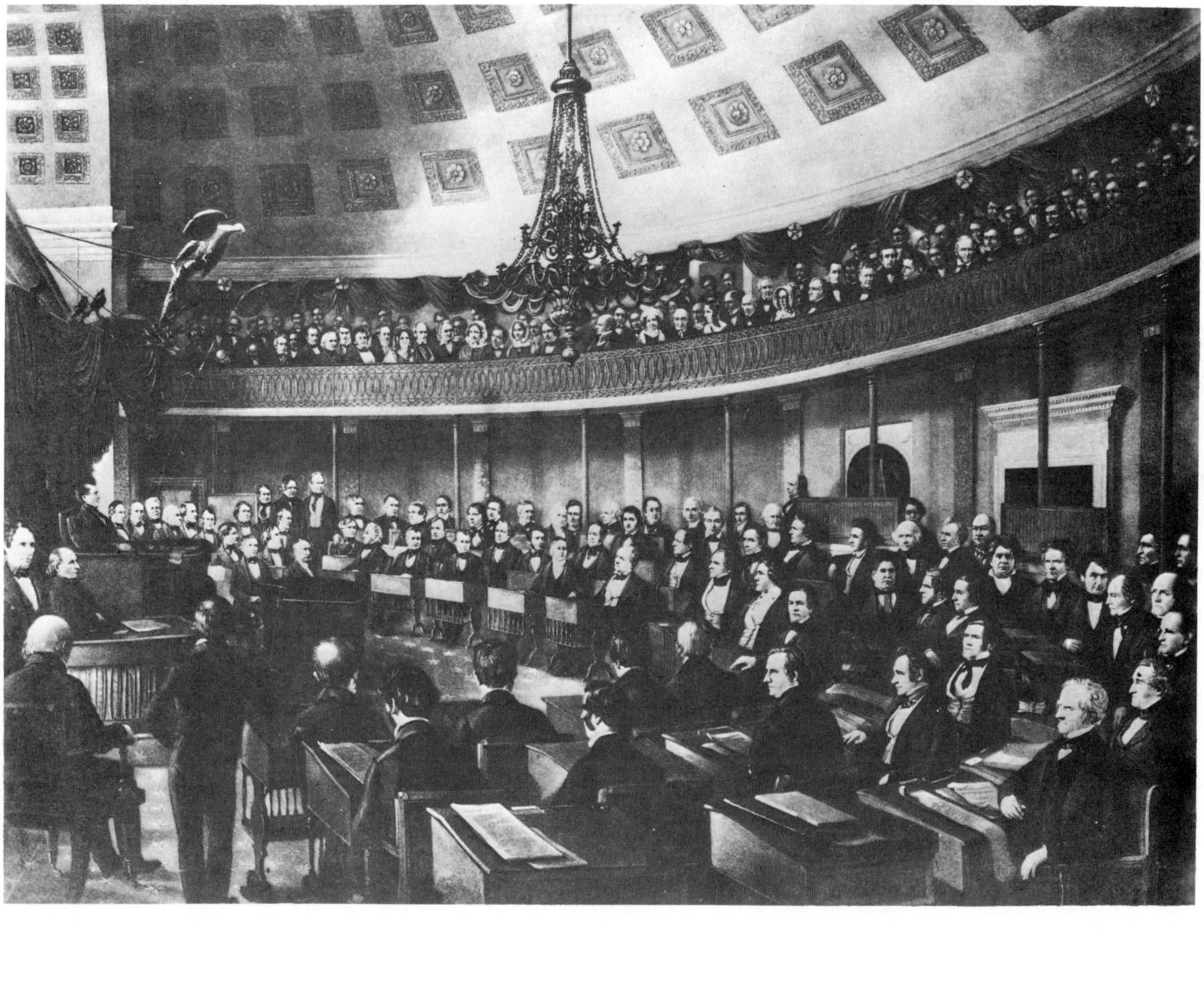

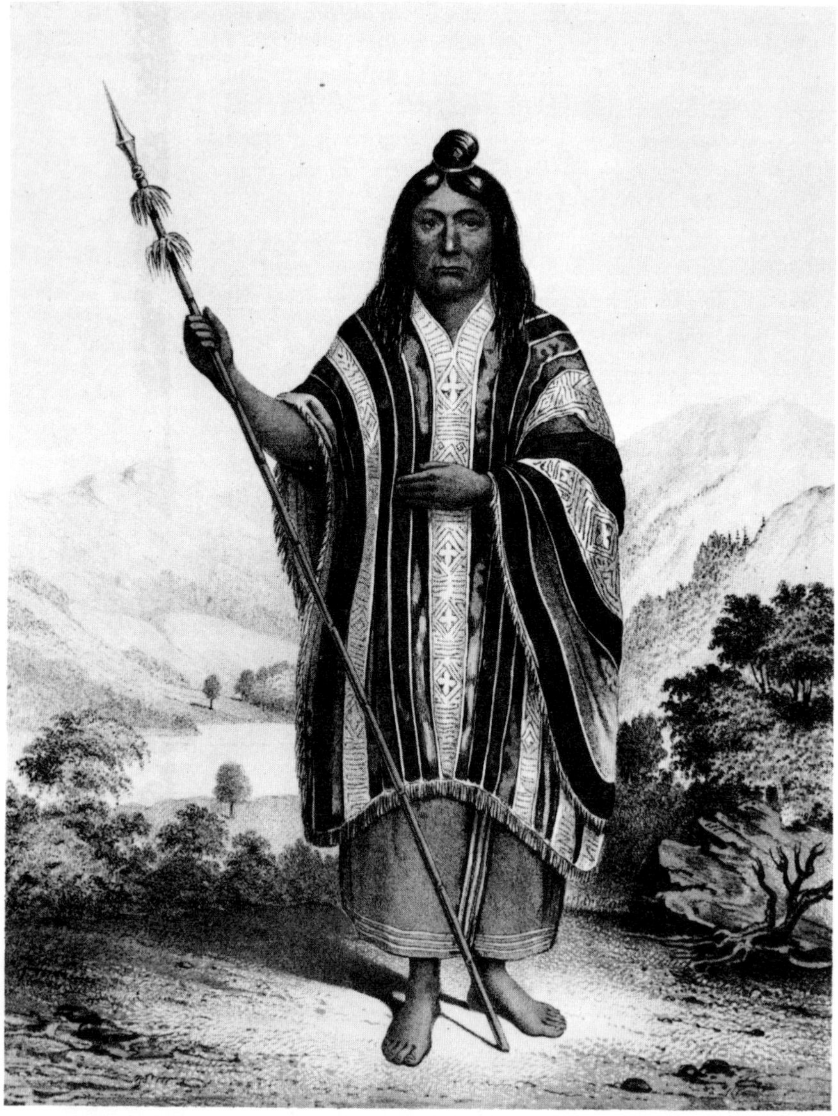

Araucanian Indian of South America, drawn by J. M. Stanley from a daguerreotype by E. R. Smith. Illustration in the report of the U.S. Naval Astronomical Expedition, 1849-52.

of other statesmen. This practice is fully explored in "Heads of States" by Milton Kaplan of the staff of the Library of Congress, published in the *Winterthur Portfolio No. 6* in 1970. By 1863 the beginnings of a modern-day concept of news relevance interfered with our earlier concern for absolute integrity in art representations.

Some of the earliest scenic views made by the daguerreotype camera in this country exist today only in the form of watercolor drawings copied from them. Many are present among records on deposit in the National Archives. On the same survey of the Northeast Boundary mentioned earlier, Edward Anthony, a 22-year-old engineer who had studied at Columbia University with Professor Renwick, was invited to go along for the purpose of trying out the daguerreotype camera. From August 1840 to March 1842, he spent a part of each year along the boundary line between the United States and Canada, principally in Maine and New Hampshire.[32]

The original daguerreotypes made on the survey are not, so far as can be discovered, still in existence; nor are there any daguerreotypes of any surveys among the government's holdings in the National Archives. The watercolor drawings done from them by sketch artists are all that remain of this early work. They are, however, important as primary evidence that the government used the daguerreotype camera to obtain accuracy in its observations of disputed territory, and they are important because they provide additional information about obscure landscape artists, among whom was Philip Harry of Boston and Washington.[33]

Other explorations of the government in which daguerreotypy played a part are the U.S. Naval Astronomical Expedition to the Southern Hemisphere, 1849-52. The published report includes an excellent full-length picture of an Araucanian Indian of South America, drawn by John M. Stanley from a daguerreotype by Prof. E. R. Smith, artist-engineer. Presumably Stanley made the illustration after the return of the expedition to this country, since there is no evidence that he accompanied it.[34]

The daguerreotypes made on Commodore Perry's expedition to Japan, 1852-54, are better known. Some 40 illustrations from them were published in the government's report, together with some account of the work of the daguerreotypist-lithographer Eliphalet Brown, Jr. None of the plates can compare in beauty and brilliance with the six large and rare lithographs separately produced by Brown after his return to this country, illustrating the dramatic events of the opening up of Japan in 1853. Fortunately, some of the original watercolors of Perry's expedition were preserved in the Middendorf Collection, and three daguerreotypes by Brown, recently discovered in Japan, were brought to this country for exhibit at the Smithsonian Institution in 1968.[35]

When at last true photography was achieved by the negative-positive process, involving glass plates and wet collodion, daguerreotypy disappeared quickly from the

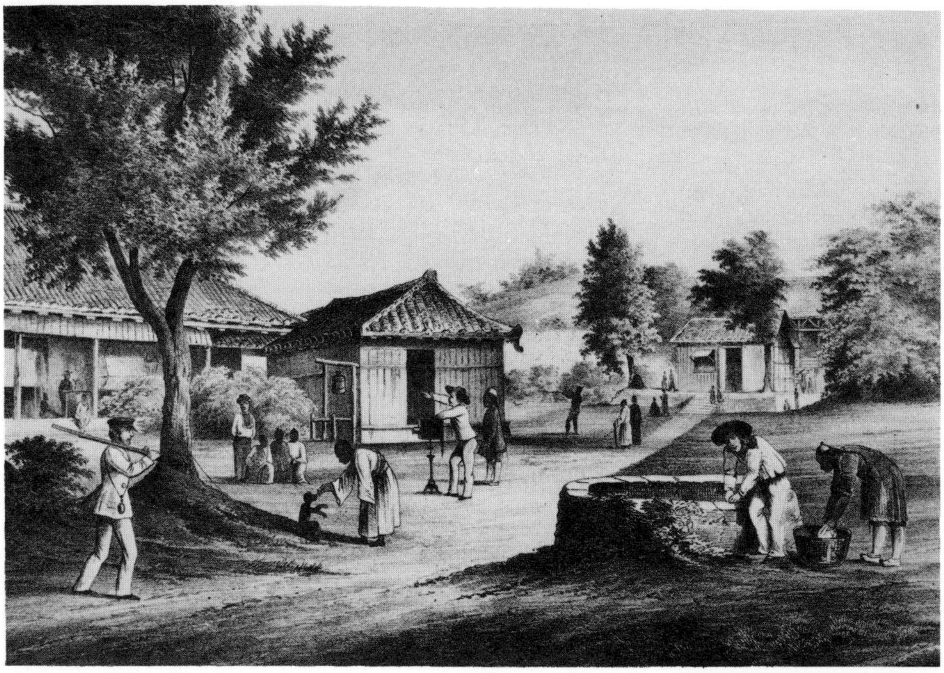

An illustration in the report of Commodore Perry's expedition, 1852-54, shows a daguerreotype camera in use in Tumai, Lew Chew, Japan.

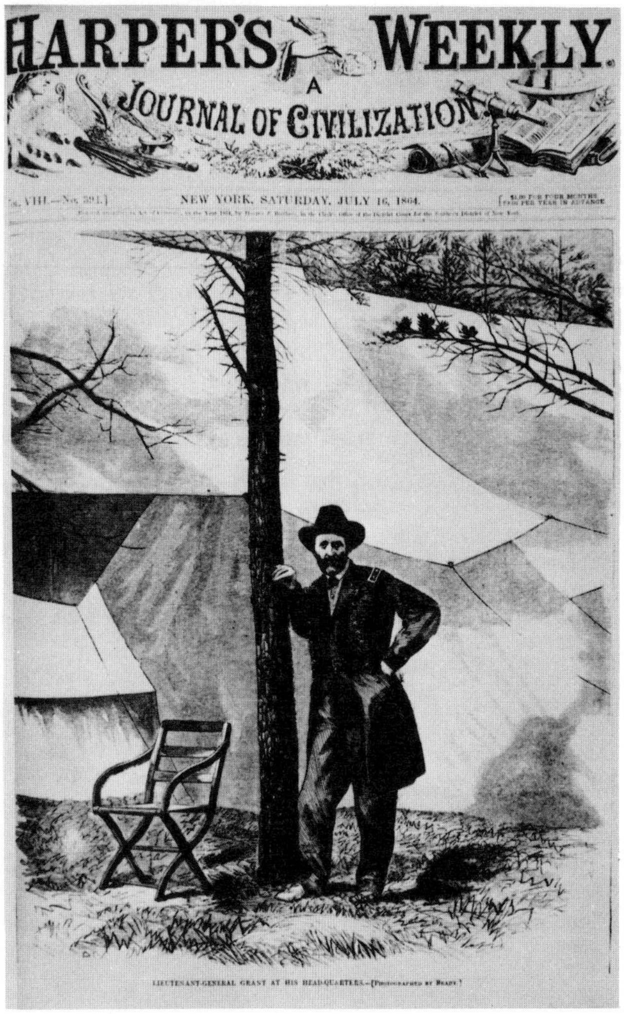

Below: Wood engraving of General Grant at Cold Harbor, Va., in 1864, made from a photograph attributed to Mathew B. Brady.

American scene, as it had already vanished in England and Europe. By the late 1850's magazine and book illustration as well as newspaper illustration occasionally employed photographs in the form of engravings derived from them.[36] To a limited extent, photographs were used for illustration of the Civil War in the weekly illustrated newspapers. Although the editors of *Harper's Weekly*, *Frank Leslie's Illustrated Weekly Newspaper* and the *New York Illustrated News* expressed a preference for photographs because of the public's confidence in their inflexible veracity, they were seldom obtainable in time to be newsworthy. William Campbell's excellent work on eyewitness drawings published during the war states that only 6.5 per cent of all the war scenes published in the newspapers were derived from photographs. All the others were from artists' drawings often made on the spot. He said, "While today these Civil War photographs are extremely important to the pictorial record of the war, it is a curious fact that at the time they were made, their influence on the populace both North and South was relatively slight." [37]

With the coming of photography and the demise of the daguerreotype, the "incredible plethora of contraptions used in the nineteenth century to guarantee the reproduction of nature with maximum precision" vanished also.[38] Ultimately, according to John Wilmerding, it would mean that artists would have to turn to nonrepresentational painting to find original expression.[39]

NOTES

[1] Columbia Historical Society, *Records,* 1957-59, p. 123 and illustration in black and white. No color reproduction of the watercolor is permitted by the society.

[2] *Image, Journal of Photography of the George Eastman House, Rochester, N.Y.,* 2, no. 3 (March 1953):11; and Arthur T. Gill, "Call back Yesterday," *The Photographic Journal of the Royal Photographic Society,* (March 1972):102-3.

[3] U.S. Patent No. 34970, April 15, 1862.

[4] Henry T. Tuckerman, *Book of the Artists,* 2d ed. (New York: J. F. Carr, 1966), pp. 97-98, 102, 105.

[5] *The Peale Family; Three Generations of American Artists,* (Detroit: Detroit Institute of Arts, 1967), p. 27. An exhibition organized by Charles H. Elam.

[6] *Cyclopedia of American Biography,* s.v., "Porter, Rufus." *Dictionary of American Biography,* s.v., "Porter, Rufus." and Nina Fletcher Little, *American Decorative Wall Painting, 1700–1850,* (Sturbridge, Mass., 1952), p. 147.

[7] Georgia Stamm Chamberlain, *Studies on American Painters and Sculptors of the Nineteenth Century,* (Annandale, Va.: The Turnpike Press, Inc., 1965), pp. 20-21.

[8] Richard K. Doud, "John Hesselius, Maryland Limner," *Winterthur Portfolio No. 5,* (1969):129-53.

[9] *The Gernsheim Collection* (Austin, 1965), Items 21, 22, 23, 24. Catalog of an exhibit at the University of Texas, June 1965.

[10] *Image* 5, No. 1 (February 1956):41.

[11] *Image* 6, No. 8 (October 1957):195-97.

[12] *Three Centuries of Niagara Falls* (Buffalo, N.Y., 1964), Item 84. Catalog of an exhibit at the Albright-Knox Art Gallery, Buffalo, N.Y.

[13] House of Representatives. House Executive Document No. 31, 27th Congress, 3d session. Serial 420. A report of the Board of Commissioners appointed to survey the Northeastern Boundary, April 7, 1842. pp. 2, 4, 9.

[14] Richard Rudisill, *Mirror Image* (Albuquerque: University of New Mexico Press, 1971), p. 100.

[15] Tuckerman, pp. 421-423; and Clara Erskine Clement and Laurence Hutton, *Artists of the Nineteenth Century and their Works* (Boston: J. R. Osgood & Co., 1885 [1884]) pp. 301-2.

[16] U.S. Govt. Print. Off., *100 GPO Years, 1861-1961; a History of United States Public Printing* (Washington, 1961) pp. 1-20.

[17] Herman Viola's forthcoming biography of Thomas L. McKenney, to be published by the Swallow Press, will have more information about the making of lithographs of the Indians than is available today.

[18] Robert Taft, *Artists and Illustrators of the Old West, 1850-1900* (New York: Scribner, 1953) pp. 7-8.

[19] The Mount Vernon Ladies' Association of the Union, *Annual Report,* 1957, pp. 11-13, 39; *American Paintings and Historical Prints from the Middendorf Collection,* Item 7, showing a likeness in rectangle, formerly owned by the family; and *Cosmopolitan Art Journal* (December 1857):24-25 re Sharples' use of the pentograph for mathematical accuracy.

[20] Helmut and Alison Gernsheim, *Creative Photography, 1826 to the Present* (Detroit: Wayne State University Press, 1963), pp. 15-16. A catalog of a 1963 exhibit.

[21] Alfred L. Bush, *The Life Portraits of Thomas Jefferson* (Charlottesville, Va.; The Thomas Jefferson Memorial Foundation, 1962), p. 20. A catalog of an exhibit at the University of Virginia Museum of Fine Arts, April 1962.

[22] Columbia Historical Society, *Records,* 1960-62. pp. 326-29. Other examples of Barlow's physiognotrace are in the Huntington Art Gallery and at Harvard University.

[23] *The Crayon* (October 1857): 307-8, and May and October 1860 as mentioned in text.

[24] *Pennsylvania Magazine of History and Biography,* 88 (October 1964):395-438.

[25] *The Papers of Thomas Jefferson,* ed. Julian Boyd, vol. 12 (Princeton: Princeton University Press, 1955), pp. xxxvi-xxxvii.

[26] National Archives. Record Group 241, Records of the Patent Office; and Alphabetical list of designs issued from the United States Patent Office from 1790 to 1873, in the *Subject-Matter Index of Patents for Inventions,* Vol. 3 (Government Printing Office, 1874), pp. 1858-1911.

[27] National Archives. Record Group 46, Records of the Senate. Committee on Patents; and Record Group 233, Records of the House of Representatives. Committee on Patents.

[28] The Arts Council of Great Britain. Catalog of an exhibit on the beginnings of photography held at the Victoria and Albert Museum, March 16-May 14, 1972, entitled *From Today Painting is Dead.* The catalog consists of 60 pages of text describing 914 items, 50 plates, and three essays on the origins of photography by the English method.

[29] Washington, D.C. *City Directory* for 1846. Includes two pages of advertisement of the Plumbe National Daguerrian Gallery, founded in 1840 but operating in D.C. from 1845. Plumbe also established a "Plumbeotype Gallery" in Philadelphia about this same time, which sold lithographic copies of his daguerreotypes. See also Beaumont Newhall, *The Daguerreotype in America* (New York: Duell, Sloan & Pearce, 1961), pp. 38-41.

[30] *American Review* (October 1846):431-32 for an account of this engraving.

[31] Steel engraving of "News of the Emancipation" among records of the Ford Museum, National Park Service, Washington, D.C. (now Ford's Theatre).

[32] National Archives. Record Group 76. Series 11 and 30 for portfolios of watercolor drawings of the Northeast Boundary Survey; Record Group 59, Misc. Letters, 1840-47 and Fifth Auditor accounts, 1840-42. See also note 13.

[33] Boston Museum of Fine Arts. *Catalog of an Exhibit of American Paintings, 1815-65* (Boston, 1956), Item 75; and Josephine Cobb, "Washington Art Association; an Exhibition Record, 1856-60," in Columbia Historical Society, *Records,* 1963-65, p. 133.

[34] 33d Congress, 1st Session. House Ex. Doc. No. 121, plate 2, facing page 68 and text, p. 68.

[35] Joe D. Thomas, "Photographic Archives," *The American Archivist,* 21, no. 4 (October 1958): 419-23; Correspondence of Josephine Cobb with Shiro Shibuya of the Hakodate City Museum in Hokkaido, Japan, 1966-68, identifying some newly discovered daguerreotypes in Japan as the work of Eliphalet Brown, Jr.; and the catalog of an exhibit at the Smithsonian Institution in 1968 on the Japan Expedition, 1852-55, for which original watercolors, daguerreotypes, and lithographs were assembled.

[36] Budd Leslie Gambee, "Frank Leslie's Illustrated Newspaper, 1855-60," 1964. Doctoral dissertation, available from University Microfilms.

[37] William Campbell, *The Civil War; a Centennial Exhibition of Eyewitness Drawings,* (Washington: National Gallery of Art, 1961).

[38] Aaron Scharf, *Art and Photography* (London: Allen Lane, 1968), pp. 1-5.

[39] John Wilmerding, *History of American Marine Painting* ([Salem, Mass.]: Peabody Museum of Salem, 1968), p. 28.

David Tatham is an associate professor and chairman of the Department of Fine Arts, Syracuse University. He has published numerous articles concerning the graphic arts in America and is the author of The Lure of the Striped Pig—The Illustration of Popular Music in America 1820-1870 *(1973).*

Pictorial Responses to the Caning of Senator Sumner

David Tatham

Early in the afternoon of Thursday, May 22, 1856, Congressman Preston S. Brooks of South Carolina entered the nearly empty chamber of the United States Senate and made his way to the desk of Republican Senator Charles Sumner of Massachusetts. After addressing a few words, Brooks lifted his cane and rained down a torrent of blows, as hard and as rapidly as he could. In less than a minute his cane was shattered and Sumner lay collapsed, insensible, and bleeding on the Senate floor.[1]

The direct cause of this violent assault upon the most outspoken antislavery member of the Senate was a long philippic Sumner had delivered earlier in the week on the Kansas question. For two days he had eloquently reviled the institution of slavery in general and the prospect of its spread to Kansas in particular. He was especially abusive to Democratic Senators Andrew P. Butler of South Carolina and Stephen A. Douglas of Illinois. Douglas was visibly perturbed, and uncordial words passed between him and Sumner at the close of the speech. (We shall sample the exchange later in this paper.) Senator Butler's reaction was not immediately known since he was absent in his own state. His cousin, Congressman Brooks, was present however, listening from the Senate gallery to the first half of Sumner's speech. Brooks's offense at the insults to his state and his kinsman deepened the next day as he read and brooded over the printed text of the speech. Convinced that the honor of his family was at stake, he determined to punish Sumner. There is some reason to believe that Brooks intended to strike only a single, token blow—to humiliate rather than harm—but as the first blow was landed, all of his contained rage burst forth with the result that Sumner, rather than being humiliated, was left a martyr to the antislavery cause.

This was not the first time that one member of Congress had physically assaulted another within the hallowed walls of the Capitol, nor was it the first time that a legislator had been caned for opinions expressed in Congress. The most notable earlier incident occurred one evening in April 1832, when Sam Houston of Texas, who was not at the time a member of Congress, thrashed Representative William Stanbery of Ohio on Pennsylvania Avenue with a hickory cane cut on the grounds of Andrew Jackson's Hermitage.[2] But this encounter was different from the Brooks assault in several regards, not the least of which was a background in 1832 of personal enmity between the two men or the fact that Stanbery's major injuries were to his feelings. There

Wood engraving The Assault in the U.S. Senate Chamber on Senator Sumner *from the cover* of Frank Leslie's Illustrated Newspaper, *dated June 7, 1856.*

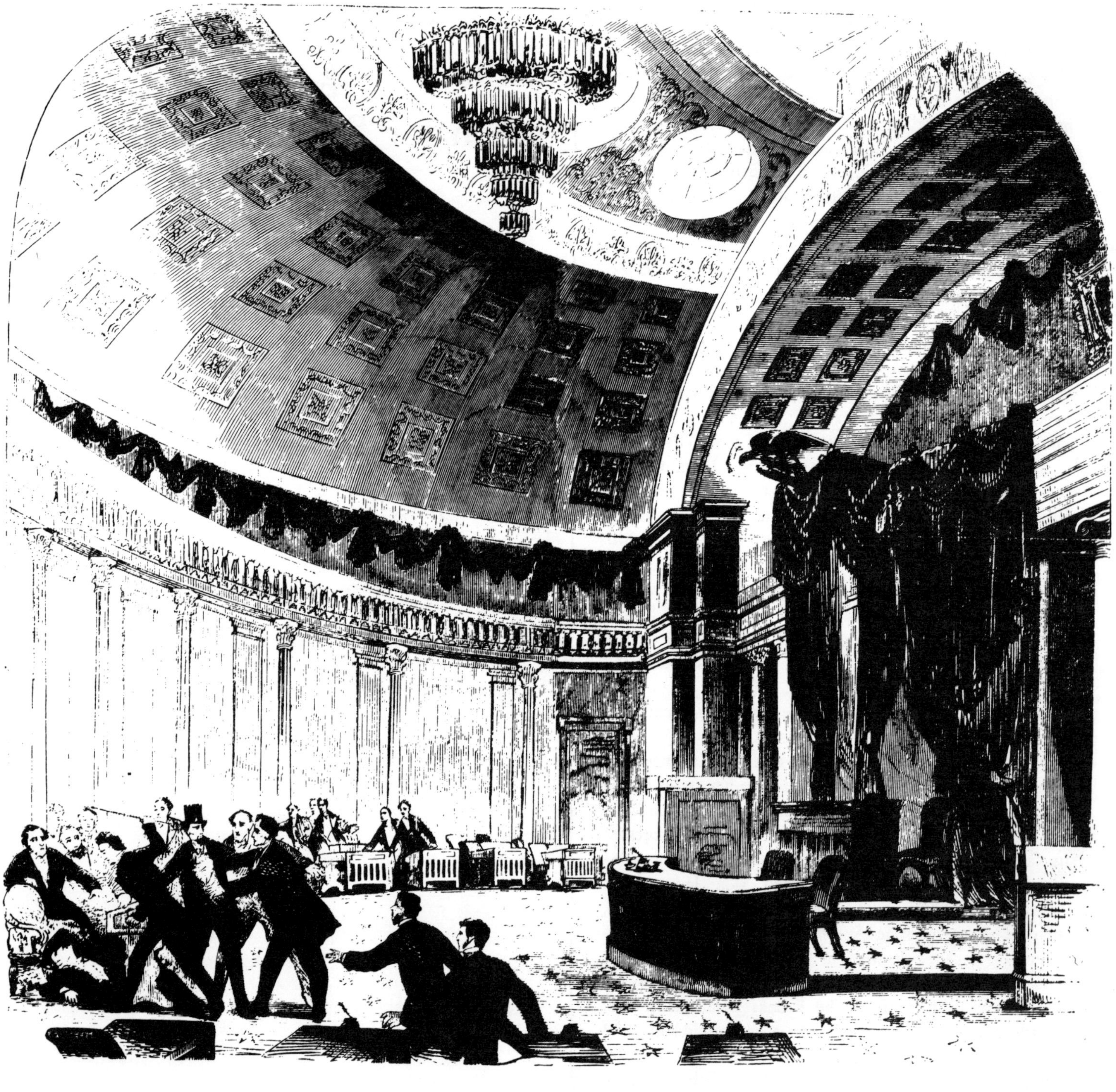

is a contemporary caricature of this incident, *Houstonizing, or a Cure for Slander,* an unsigned lithograph. It is not listed in Weitenkampf, and the only impression I have located is at the Essex Institute.

But the major difference between the Houston and Brooks canings rests with the tempers of their respective times. The issues at stake in the 1832 fracas were mostly personal, of small scale, and short lived. The assault on Sumner, on the other hand, stood in relief against a background of more than two decades of unrelieved national torment about slavery. Brooks's act was a virtual sloshing of kerosene into already dangerously overheated furnaces of partisan rancor on the issue.

Within days prints appeared, all in the north and all using Brooks's assault to promote and intensify antislavery feeling. I have located eight prints which in whole or part are direct and immediate pictorial responses to the incident. Most seem to have been executed within three weeks of the event. Of the lot, one offers something akin to objective documentation, three are free flights of comic imagination, and the remaining four are sober caricatures, as humorless as Sumner himself. In their variety, the eight constitute an illuminating cross section of popular printmaking at midcentury. If there are other contemporary prints on the subject, they have eluded me, and I would be grateful for information about them. It would be interesting to have a pro-Brooks caricature, though I am not surprised that I have not found one. In the North, though Sumner was certainly not universally admired, there was close to universal disapprobation of the assault on him. In the South, where the business of caricature publication was far less well established, there was no very good subject for a comic artist, for Sumner had been roundly punished in actuality, and Brooks, who overnight became a southern hero, was certainly not to be ridiculed. The one or two printed portraits of Brooks which date from about 1856 are straightforward hagiography and may have been published before the assault.

If in fact printed portraits of Brooks were in existence before the assault, copies were scarce enough in the North so that those graphic artists wishing actually to portray the key figures of the incident were at a loss for a likeness in his case, and this seems to have influenced the design of one print as we shall see. Likenesses of the other principals were all readily available in one printed form or another, and this was especially true for Sumner. From the start of his career in the Senate in 1851, wood engravings and lithographs adapted from daguerreotypes were everywhere available and had been put to good use by caricaturists. A prime example comes from 1852. In April of that year, William Lloyd Garrison was impatient with Sumner's failure after four and a half months in office to speak out boldly against the proslavery forces and inquired in the *Liberator* as to whether the good Senator had a backbone.[3] The Boston comic artist David Claypoole Johnston utilized this jibe as he satirized a constellation of Bay State politicians, and P. T. Barnum's baby contests as well, in his lithograph, *Massachusetts Baby Show.* Sumner is portrayed as the "Baby without a Backbone." For more than 30 years thereafter, Sumner remained a regular target of political cartoonists, except of course for the period embracing the assault and the long convalescence which followed.

The first of our series was certainly the best-known picture of the Brooks assault in its own time. It is a wood engraving by unknown hands after a drawing by an unknown artist and is titled *The Assault in the U.S. Senate Chamber on Senator Sumner.* It occupied most of the cover of *Frank Leslie's Illustrated Newspaper,* a weekly, in the number dated June 7, 1856, which actually was published on May 30.[4] Unlike the partisan story that accompanies it and unlike the other prints in our series, this print represents an attempt at objective reporting. The figures are relegated to the lower left quadrant with the result that the noble grandeur of the chamber itself, rather than the sullying behavior of its occupants, becomes the chief subject of the picture. There are good reasons for this. It was difficult in the heated aftermath of the assault to determine accurately the locations and movements of all those present, but it was not at all difficult to portray the setting with great accuracy. Any well-established pictorial printmaker would doubtless have had one or more views of the Senate Chamber on file, to be borrowed from as jobs required. Of those available, one of the most detailed was Thomas Doney's large engraving ca. 1848, *U.S. Senate Chamber.* But it is just as likely that *Leslie's* commissioned a special artist in Washington to produce its view.

The accuracy with which the great room and its allusions to Rome are depicted in the *Leslie's* wood engraving lends a sense of authenticity to the figures, though in fact they are too small for the scale of the chamber. There are no specific portraits, and the location of the key figures is faulty, for after freeing himself from his back row desk, Sumner actually got no farther than a few feet before collapsing under the continuing barrage of blows, never reaching the first row where he is shown here. But these inaccuracies, which would not have been apparent to any but a handful of the thousands who saw this print, do not diminish the general impression of objective documentation.

Leslie's Illustrated was rounding out its first six months of publication with this issue and had gained in that time a solid reputation for the rapid pictorial reporting of eyewitness accounts of disasters and other newsworthy events. This print is a typical example of what timeliness meant at midcentury. The assault occurred on a Thursday afternoon; a week and a day later *Leslie's* began distribution of its run of probably somewhere over 10,000 copies, each with this wood engraving dominating the cover page.[5] The printing, of course, was from metal electrotypes and not from the wood block itself.

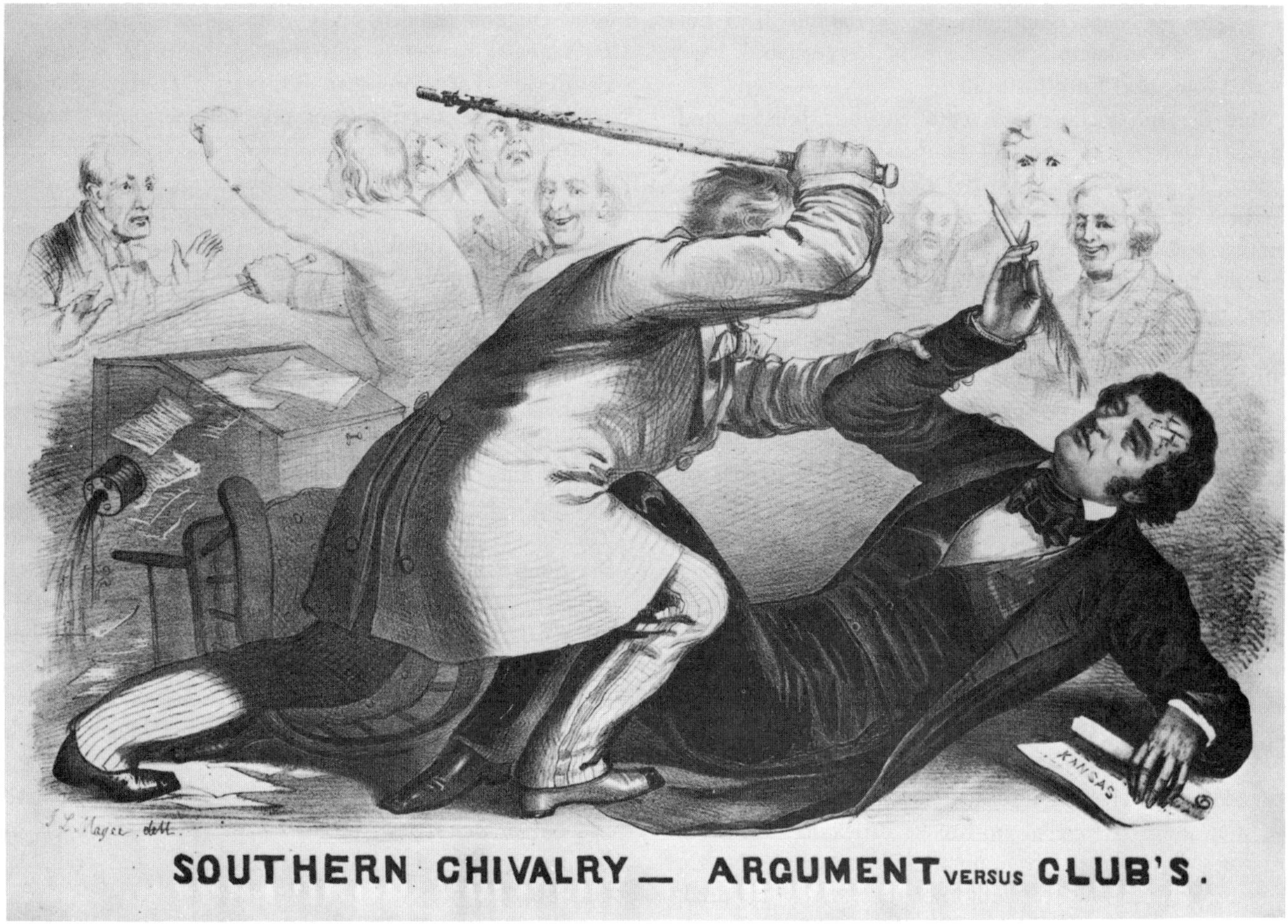

John L. Magee's lithograph of the caning. Courtesy Chicago Historical Society.

There is a long history of re-use of this print by photographic reproduction, though in most instances only the detail with the figures has been reproduced. This disregard for the integrity of the original design robs the print of one of its chief meanings; that the Senate as an institution, here exemplified by the great chamber, endures despite the imperfections of its members.[6]

To the modern viewer, perhaps the best-known representation of the assault is John L. Magee's lithograph, *Southern Chivalry—Argument versus Club's,* a caricature which has been reproduced in a number of popular histories of the era, and with good reason, for it is among the most dramatic and effective of American political cartoons. The main figures need no identification. The man shown brandishing a cane in the background is Congressman Lawrence Keitt of South Carolina, a friend of Brooks who accompanied him to the Senate to ward off anyone who attempted to come to Sumner's aid. Keitt had little enough to do in this regard since most of the dozen or so persons who observed all or part of the assault made no attempt to stop it. Indeed, some looked on approvingly, and the grisly irony of the nation's lawmakers grinning in amusement at the savage beating of a colleague did not escape Magee. In giving us Sumner overcome by Brooks, he gives us, in a larger sense, reason overcome by violent impulse, gentility overcome by ruffianism, and, indeed, all civilized values overwhelmed by brute barbarism. That constant and consistent thread of violence which has been so prominent in the fabric of our national life has, from time to time, found an artist willing to portray it. David Gilmour Blythe was certainly one such limner of the darker elements of our national character, and Magee, from the evidence of this print, was another. It is regretable that we know so little about Magee. In the 1840's he exhibited paintings at the National Academy and the American Art Union. The single oil I have seen is sufficient to prove that he was a very able professional painter, though what little attention he has received in the 20th century has been as a graphic artist.[7]

Brooks' face is hidden by his pummeling arm—this is Magee's solution to the lack of a proper likeness—but nothing is lost since the figure is as much a personification of uncontrolled rage as it is of Brooks. There is some very accomplished draftsmanship here, especially in Brooks' head and arm. Though we cannot see his face, the streaking hair, jutting chin, and tightly gripped paw of a hand tell us all we need to know of the emotions involved. In the general design, the sweep of the great

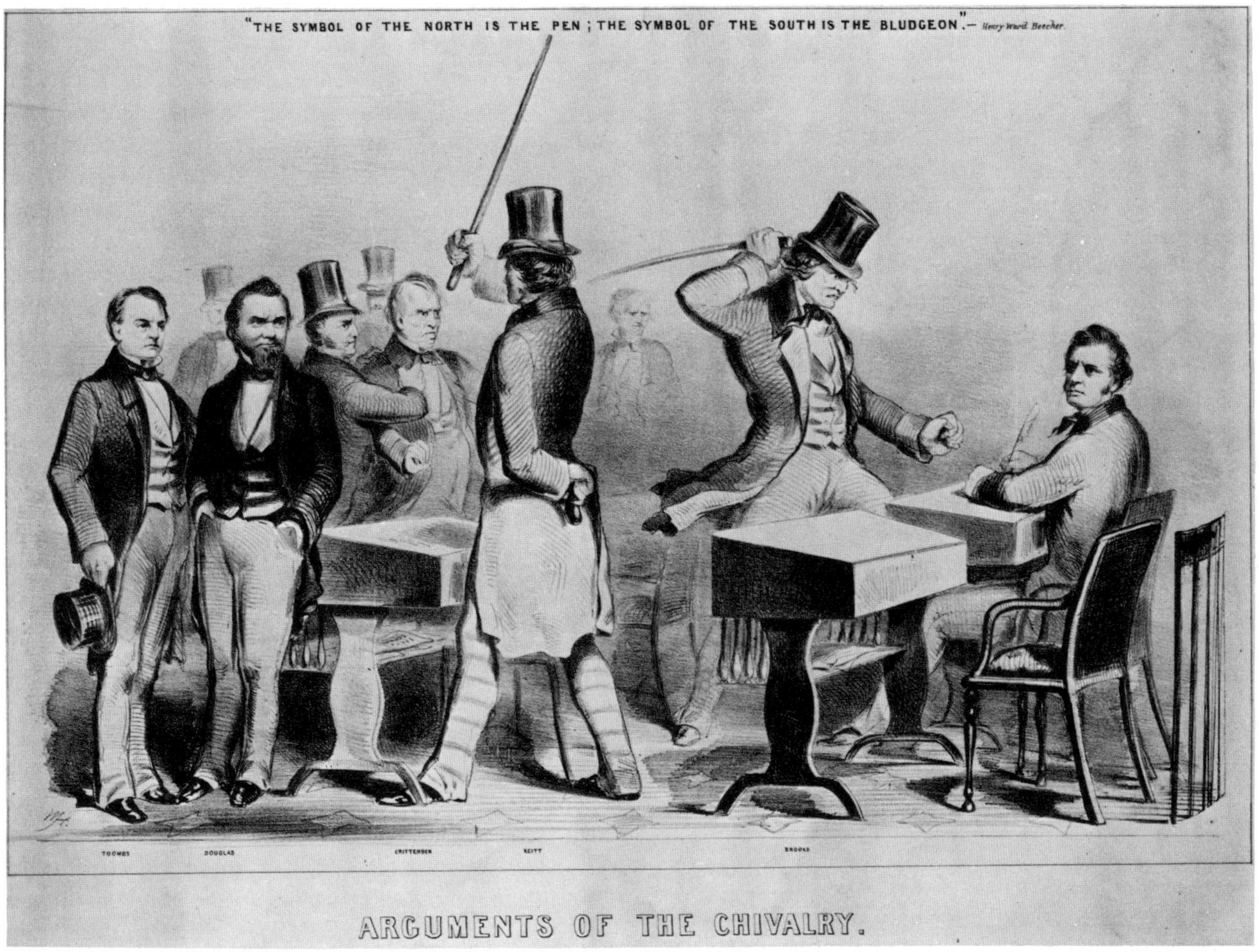

Winslow Homer's only political caricature, Arguments of Chivalry.

forms of the bodies, the purposeful exaggerations, and the animation of the lightly drawn frieze of background figures, we have the hand of a master illustrator. The print was advertised for sale at 12½ cents a copy.[8]

The word "chivalry," used here and in the title of the next print as well, is a sarcastic expression of the northern view which held that the elegant plantation manners and aristocratic courtliness of the southern gentleman veiled an intolerable hypocrisy. Delicate sensitivity about family honor must be a sham in any man who practices slavery, it was argued, for gentility and slavery are mutually repellent. As well, these scornful references to southern manners and codes of honor probably reflected some residue of old Puritan New England anti-aristocratic feeling. But it was Sumner himself who, in his speech on Kansas, bathed the word in sarcasm. Referring to Butler he said:

> The Senator from South Carolina has read many books of chivalry, and believes himself a chivalrous knight, with sentiments of honor and courage. Of course, he has chosen a mistress to whom he has made his vows, and who, though ugly to others, is always lovely to him; though polluted in the sight of the world, is chaste in his sight;—I mean the harlot, Slavery.[9]

And of course the northern press made much of the great gulf between Brooks' purported chivalrous motives and the actuality of his deed.

The least known caricature of the caning was, I suspect, the large folio lithograph *Arguments of the Chivalry* on stone by Winslow Homer. It is Homer's only political caricature and the rarest of all his lithographs. My census of most major American print collections persuades me that the only copy of record is at the Library of Congress. Until two years ago when Milton Kaplan uncovered and identified this impression, the print was unknown to Homer scholars.

The print is a product of Homer's apprenticeship to John H. Bufford, the Boston lithographer. Since Homer was probably executing a customer's commission, the political bias does not necessarily reflect his own views. In matters of design, on the other hand, there is probably a great deal original with Homer, for he seems to have taken pride in the completed drawing and signed it prominently with his initials on stone, lower left. The LC impression dates from after May 31, on which date Henry Ward Beecher, speaking at a Sumner rally at the Tabernacle in New York, declaimed the motto which tops the print: "The symbol of the North is the pen; the symbol of the South is the bludgeon." [10]

More than any of the other pictorial comments on

the assault, Homer's picture presents a narrative of the events, and he accomplishes this by telescoping time. At the right we have Sumner seated, so close to his desk that when he attempts to rise after the first blows have fallen, he rips the desk from the floor. In the center we have Brooks about to strike (his face is an imaginary portrait) and Keitt, seconds later, warning off those who would intercede. The two figures at the left, representing perhaps a still later point in time in the sense that they graphically portray the postassault opinions of each man, are Senator Toombs of Georgia, hat in hand, who was quoted as approving of the beating, and Douglas of Illinois, to whom we shall return shortly. In the background, showing a visage of concern, is the portly figure of Crittenden of Kentucky, the only Senator from a southern or border state to speak out against the assault. The naturalism of Homer's drawing gives a sense of reality not often found in caricature, and it is perhaps less expressive of the violent mood and acts of the occurrence than Magee's exaggeration.

The source for Homer's characterizations is certainly an item which appeared in a number of newspapers, including the *Liberator,* soon after the event. This item reports the comment of a Dr. Bunting of Montreal who claimed to have witnessed the assault from the Senate gallery and to have seen Keitt "holding a pistol behind him, partially under the flap of his coat . . . ," and Homer has included that detail. Bunting also claimed that, "During the attack, Senator Douglas stood within five feet of Mr. Sumner in a free and easy position, both hands in his pockets . . . and making no movement toward the assailant." [11] Homer has portrayed this as well. But Bunting was wrong in this instance because Douglas, in fact, was not present. It seems to me that this major inaccuracy in a print which verges on documentary realism may have resulted in a decision not to print or publish it, and this is one way to account for its rarity. If this rationale seems farfetched, consider that Bufford was not in the business of caricature publication and that the publisher was very possibly an abolitionist. Reflecting on the abolitionist mind with its determined sense of fair play and truthfulness, even in dealing with representatives of such loathsome policies as it was felt Douglas nurtured, encourages me to think that the LC impression is a trial proof and that the print was withheld from publication. There are other conjectures, of course, to account for its rarity but not a bit of evidence to bias any argument. Indeed, the argument I have presented is whittled down by the suggestion that Homer's characterization of Douglas fairly represents the man's attitude following the incident, if not his location during it. Douglas was conversing in a room adjacent to the Senate Chamber when he was notified that Brooks was beating Sumner. Later, in a statement widely printed, he commented that his "first idea was to come in and endeavor to restore quiet, but, upon reflection, he thought his motives in interposing might be misconstrued and so did not enter the Senate Chamber until the affray was over." [12] This attitude of deliberate inaction is just what Homer has drawn.

Homer was 20 in 1856, and his budding talents are amply evident. The draftsmanship and technique on stone are equal to the work of any other lithographic artist then active in Boston. The portraits are especially well done; he had become expert at copying likenesses during the previous year at Bufford's, and his skill in this art may have netted him this assignment.[13] Except for Brooks, the portraits here are adapted from printed sources, though it should be noted that in the cases of Crittenden and Douglas, Homer has invented emotional states. Stylistically, these hang between the exaggeration of caricature and the straightforward naturalism which was Homer's métier. Also worth noting is Homer's concern with authenticity in detail. The design of the desk (though not of the chair), the placement of the railing, and the star pattern of the carpet are all generally correct. Since there is no reason to think Homer had ever been to the Senate, it is likely that his details were adapted from such sources as the Doney engraving.

Our first three prints have shown the assault itself. A different sort of pictorial response was to punish Brooks, figuratively at least, an impulse strengthened no doubt by the reluctance of both houses of Congress to effect much more than token penalties (though in time Brooks was censured and resigned his seat, only to be re-elected to it). The lithograph *The Right Man in the Right Place* takes its title from the American party's presidential campaign slogan for the Know-Nothing candidate, ex-president Millard Fillmore. There is no imprint, but the lithograph was probably published in New York or Philadelphia. The artist is unknown.

As a flight of fancy, *The Right Man in the Right Place* does not rise much above the tree tops. Soaring far higher as imaginative inventions are two lithographs by Johnston which reflect with mordant wit on the aftermath of the caning. In *Indignation Meeting in Skunkdom—Great Excitement!* we have a meeting modeled after those which packed Faneuil Hall in Boston and the Tabernacle in New York with citizens expressing support for Sumner and contempt for Brooks. Here the meeting is of skunks, and Sumner himself has provided the imagery in his impromptu exchange with Douglas on the Senate floor immediately following the close of his speech on Kansas. Referring to Douglas he commented: "No person with the upright form of man can be allowed, without violation of all decency, to switch out from his tongue the perpetual stench of offensive personality. . . . The noisome, squat, and nameless animal, to which I now refer, is not a proper model for an American Senator."

Douglas answered that he would not model himself after Sumner.

Sumner thundered back, "Again the Senator has switched

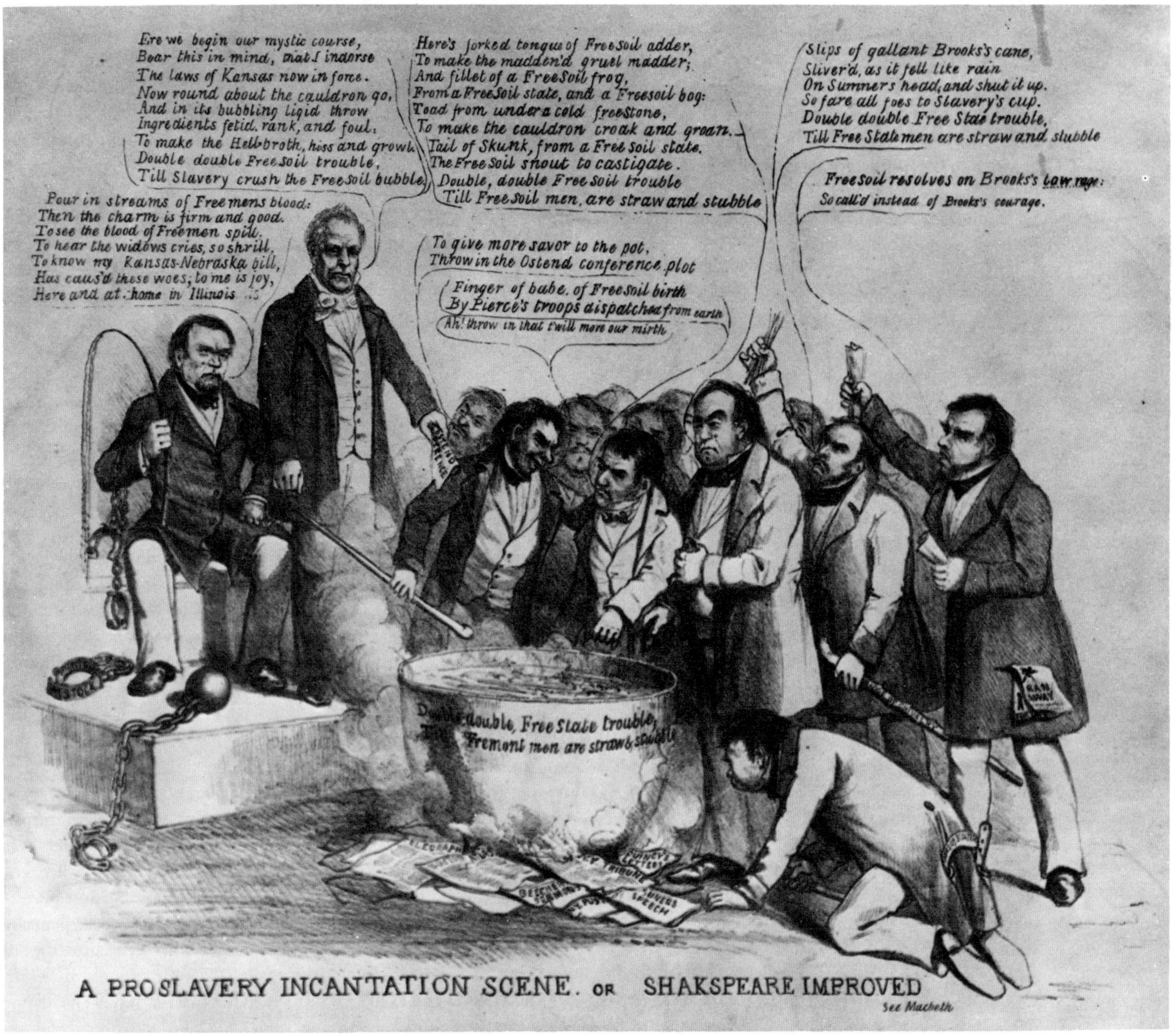

A cartoon by David Claypoole Johnston satirizing the Democratic Party convention which nominated James Buchanan for the presidency.

his tongue, and again he fills the Senate with its offensive odor."[14]

From this exchange, Johnston conjured an outraged skunkdom making endless resolutions—in the manner of the Sumner support meetings—including:

> Resolved that the Hon. Chas. Sumner in attempting to institute a comparison between an unsavory and venomous senator from Illinois and one of us, has thereby—unwittingly it may be—grievously wounded our feelings, and grossly libeled & insulted our whole race . . . it is the imperative duty of the Honl. senator to employ the earliest moments of his convalescence in framing . . . an apology . . . That in the interval . . . no skunk will be found so void of decency and self-respect, as to imitate either in action or language, the foul-mouthed ruffians of the national capitol. . . .

This is a typical example of Johnston's blend of comic writing and comic art.

The print is not signed. Johnston was well enough known to his contemporaries in Boston that during the final three of his four decades as a comic artist in Boston, he rarely signed his work, but most of it, including these prints, is easily identifiable by his drawing style, his phraseology, and his clever uses of literature. It is unfortunate that the misattribution of several lithographs to him—notably the *Old Soldier* portfolio which was suggested to be Johnston's work by William Murrell—has obscured the recognition of a singular and consistent graphic style which spanned four decades.[15]

The next print we see by Johnston concerns the results of the Democratic Party convention which met during the first week of June and nominated James Buchanan for the presidency. *Proslavery Incantation Scene. or Shakspeare Improved* is a political burlesque of the witches scene which opens the fourth act of *Macbeth.* The bubbling cauldron here is fired by, among other fuels, a copy of Sumner's speech. Presiding as the chief warlock is Buchanan, brewing trouble for free men, free soil, and Fremont. His right hand man is Douglas, portrayed by Johnston to be as unsavory as his skunks envisioned. The figure second from right holds a cane labeled "Badge of Chivalry" and raises high a handful of splinters while chanting this bit of Johnstonian doggerel:

Slips of gallant Brooks' cane,
Sliver'd, as it fell like rain
On Sumners head, and shut it up.
So fare all foes to Slavery's cup.

It is a basic rule of political caricature that a successful cartoon must patently be against more things than it is for, and Johnston's compendium of Democratic Party sins and failures greatly outweighs the tepid pro-Fremont sentiment of the print. Within this context, the assault on Sumner is simply one further proof of the inherent and pervading baseness of the party. Johnston's wholesale consignment of the Democrats to perdition was essentially on moral rather than political grounds. This was Sumner's view, and it was rapidly becoming a majority view in the North. We see it expressed pictorially, though with less imagination, in an unsigned lithograph, *Democratic Platform Illustrated,* published in Portland, Maine. The caning of Sumner is a prominent vignette set against a distant view of a sacked Lawrence, Kans. The attack on Lawrence occurred the day before Brooks' assault, and references to both incidents served to remind the viewer of the violence which had so recently served the causes of the Democratic platform. The Sumner vignette would seem to be an adaptation of Magee's design. A still smaller vignette of the assault, different from all others we have seen in that Brooks approaches from the rear in a sneak attack, is one of a jumble of images to be found in the unsigned lithograph *Buchaneer Pacification.*

Sumner does not emerge from these prints as a hero. The circumstances of the event provided no opportunity for heroics, for as we have seen, from the first blow Sumner was stunned. Then too, despite his very great abilities and accomplishments, he had few of the personal qualities which seemed necessary in some combination for apotheosis to popular heroism in mid-19th-century America. Though he was handsome and had no superiors in morality (as he would not hesitate to affirm), he had none of the folksiness so admired in American politics. He was respected more than he was liked, and many who were friendly to him thought him cold and too often imperious, humorless, and deficient in the arts of small talk and other means of relaxing and reassuring one's acquaintances. Committed to principles rather than practical programs and policies, he saw compromise as a failure of principle and views opposed to his own as intolerable. It is not surprising that he regularly offended other Senators. He was often enough an embarrassment to the fledgling Republicans, so that we can wonder if a few of his party colleagues might not have thought it typically disagreeable of the man not to die from the caning when he had the perfect opportunity to further his own and the party's causes by doing so. Indeed, the circumstances of the assault were far more propitious to martyrdom than heroism.

But Sumner failed even to satisfy the ultimate requisite of martyrdom. He didn't die. And when it became clear about a week after the assault that he would recover, he was left more to be pitied than hallowed and was, in that state, worth little attention from caricaturists. He received none. There were, to be sure, a flurry of lithographed portraits published, but these were commercial props for acts of personal homage and had nothing to do with the narrative and imaginative tasks of reportorial and comic artists.[16]

Sumner was convalescent for three and a half years. During that time Brooks and Butler died, and the nation moved inexorably toward war. With the close of the war and the triumph of his causes, Sumner could honorably have continued on in the Senate as a mellowed elder statesman, full of years, honors, and seniority. Instead, and characteristically, he embroiled himself in the new issues of Reconstruction, inflexible as ever in pursuit of principle. He became a prime target for satiric treatment at the hands of a new generation of comic artists. When the most talented of these, Thomas Nast, turned against the Liberal Republicans in 1872, Sumner was cruelly ridiculed week after week in *Harper's Weekly.* After a four-hour tirade in the Senate against President Grant, Sumner was portrayed by Nast as a paunchy warrior in classic garb, launching arrows of malice toward the president so ineffectually that the figure of Truth needs not even lift her shield to protect him. The happy incongruity of antique tunic, medieval crossbow and redesigned White House makes *The Last Shot of the Honorable Senator from Massachusetts, or He Pulled the Long Bow Once Too Often* rather more humorous than most of Nast's caricatures of Sumner. George William Curtis, publisher of *Harper's,* pleaded with Nast to spare his old friend, but Nast persisted, culminating his attack in the issue of August 17, 1872, with a cartoon which resurrected the Brooks incident of 16 years earlier.[17] Taunting Sumner's efforts to heal some of the wounds of war and reconstruction, the wood engraving *Will the Senator from Massachusetts Do This, To Make His Words Good?* has Sumner kneeling "in memory of Bully Brooks" as he places a lock of his hair on the grave of his old assailant. And so in his final, bitter years, Sumner took a beating from Nast's pen in some ways more damaging and painful than that he had received from Brooks' cane.

But to return to the eight prints which are our chief

interest, I offer three observations by way of a brief conclusion.

First, it seems to me that we do not have a group of pictures which adds any significant degree of new understanding of Sumner himself. The sum of our knowledge of this very complex and crucially important man has not been augmented in any important way. The same applies to Douglas.

Second, we do have a group of pictures each of which helps our understanding of the public reaction to the caning. A variety of aspects of northern feeling are reflected. I use the word "reflect" cautiously because it is often too limiting a description of the value of popular art to scholarship, as though popular art were no more than a mirrored globe, ever turning in the dance hall of history, casting an array of uneven flashes of occasionally brilliant insight, but basically worth little except as colorful decoration. Certainly some popular art is worth more.

And so third, we do have a group of pictures some of which I suggest have intrinsic merit as works of art. I refer particularly to the Magee, Homer, and Johnston cartoons. Because these are caricatures, and it is difficult to articulate their merits beyond the immediate responses of laughter, delight, and wonder, we necessarily fall back on historical fact and treat these and other cartoons as reflections of attitudes toward the fact. They are that, of course, but the best caricatures "work" even when the specifics they satirize are unknown. Since the critical apparatus of the fine arts does not serve comic art well, the standards of connoisseurship we apply to fine prints fail us with these, and other measures will need to be found.

NOTES

[1] Except where otherwise noted, my references to Sumner and his career are drawn from David Donald's biography in two volumes, *Charles Sumner and the Coming of the Civil War* (New York: Alfred A. Knopf, 1960) and *Charles Sumner and the Rights of Man* (New York: Alfred A. Knopf, 1970). The circumstances of the assault are described on pp. 278–97 of the earlier volume.

[2] On Nov. 27, 1809, Representative I. A. Coles struck Representative Roger Nelson. On April 17, 1850, Senators Benton and Foote had an altercation. I am indebted to Mrs. Florian H. Thayn, art and reference librarian of the office of the Architect of the Capitol, for information about these incidents and about the furnishings of the Senate in 1856 as well. A good summary of the Houston-Stanbery encounter appears in Marquis James, *The Raven* (Indianapolis: Bobbs-Merrill, 1929), pp. 162–72.

[3] *Liberator,* April 23, 1852, p. 66.

[4] The actual publication date of each issue of FLIN was a week earlier than the date shown; in New York City, publication occurred a day earlier yet. FLIN June 7, 1856, p. 408.

[5] The letterpress portions of FLIN were as timely as the day of publication; for example, the issue actually published in New York on May 30, 1856, reported Sumner's medical condition as of that day. Pictorial matter took longer to ready for the press, but I cannot say how much time was required from receipt of a drawing to the printing of the cut made from it except to observe that in its first year (1855–56) FLIN published no picture of a news event which was less than a week old. There are no circulation figures for FLIN for 1856, but two years later the paper claimed a run of over 100,000 copies each week. This was noted as a great improvement over the early months of 1856 when the paper almost failed. Frank Luther Mott, *A History of American Magazines,* vol. 2, 1850–1865 (Cambridge, Mass.: Harvard University Press, 1938), p. 454. Ten thousand copies seems to me to be a reasonable minimum run for an American pictorial weekly, but a closer estimate of how many copies of the June 7 issue were actually printed is anyone's guess.

[6] For an early instance of the use of the detail see C. Edwards Lester, *Life and Public Services of Charles Sumner* (New York: United States Publishing Co., 1874), plate facing p. 248. I am indebted to Mr. James Ketchum, curator of the Senate Commission on Art and Antiquities, for the opportunity to examine the old Senate Chamber (Room S–228) in the Capitol.

[7] *Reading of an Official Dispatch (Mexican War News).* repro. *The American Scene,* exhibition catalog, (New York: Hirschl and Adler, 1969), p. 51.

[8] *Liberator,* June 6, 1856, p. 91.

[9] Charles Sumner, *The Crime Against Kansas,* (Washington: Buell & Blanchard, 1856), p. 5.

[10] *The New York Tribune,* May 31, 1856, p. 8.

[11] *Liberator,* June 6, 1856, p. 91. For another report that Douglas was present see *Boston Courier,* May 24, 1856, which quotes a *New York Tribune* correspondent.

[12] *Boston Transcript,* May 28, 1856.

[13] Homer's best known work as a portrait copyist is *Massachusetts Senate 1856,* repro. Lloyd Goodrich, *The Graphic Art of Winslow Homer* (New York: Museum of Graphic Art, 1968), pl. 3. This large folio lithograph, which contains 42 separate likenesses, may however date from after *Arguments.* Earlier lithographic portraits by Homer include more than a dozen published in the various genealogical publications of Abner Morse in Boston in 1855. These are discussed in my *Winslow Homer in Boston,* forthcoming.

[14] Donald (1960), pp. 287–88.

[15] William Murrell, *A History of American Graphic Humor,* vol. 1 (New York: Whitney Museum of American Art, 1933), p. 188. The most comprehensive listing of Johnston's separately published prints is Malcolm Johnson, *David Claypool Johnston, American Graphic Humorist* (Lunenburg, Vt.: Printed at the Stinehour Press, 1970).

[16] The *Boston Advertiser* for May 30, 1856, reported that C. H. Brainard, a print publisher, being unable to keep up with the demand for Sumner portraits, had a new print in preparation, on stone by the Boston lithographic artist Leopold Grozelier, copied from a Southworth and Hawes daguerreotype. An impression is in the collections of the American Antiquarian Society.

[17] Albert B. Paine, *Th. Nast* (New York: Harper, 1904), pp. 241–44.

Nancy R. Davison was assistant to the Keeper of Prints at the Boston Public Library and has worked with the print and sheet music collections at the William L. Clement Library, Ann Arbor, Mich. Her article about early American sheet music was published in Prints in and of America to 1850. *She has exhibited her own etchings and woodcuts.*

Andrew Jackson in Cartoon and Caricature

Nancy R. Davison

Andrew Jackson, thanks to an expanding country, a new printing process, and his own colorful and controversial nature, received unprecedented attention from the political cartoonists of his day. This pictorial commentary was often unfriendly and frequently crude in inspiration and execution, but it marked the first major flowering of American political caricature.

One of the earliest cartoon references to Andrew Jackson appears in William Charles' etching of 1815, *John Bull Before New Orleans,* in which an American and a Frenchman pull a wigless, bedraggled John Bull out of a swamp by his ears. "Come along you old rascal," says the American, "you did not know the brave Americans and their old Hickory." [1] This refers, of course, to Jackson's victory over the British in the Battle of New Orleans.

Few political cartoons were produced in America during this period. English engraved caricatures had been popular before and during the Revolution, and after the war a few men such as Charles and Amos Doolittle produced, etched, and engraved cartoons in America. It was not until after the successful establishment of lithography in the United States in the mid-1820's that American political caricatures became numerous.

Jackson's next appearance in popular caricature came during his first campaign for the presidency in 1824. D. C. Johnston's etching, *A Foot-Race,* shows John Quincy Adams nosing out William Crawford, while a tall, thin Jackson runs a close third. Henry Clay, a distant fourth, has dropped out of the race. The stakes—The White House and the Presidential Chair—are seen in the background, and the spectators' voice balloons are filled with innocuous and dubious puns. Jackson had the most popular votes, but the electoral votes were split among the four candidates. Adams, with Clay's support, won the election in the House of Representatives. General Jackson and his backers immediately charged Adams and Clay, who became secretary of state, with a "corrupt bargain."

This accusation struck a bitter note for the election of 1828 when Jackson was elected President. Pictorial propaganda was used by the supporters of the two candidates, as well as slanderous newspaper articles. John Binns, a pro-Adams editor, published the "coffin handbills"—broadsides with six coffins printed at the top, one for each of six volunteer soldiers who were shot for desertion in Florida when they attempted to return to their homes.

They believed that their terms of service had expired, but the War of 1812 was not yet over. Jackson offered no leniency when the case was brought to his attention. The Adams men depicted him as a violent "military chieftain" who was unfit to govern and who had done vile deeds as governor of Florida. The Jackson forces responded in print by accusing the staid John Quincy Adams of having procured an American girl for the Czar while he was minister to Russia,[2] and in a caricature *The Pedlar and his Pack . . .* Binns, whose coffin handbills had boomeranged in Jackson's favor, is shown staggering under the combined weight of several coffins, the Presidential Chair, Henry Clay, and Adams.

A New Map of the United States with the Additional Territories . . ., which is generally accepted as the first lithographed cartoon in America,[3] portrays the contest as a tug-of-war between Jackson's western alligator and Adams' eastern tortoise. The two are tied tail to tail and stretch across a map of the United States. The tortoise, who first appears in American caricature as the *Ograbme or American Snapping Turtle* in honor of the Embargo of 1807, here represents Adams. In 1836, however, the tortoise appears with Jackson's head as it slides into a "Pool of Corruption."

Jackson's first Cabinet was politically and socially unstable. Several of its members were more loyal to John C. Calhoun, the Vice President, than to the President. The immediate and obvious problem, however, was Margaret O'Neale Timberlake Eaton, the new wife of Jackson's good friend and secretary of war, John Eaton. Mrs. Eaton had had a rather strange marital career for a Cabinet lady, and the other wives, led by Mrs. Calhoun, snubbed her. No amount of pressure and pleading by the President could budge the ladies. Finally Martin Van Buren, a widower, suggested that he resign as secretary of state, clearing the way for a full Cabinet shake-up. Jackson accepted, and the Cabinet resigned. This affair was the subject of considerable pictorial comment. At least a dozen different cartoons and their variants were printed. The best-known, E. W. Clay's lithograph of 1831, *The Rats Leaving a Falling House,* was widely distributed and copied. Jackson, with his glasses pushed up on his forehead, sits bemused in a collapsing chair, while the Altar of Reform topples over beside him. Three rats with the faces of Cabinet members scamper away, but the fourth, Martin Van Buren, is restrained by Jackson's foot, which is clamped firmly on his tail. This use of animals with human faces was common at least up until the Civil War. John Quincy Adams describes the caricature in his diary entry for April 25, 1831, and comments upon its sale.

> Two thousand copies of this print have been sold in Philadelphia this day. Ten thousand copies were struck off, and will all be disposed of within a fortnight. This is an indication of the estimation in which Jackson and his Administration are held.[4]

The Exhibition of Cabinet Pictures, an 1831 etching by D. C. Johnston, summarizes the problems of the administration during the early 1830's. It contains references to broken Indian treaties, nullification, the Bank of the United States controversy, the Democrats' new newspaper the *Globe,* and the "Eaton Malaria." One of the center pictures shows a lion attacking a jackass. The Democratic donkey may well date from this period. It is also curious that Jackson's opposition is represented by an elephant in an 1833 cartoon called *Congressional Elephant or Last Desperate Pull for Power.* The *Cabinet Pictures* caricature requires a great deal of study if one is to catch all of the references. For example, Jackson is tripping over Peggy Eaton's petticoat in a picture at the lower right. Many 19th-century cartoons were meant to be read and digested rather than seen and recognized.

A Political Game of Brag. or the Best Hand Out of Four is one of many caricatures printed for the election of 1832. This cartoon shows the three official candidates and Calhoun playing a form of poker with cards that describe each player's platform. Jackson's cards read "Corruption, Imbecility, Intrigue," and Calhoun holds nullification and antitariff cards. Clay has just laid down a hand of internal improvements, domestic manufactures, and U.S. Bank. William Wirt holds only anti-masonic cards. The portraits are excellent as are many portraits in 19th-century caricature. Only Jackson is ridiculed at all, and the point of the cartoon is contained in his cards. This theme, the poker game, was repeated with some of the same players in 1848.

The election itself was overshadowed, at least in the cartoons, by Jackson's battle with Nicholas Biddle's Second Bank of the United States. Jackson had expressed his doubts about the constitutionality of the bank in his annual message to Congress in 1829, and his distrust of banks was well known. When Clay and Biddle sought to embarrass him in an election year by applying for a premature renewal of the bank's charter, the President vetoed the charter renewal and convinced the electorate that he had done a just and democratic thing. Although the bank and its stabilizing influence on the economy could have been saved by compromise, both Jackson and Biddle were stubborn, arrogant men who preferred confrontation. Feelings ran high on the issue, and the Bank War was a popular subject with caricaturists during the early 1830's.

Set To Between Old Hickory and Bully Nick, although copyrighted in 1834 after the bank had been destroyed, shows Jackson and Biddle squaring off for a fight. Van Buren and Major Jack Downing back the President, while Long Harry Clay and Black Dan Webster second Biddle. A woodsman called Tammany holds a bottle for Jackson. A fat, richly dressed Mother Bank holds a bottle of port for Biddle. The same well-fed figure is shown vomiting government deposits from her sickbed in an 1833 caricature.

One of the funnier Jackson cartoons is *Let Everyone*

Take Care of Himself (as the Jackass said when he was Dancing among the Chickens.) The jackass is, of course, Jackson. He is characterized not only by his appearance but by his speech as well. "This is a capital Experiment," he says gleefully, "By the Eternal." Biddle is a frantic hen running after her Branch Bank chicks; Van Buren, the fox, and Major Downing, a cock, look on. Francis P. Blair, editor of the *Globe,* is shown as a hog who says "I feel quite at home on this Dung heap." This lithograph was published and for sale at Imbert's caricature shop about 1833.

Jackson's own words and expressions were often used in caricatures. Such phrases as "By the Eternal," "I take the responsibility," and frequent references to hanging people and the veto often identify Jackson even in poorly drawn works. At one point he referred to the bank as a "hydra of corruption." [5] A short time later the hydra appeared as a personification of the bank in several cartoons.

The Downfall of Mother Bank. Draw'd off from Natur by Zek Downing. Neffue to Major Jack Downing celebrates the removal of government monies from the Bank of the United States in 1833 and is quite favorable to Jackson. Biddle, distinguished by a devil's head, and Webster and Clay are caught amidst the falling columns of the bank, while Jackson watches and the Major cheers. There were many cartoons "draw'd off from Natur by Zek Downing." Zek in this lithograph is E. W. Clay, but most Zeks are anonymous and the draftsmanship varies greatly in quality.

Major Jack Downing, the Down East creation of Seba Smith, a Maine newspaperman, made his first appearance in 1830. This "hoss-sense" character or backwoods philosopher wrote letters to the newspapers concerning the doings of "Jinral" Jackson during the '30's. A popular and much plagiarized character, he appears in several of the Jackson caricatures either alone or with his "Neffue" Zek.

An English nursery rhyme serves as the basis for another bank cartoon in 1834. *This is the House that Jack Built,* which also appears in English political caricature, deals with the removal of the deposits and the Senate's reaction. The very end of the sequence sees Jackson as the dog that worried the cat (W. J. Duane, a noncompliant and soon ousted secretary of the treasury) that caught the rat (Amos Kendall and the Kitchen Cabinet) that ate the malt (government deposits) that laid in the house that Jack built (the Bank of the United States.)

Uncle Sam Sick with la Grippe deals with the currency and monetary problems of the country after the destruction of the bank. An ailing Uncle Sam in a star-spangled dressing gown is being tended by Doctor Jackson who is dressed in very fine, if old-fashioned, clothes. He is assisted by a nurse, Aunt Matty Van Buren, and by Apothecary (Thomas Hart) Benton who prescribes his famous mint drops or hard money policy. On the left is a broken bust of Washington. To the right Brother Jonathan pleads with Nicholas Biddle to relieve Uncle Sam's illness. Murrell notes that it "is the only cartoon so far discovered in which both Uncle Sam and Brother Jonathan are presented at the same time." [6]

The nullification crisis of 1832–33, serious as it was, seems to have drawn little pictorial comment. One exception, a cartoon entitled *Despotism* shows John C. Calhoun mounting the steps of treason and disunion to grasp the crown of despotism.

Boston and the North approved of Jackson's firm resolution of the nullification problem, and in 1833 Jackson made a pleasant tour of the Northeast. Commodore Jesse D. Elliott, Commandant of the Boston Navy Yard and an ardent Jackson supporter, proposed that a figurehead of Old Hickory be carved and mounted on the U.S.S. *Constitution,* which was then undergoing repairs. The Navy Department agreed, and the figurehead was being carved when Jackson ordered the removal of the deposits from the Bank of the U.S. and its branches. Proper Bostonians were outraged, and opposition to the figurehead grew. Commodore Elliott decided that he would not back down in the face of threats. The figurehead was completed and mounted on Old Ironsides. One dark night in early July 1834, however, someone sawed off the head of the Jackson figurehead. It was never found, although stories of its mysterious appearance in strange and wonderful places were told for years.[7] A cartoon, *Fixing a Blockhead to the Constitution . . .* shows the carving, intact but with a covered face, being hauled into place. A drummer berates a fifer in the lower right corner saying ". . . . didn't I tell you to play Hail Columbia and you've struck up the rogue's march."

One of the simplest, most effective caricatures of the era, to modern eyes at least, is D. C. Johnston's *Symptoms of a Locked Jaw,* which shows Henry Clay smugly sewing Andrew Jackson's mouth shut. The occasion was Jackson's attempt in 1834 to publish a protest in the *Senate Journal* concerning the Senate's resolution of censure against him for the removal of the deposits. Clay blocked publication of the protest.

Most caricatures of this period were issued anonymously. Often not even the publisher is known. H. R. Robinson, E. W. Clay, and D. C. Johnston are the best-known caricaturists of the era. Very little is known of Robinson, however, other than that he was active as a caricaturist, lithographer, and print publisher in New York from 1836 to 1851. Edward Williams Clay, who was admitted to the Philadelphia bar in 1825, became an artist instead. He was already well known for his pictorial satire when he moved to New York in 1837, where he did work for Robinson and other print publishers. Later he went to Europe to study art, but because his eyes eventually failed, he finished his career as a minor public official in Delaware.[8] D. C. Johnston's increasingly well-documented career as a satirical engraver, lithographer, and comic illustrator centered around Boston and covered the years from 1825 to the Civil War. The bias of most caricatures is definitely against Andrew Jackson, and it would be interesting to know more about the people who drew and distributed these prints and to know also how widespread and representative these opinions were.

The cartoonist represented Jackson in several ways. He often appears as a soldier, particularly in the early months of his presidency, during the second Seminole War in 1835, and during the dispute with the French. *King Andrew the First,* a lithograph of about 1832, represents him as a crowned tyrant trampling the Constitution. Jackson made bold use of executive power, and he contrasted sharply with his predecessors. He is sometimes compared to Napoleon, both favorably and unfavorably, in caricature. Jackson is shown also as a doctor, a pugilist, a jackass, and an old woman. His clothes and the general figure as President seem to have been taken from one of Ralph Earl's full-length portraits of Jackson. The painting shows him wearing a large, white beaver hat, steel spectacles, a full-skirted coat, and carrying a cane. In caricatures he sometimes carries a long-stemmed churchwarden pipe. In later cartoons, such as E. W. Clay's *The Times,* the big white hat and the glasses alone are used as a symbol of Jackson's presence.

There are many literary references in these cartoons. Martin Van Buren plays Sancho Panza to Jackson's Don Quixote in an 1834 etching entitled *Illustrations of the Adventures and Achievements of the Renowned Don Quixote and His Doughty Squire Sancho Panza.* D. C. Johnston, borrowing from both his early theatrical background and possibly from a current caricature of Napoleon, drew a vicious portrait of Jackson ca. 1830 entitled *Richard III.* His face is composed of nude figures, as are his epaulettes, and a cannon forms his uniform collar. This representation of a murderous military chieftain is captioned with a quotation from Shakespeare's *Richard III,* Act 5, Scene 3, "Me thought the souls of all that I had murder'd came to my tent." In 1832 Jackson again appears as Richard in Act 4, Scene 4 in the confrontation between the king and the two women who name his victims. In the caricature the women are Justice and Liberty, and they ask after "Public Confidence, Honor, Reputation [and] Credit."

On most issues and incidents the cartoons were unfavorable to the President. The exception, however, was the French spoilation payments problem. In 1834 Jackson, angered by French procrastination, demanded payment of the 25 million francs that France owed the U.S. for damage done to American property during the Napoleonic Wars. The French responded indignantly, but finally English mediation, as shown in *Apology. Mediation. Satisfaction,* eased the threat of war, and payments were begun in 1836. The cartoon shows William of England in his regal robes trying to mediate between Jackson who wants to fight and Louis Philippe who wants a seven percent discount for paying cash. American thinking on these events is summed up in the title of the lithograph *"The Debilitated Situation of Monarchal Government . . . (vs.) the Flourishing Condition of a Well-Formed Industrious Republic.* A French caricature on the issue appeared in *Charivari,* May 21, 1835. It shows Jackson calmly leaning on his sword, watching Louis Philippe count out coins on a table. In the background magistrates and other officials are taking money from ordinary people. The title is "Qui Paye ses dettes s'enrichit." [9] In *A Hickory Apology,* Jackson backed by Neptune challenges Louis Philippe to a bare-knuckle "set to."

In 1835 Jackson declined to run for a third term and Vice President Martin Van Buren became the Democratic candidate. William Henry Harrison was the major Whig candidate, although from cartoon evidence he appears to have been running against Jackson as well as Van Buren. In the *Set-to Between the Champion Old Tip and the Swell Dutchman of Kinderhook* the antagonists square off in the manner of Jackson and Biddle in an earlier fight. A "Western Lad" and a Revolutionary War veteran who resembles Washington back Harrison. Jackson encourages Van Buren. Van Buren apparently needs the encouragement for he says, "Stand by me Old Hickory or I'm a gone Chicken." Van Buren's bottle holder, Amos Kendall, has tapped the bottle and makes reference to the surplus treasury funds that were distributed to the states in 1836. Jackson also supports Van Buren in several races and games of cards and pool in later cartoons.

Van Buren took office just in time to inherit the Panic of 1837, a severe economic depression that was due in part to Jackson's destruction of the Second Bank. After most banks suspended specie payments in 1837, various concerns printed paper money in small denominations to be used to make change. These "shinplasters" had their comic counterparts in D. C. Johnston's *Locofoco Shinplaster* and a note issued by H. R. Robinson, which promised to pay the "bearer Fifty Cents in Counterfeit Caricatures at my store. . . . " [10] These bogus bills usually ridiculed Jackson, Van Buren, and Thomas Hart Benton.

The presidential campaign of 1840 was a propaganda battle of unprecedented proportions. William Henry Harrison was finally turned into a true candidate by using many of the devices and appeals that had elected Jackson in 1828 and 1832. Van Buren was castigated for high living and aristocratic ways, and "Old Tippecanoe," the log cabin candidate, was praised for his republican virtue. Van Buren was forced to share the responsibility for hard times with Jackson. In *The Illustrious Footsteps* he is being led away from the White House by a jackass with Jackson's face. The jackass, in turn, is being led by the Devil, who not only wears a frock coat and top hat but plays the fiddle as well. Another caricature *The Salt River Invincibles* shows Van Buren, Blair, Benton, Amos Kendall, and other Democratic stalwarts sitting unhappily on a fallen hickory tree by the shores of Salt River, a ubiquitous symbol for political defeat. The Old Hero's white hat hangs in a nearby tree, and Blair poignantly parodies Psalm 50 from the Ainsworth Psalter. "By the waters of Salt river there we sat down, yea we wept when we remembered our salaries! "

The Whigs won the election handily, but the candidate, plagued by officeseekers, died, and Tyler was not popular as President. Jackson backed James K. Polk, also known as "Young Hickory," for the presidency in 1844. In the *Political Climbing Boys* the quadrenniel candidate Henry Clay and Polk are shown climbing poles. Clay is ahead and climbing easily. Polk is being assisted from below by Jackson and Thomas Hart Benton. The latter "polks" him with a mop to prevent the candidate from sliding down the pole altogether. This mop, incidentally, is the one that Benson used to expunge the resolution of censure against Jackson from the Senate records.

Although Jackson died in 1845, he continued to appear sporadically in caricature until the Civil War. He had been a strong President for better or for worse, and this strength was referred to in *Little Bo-Peep and her Foolish Sheep,* a wood engraving of 1861. Columbia's sheep, the Southern states, are running off into the woods where the European wolves wait. The sheep dogs are no help. "Old Buck" Buchanan runs away with his tail between his legs, and "Hickory" is dead. The cartoon wistfully observes that Jackson might have been able to save the Union.

Several themes are conspicuous by their absence in Jacksonian caricature. Jackson's wife Rachel, a much slandered and vigorously defended lady who died a few weeks before Jackson's first inauguration, is not mentioned. The important tariff question and Indian removal are referred to only in passing, and there is no pictorial comment on the assassination attempt against Jackson in 1835. Seba Smith's Major Jack Downing wrote a lengthy description of the ceremonies in which the President received an honorary regree at Harvard, but no print commemorates the event. Few prints mention slavery, although that issue was ever present.

The Kitchen Cabinet and the spoils system, terms synonymous with Jackson's presidency, were caricatured, however. The Kitchen Cabinet was a name given to an informal, unofficial group of friends and advisors that surrounded Jackson. At least four caricatures mention the Kitchen Cabinet by name, primarily in connection with the removal of the deposits. *Office Hunters for the Year 1834,* one of the best-known Jacksonian cartoons, depicts Jackson as a half-naked demon, complete with wings and tail, hovering over a crowd of officeseekers. He dangles honors, offices, and other spoils on strings just out of reach of the eager and greedy crowd below. Weitenkampf and Nevins note that the cartoon "was possibly inspired by E. LePoitevin's lithographs, 'Diableries,' which had a great vogue in this period; and perhaps the artist had seen the lithograph of Satan floating in the air which Eugene Delacroix had drawn for Goethe's *Faust.*" [11]

The coincidence of Andrew Jackson's controversial presidency and the introduction of lithography to America was a fruitful one. Single-sheet, lithographed caricatures were popular in the United States from Jackson's time until after the Civil War when they were displaced by the cartoons in the new weekly magazines. These lithographed cartoons were often crude and uninspired, especially compared to the sophisticated caricatures of Daumier and other Europeans, but they were often lively and always interesting. This small but representative selection of caricatures of Andrew Jackson illustrates many of the interests and opinions of Americans during the Jacksonian era. These cartoons represent the first bloom of a vigorous American tradition of political caricature.

NOTES

[1] William Murrell, *A History of American Graphic Humor* vol. 1, (New York: Cooper Square Publishers, Inc., 1967 [© 1933]), #83.

[2] John A. Garraty, *The American Nation: a History of the United States to 1877,* 2d ed. (New York: Harper & Row, American Heritage Publishing Co., Inc., 1971), p. 310.

[3] Murrell, p. 110.

[4] *The Diary of John Quincy Adams,* ed. Allan Nevins (New York: Charles Scribner's Sons, 1951), p. 419.

[5] Garraty, p. 326.

[6] Murrell, p. 133.

[7] John William Ward, *Andrew Jackson: Symbol for An Age* (New York: Oxford University Press, 1962), pp. 115–119.

[8] George C. Groce and David H. Wallace, *The New York Historical Society's Dictionary of Artists in America 1564–1860* (New Haven & London: Yale University Press, 1957).

[9] "Who pays his debts enriches himself."

[10] Frank Weitenkampf, *Political Caricature in the United States in Separately Published Cartoons. An Annotated List . . .* (New York: The New York Public Library, 1953), p. 50.

[11] Allan Nevins and Frank Weitenkampf, *A Century of Political Cartoons: Caricature in the United States from 1800 to 1900* (New York: Charles Scribner's Sons, 1944), p. 42.

Frank H. Sommer III is the Head of Libraries at the Francis du Pont Winterthur Museum, an adjunct professor at the University of Delaware, and the librarian of the Waldron Phoenix Belknap, Jr., Research Library of American Painting. He has written many articles about early American art and the Winthergthur collections and is the coauthor of two books on archeology.

Prints As Documents of Early American History

Frank H. Sommer III

Introduction

Dr. Edgar Breitenbach on December 13, 1971, wrote a letter in which he suggested that the speakers at the print conference sponsored by his division at the Library of Congress address themselves to the question of the ways in which the print could be used as historical source material "and to what extent the evidence of the graphic arts reveals important insights into the social life, politics, and topography of the American Colonies and the early United States." I propose to outline my own efforts to use prints as historical source material.

The vast majority of the prints I shall discuss belong to Winterthur and are available for study by the participants in the print conference. Before proceeding to the body of my talk, I should like, in the interest of the sociology of knowledge, to tell you that I am an archeologist by training, and I am a book collector both by avocation and as a librarian. Most of the prints which I shall discuss, I myself have collected, and I have collected them for reasons which I trust will be more apparent as this paper develops.

Twenty years ago, in October 1951, it was decided to establish in connection with the Winterthur Museum a program on the graduate level for the study of the arts of early America. I was then a 28-year-old instructor at the University of Delaware with recently acquired degrees from Yale and Cambridge Universities. At the latter I had studied both prehistoric British archeology and the archeology of Roman Britain. The curator of the museum was the late Joseph Downs. The secretary was Charles F. Montgomery. The founder of the museum was Mr. Henry Francis du Pont. Mr. Montgomery approached the president of the University of Delaware, then John Alanson Perkins, to discuss the possibility of starting this formal program of graduate studies. Since I had been teaching an extension course at the old Wilmington High School attended by the Montgomerys and quite a few guides at the museum, President Perkins asked me to draw up a proposal for submission to a foundation to finance such a graduate program. Dr. Ernest Moyne and I drew up the proposal. It was revised by Dr. Perkins and Mr. Montgomery and submitted to the Rockefeller Foundation. The university was awarded the requested funds for a period of three years, and the program was launched.

As a student of Roman Britain, my idea was that our program set out to study and to teach the early history of the art of North America as though we were dealing with the history and archeology of the Roman Empire in Britain but studying in fact the antiquities of the British Empire in North America. The period after the United States' breaking of British Imperial rule over the new nation seemed to me roughly analogous to the period after which Britain had lost contact with Rome, called "The English Settlements." It had been defined by Myres, the Oxford historian, as "The period of some two centuries which lies between the collapse of Roman government in Britain and the arrival of St. Augustine," i.e., the period in which Britannia turned into England. I could see no reason why the concepts and techniques used by Collingwood and Myres in their classic work *Roman Britain and the English Settlements* would not work for the history of the United States. True, I had no St. Augustine for a cut-off date but could use the cut-off date of Mr. du Pont's collections. I was somewhat surprised when the proposal was accepted. I was even more surprised when the Rockefeller Foundation made its grant, particularly after we had subjected its representative on a very hot day to absolutely fruitless archeological "ground-scratching" at the site of Caspar Wistar's glass factory.

We at the University of Delaware and Winterthur realized some of the pitfalls which lay before us when we started the program. (Had we realized all of them, I doubt we would have ever got going.) One of the obstacles we did realize we had to face was the fact that neither the museum nor the University of Delaware had a library that was adequate to the task that lay ahead of us. Mr. Montgomery and I set out to remedy this situation in a way which resembled the onslaught of the Angles, Saxons, Jutes, and Danes on a prostrate Roman Britain. In the fateful summer of 1951, Mr. Montgomery and I descended on the London book trade and bought on a scale which still brings to a member of the staff of Quaritch's shop an unflattering, polite shudder of remembered horror every time I see him. The invasion of Britain by Winterthur and Delaware had begun and has continued—although in, I hope, a more discreet way—ever since.

The lack of a library forced me in 1951 to become a professional book collector, having been an amateur before. My hunt has continued ever since, first at the University of Delaware and since 1958 at the museum. What started with Mr. du Pont's private library, a librarian, Miss Helen Belknap, and a small collection of books, has in the past 20 years, thanks to Mr. du Pont's extraordinary generosity, been housed in a new five-story building containing three library floors for 140,000 books, 1,000,000 photographs, 200,000 slides, a large number of manuscripts, and microfilm, and two floors of laboratories. Thanks to Mr. du Pont, the Friends of Winterthur and many other donors, such as Mrs. Belknap (late of Beacon Hill) and Mrs. Edward Deming Andrews, we now have several libraries in that building. Thanks to the volunteer efforts of Mr. and Mrs. John J. Evans, the most friendly of Friends, we have among our libraries the finest collection in the world of photographs of American decorative art—and one indexed with the most sophisticated indexing yet devised for handling material objects.

Behind the collecting of books, periodicals, manuscripts, photographs, and slides, which the staff and I have been doing, has been a plan. The plan was to create the libraries we should have had when the Winterthur Program started in 1951. Today the advanced collector, the historian, and the graduate student can come to Winterthur and find under one roof a very large part of the material they need for research in the history of the English Empire in the United States, and they also can study the antiquities produced or used in our country from after the Revolution to 1913—though the libraries' primary slant on collecting is still up to 1840.

When Mr. du Pont collected, he found that there were many kinds of objects made and used in North America before 1840 which did not interest him. Unlike Electra Webb he had no desire for carriages and steamboats (or if he did, as a gentleman, he let her have priority). Unlike Mr. Rockefeller he did not collect cities, and unlike Mr. Ford he did not collect machinery. But all of those things, including machinery, are part of the whole story.

In the form of prints, drawings, posters, photographs, slides, and manuscript bills and account books, we in the libraries at Winterthur have been trying to round out the whole picture of early American life so that the collector and the researcher can see the history of its arts and skills both as widely and as deeply as possible. Together, the museum collections and the libraries make possible an examination of the history of American art not possible under anybody else's roof.

I should now like to illustrate the way in which we have been collecting by briefly discussing examples of our acquisitions, collected over the past 20 years. I have attempted to choose topics to show that life in the 18th and early 19th centuries was, if anything, even more remote from that of the United States in the 1970's than life in Roman Britain was from that of the English settlements (and certainly better documented).

Architectural Prints and Books

When I was an undergraduate at Yale early in the 1940's, the School of Art and Architecture destroyed its casts of Greek and Roman sculpture and sold its antique art books, presumably on the grounds that modern, young artists and architects needed no truck with the ancients and no *Beaux arts* reference library from which to cull ideas.

Life was very different in the 18th century in general, and especially so in architecture. Both the artist and the architect had to be "learned" to succeed with the fashionable. Learning involved an acquaintance with the great

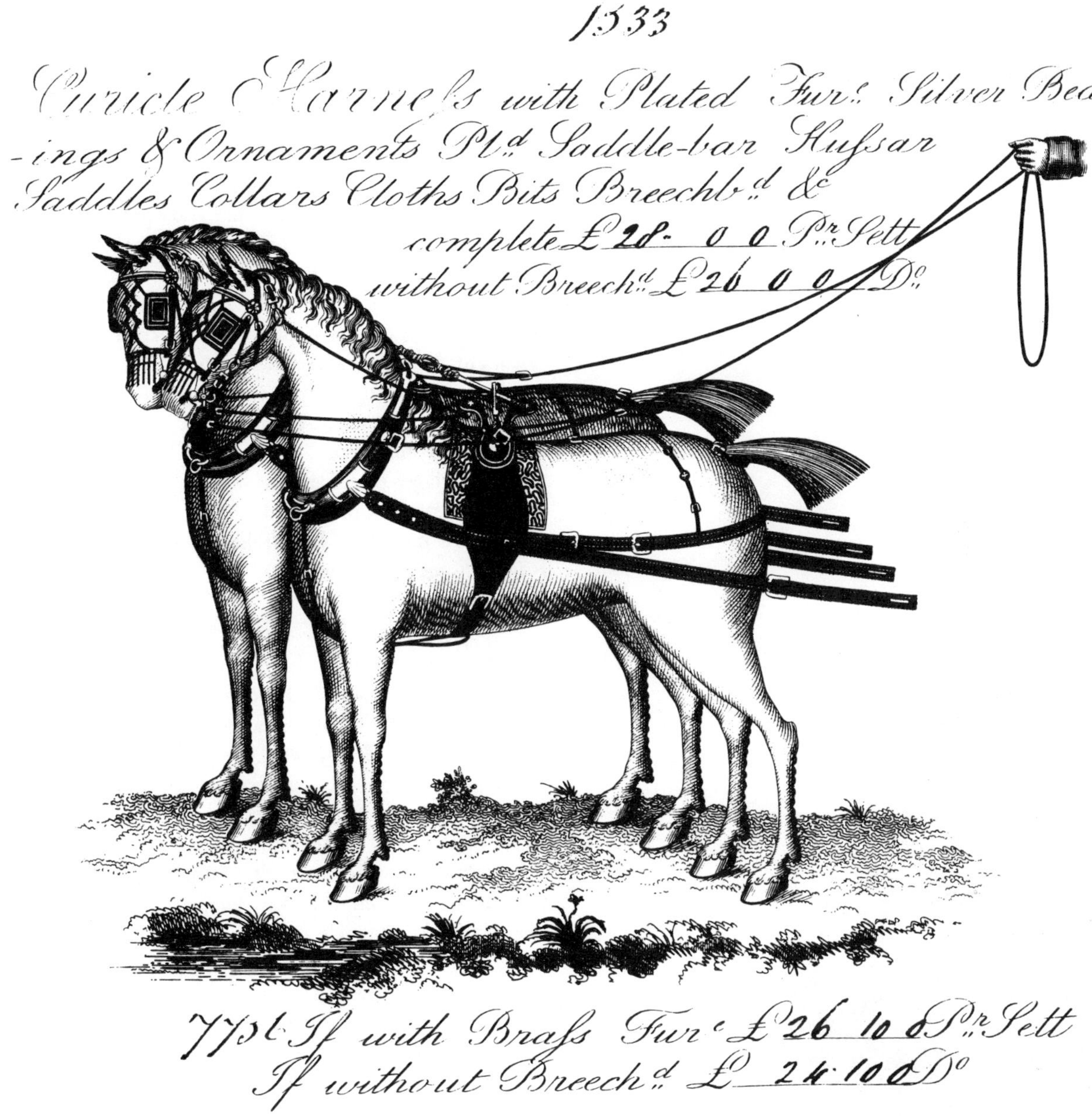

"Curicle Harness" from a late 18th-century, British leather goods catalog.

sculpture and buildings of ancient Rome and what the 18th-century gentleman for the most part thought was Greek art. Learning became more diversified as the century wore on, gained an acquaintance with true Greek art, and began to cultivate the thrills of the Gothic, so important in the 19th century.

It was no accident that two of the most important architects of the early 19th century, Ithiel Towne and A. J. Davis, owned large architectural libraries containing the books and prints they used as the reference sources for their own designs. Laugier's *Essai sur l'architecture,* a study of architectural theory by the 18th-century Jesuit was owned by Sir John Soane, in all its editions, and in the United States was used by Davis as the basis of his design for "The American Cottage." Near Philadelphia, Nicholas Biddle lived in a house designed to look like a Greek temple, and to the south, Thomas Jefferson designed and built the University of Virginia, in part at least, to supply his undergraduates with "proper" examples of the orders—Doric, Ionic, and Corinthian. To his very 18th-century mind, novelty was horrifying, and good architecture had to speak Latin (although it must be admitted that the Latin consisted of tags dropped into structures that in plan owed nothing to ancient Rome).

Travel and Transportation

Those of us over 50 can remember the last days of the horse as part of the American way of life and the pleasures of stealing ice from the back of a horse-drawn wagon. To permit the researcher to recapture the past and to reconstruct the way of life in 18th- and 19th-century America, the illustrated books and prints on the subject of "equitation" are vital. A gentleman had to be able to ride a horse and do it with style. He needed a learned stable to go with his learned house. Ladies demanded car-

Garden roller from Descriptions of some of the Utensils in Husbandry, Rolling Cariages, Cart Rollers, and Divided Rollers for Land or Gardens, *by James Sharp (London, ca. 1777).*

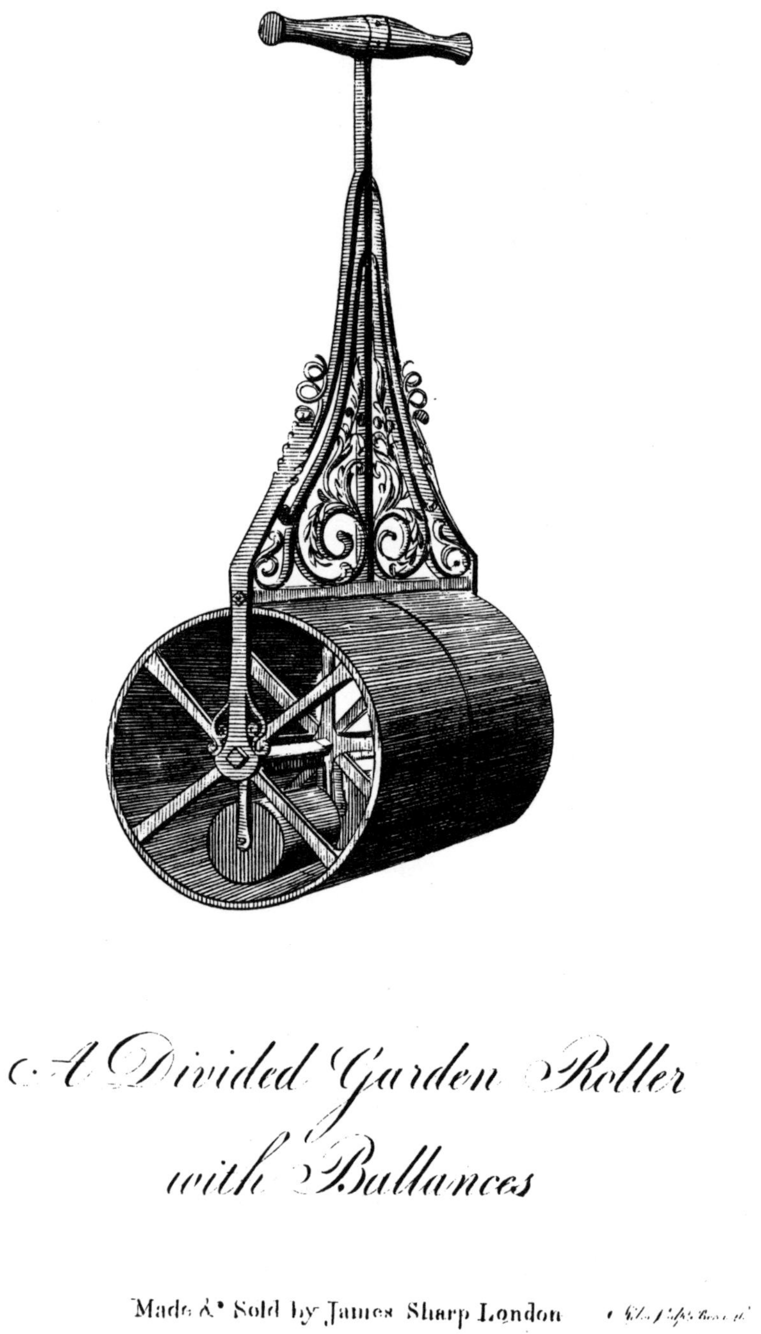

riages and coaches, and they could be status symbols far more expensive to buy and operate than a Rolls. They demanded coachmen, footmen, and postilions, and all of those servants had to be uniformed in the latest fashion. Trade catalogs document all these things visually from the 18th century up to our cut-off date of 1913—even the 18th-century harness. F. M. L. Thompson delivered as his inaugural lecture as the recently appointed professor of modern history at Bedford College of the University of London a talk called *Victorian England: the Horse-drawn Society,* but, as published, the lecture lacks illustrations. An American audience—especially those under 40—would profit greatly from a comparable lecture on American horse-drawn society, if illustrated. I wonder how many members of the Pepsi generation even know what the term "carriage trade" means or what those rectangular blocks of stone with initials found on American street curbs were used for—both relics of the dead and largely forgotten age of the horse.

The World of Agriculture

In our contemporary world in which the population of the city grows and that of the countryside decreases, a life dominated by agriculture is necessarily strange. There is a story about a little boy who, on his return from a Fresh Air Fund visit to the country, complained that in contrast to the city where milk came in bottles, in the country it came out of large, hulking beasts.

A world in which the city fathers provide a zoo so that urban children can see domestic animals is rather like Marie Antoinette's *hameau* at Versailles.

Early American prints or drawings illustrating 18th-century farm life are hard to come by, perhaps because the country was so familiar to urban man and the farmer that they took no interest in it. Even landscape paintings of the period are very rare. We have tried especially hard to find pictures that show how stables and barns looked, the farm tools and wagons used, what beehives were like, and the appearance of slave quarters. We even have an 18th-century work illustrated with plates of chicken incubators. There are very few plantations left where one can see the original outbuildings as one can at Shirley near Williamsburg. For the most part the scholar interested in early American, rural life must reconstruct from documents, and prints are an important part of that documentation. The home industries of canning and preserving, milking, making of cheese and butter, cider pressing, and smoking meat all are as difficult to document for the 18th century as are the long-gone street cries of the farmers and farm wives come to peddle their goods in town.

The world of the plantation slave is especially hard to document since, like the slum dwellers of the 18th century, he was portrayed normally only when he was picturesque. Perhaps now that black studies are fashionable more material will come to the surface. Paul Revere's engraving of the Boston Massacre documents the

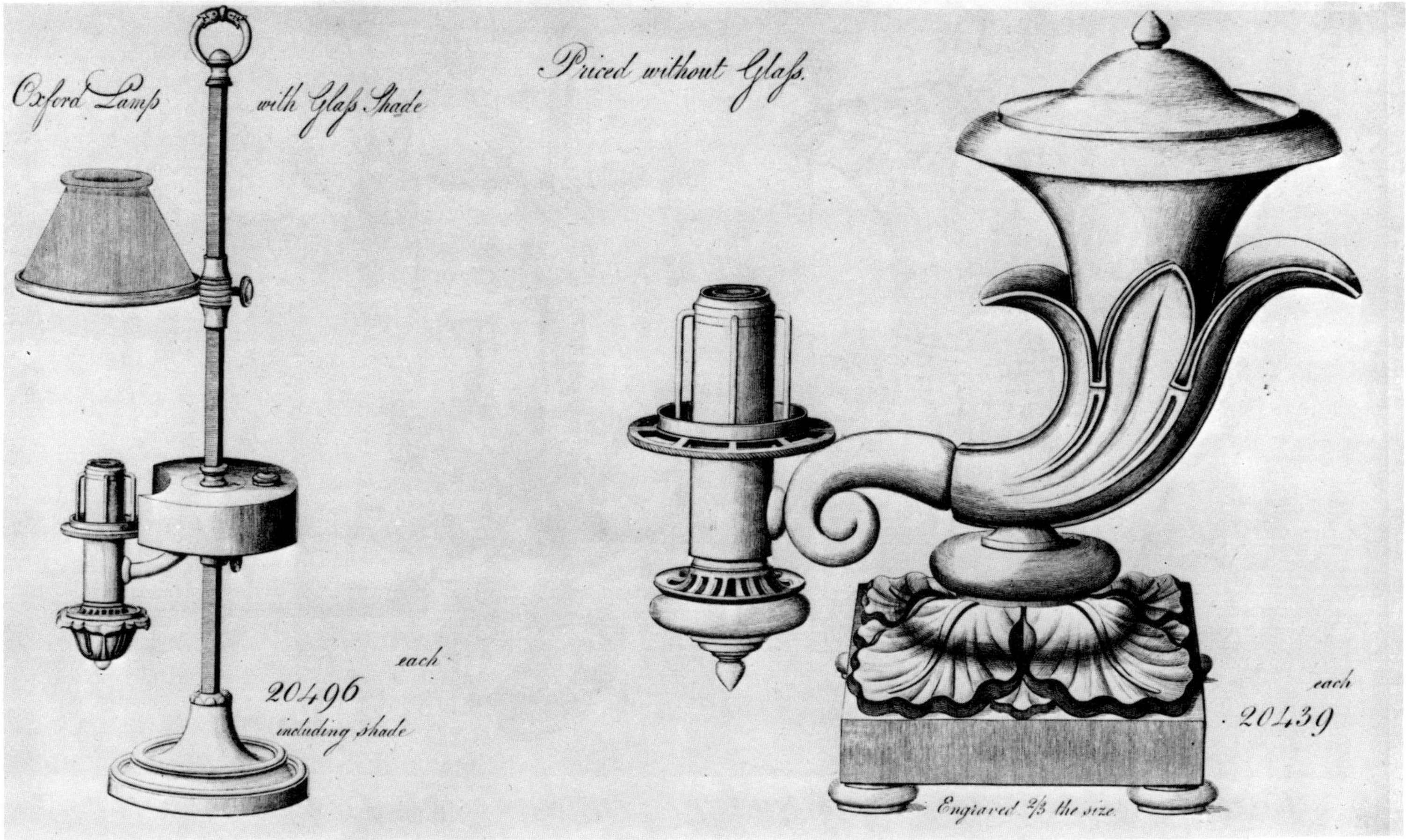

Argand lamps, engraving after unknown artist, from Lamp Book *(England, ca. 1840).*

first scene of mob violence known to me in which an American Negro took an active part. Visual material on the slave trade which supplied the farm laborers to America, on the other hand, is easier to find, since quantities of it were generated to illustrate the abolitionist literature of the 18th and early 19th centuries.

The World of Darkness and Cold—and Heat

Only the camper and the traveler whose masochistic pleasures lure him to the less civilized parts of our planet can fully appreciate some aspects of 18th-century life. I once spent a year in a building erected about A.D. 1352. My quarters consisted of a sitting room perhaps 25 feet long, a small bedroom, and a tiny "gyp" room (a sort of butler's pantry). Other than a two-burner stove in the pantry, the sole source of heat was a fireplace grate some two feet wide and perhaps 10 inches deep which had as its fuel wood kindling and coal. The fire heated the room for a distance of some three feet. In the evening I used to sit reading by the fire wrapped in blankets, while spread over chairs my sheets steamed picturesquely before the grate until dry enough so I could make up my bed and retire for the night armed with a hot water bottle (invariably stone cold by early morning). The Anglo-American world of the 18th century was perplexed by the problem of cold. Franklin and Rumford published proposals for using stoves much like those employed by the Pennsylvania Germans in America and widely used on the Continent. Winterthur's collection of trade catalogs shows that a London ironmonger named James Sharp manufactured in the 1780's a line of "American stoves." Though they may exist, I have never seen one in use in England. As an incautious student, I once suggested to my tutor that stoves would be more practical than open fires only to be told that one would lose the beauty of burning wood.

Beauty is undoubtedly supplied by what one American writer has injudiciously titled "flickering flames." But firelight and candlelight are of little help to a serious reader. A painting attributed to Rembrandt Peale in the Detroit Institute of Fine Arts shows a man painfully engaged in trying to read a manuscript by candlelight while wearing green-lensed spectacles to shade his eyes. It is a sobering thought to remember that it was not until late in the 18th century that the French produced the Argand lamp, the first major innovation in lighting since some unsung genius invented the wax candle.

The world of darkness and cold—fortunately—today needs intellectual reconstruction by most people, but anyone over 40 can remember life before air-conditioning. How the French, dressed in 18th-century clothes, survived in New Orleans boggles the imagination. But Captain

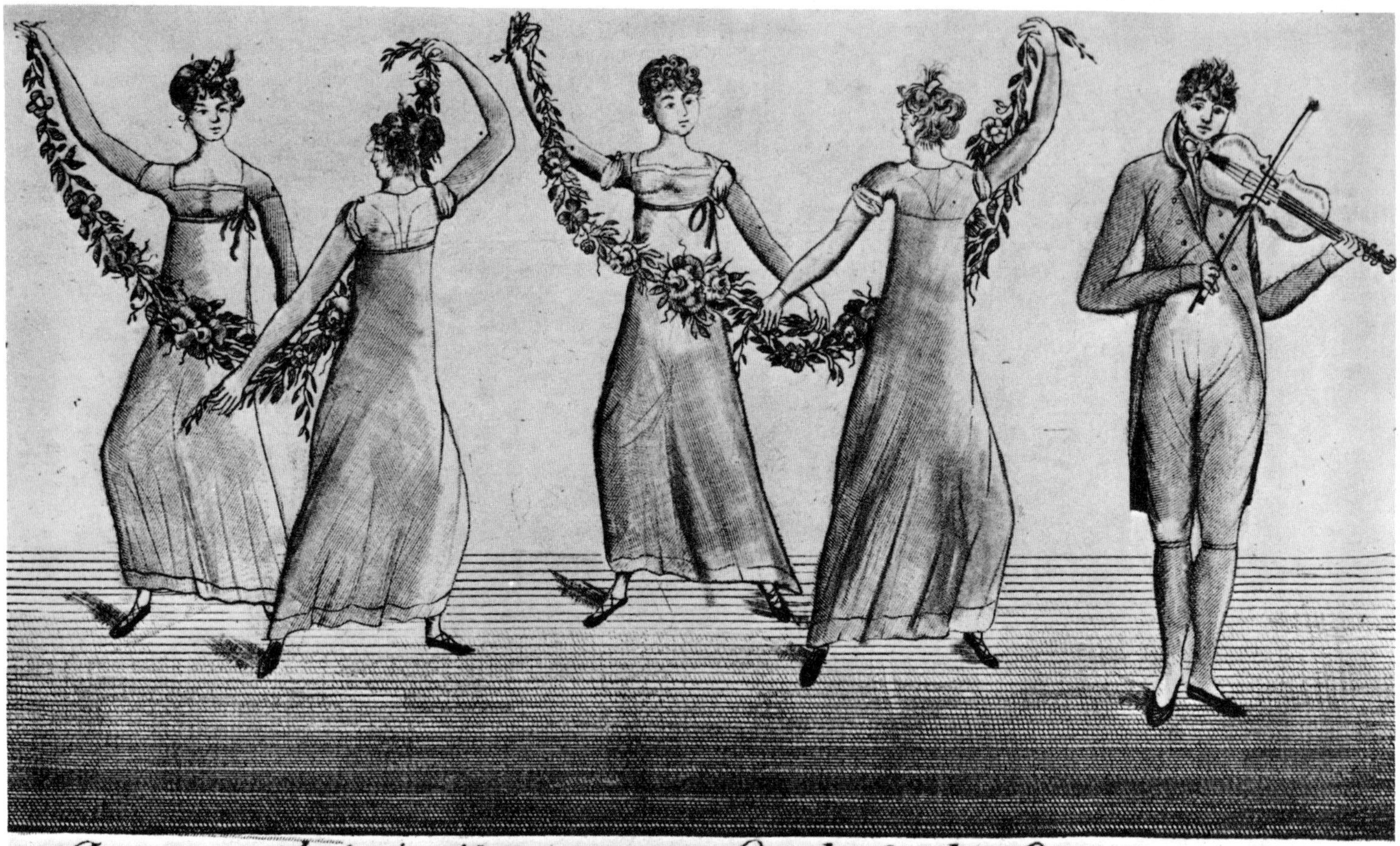

'Come, and trip it as you go': On the light fantastic toe."

Plate from Francis D. Nichols, A Guide to Politeness . . . *(Boston, 1810).*

J. G. Stedman's book on Surinam illustrates how the Dutch managed during the years 1772 to 1777 in a similar climate. Trousers rather than knee britches were a partial answer for the white; total or near nudity was the answer of the Indian and the Negro.

The Veiling of the Skin

Since Winterthur does not collect costumes, it is necessary for us to search for prints and photographs to provide the scholar with research material on this topic. Before 1913 the only Americans to be seen in public even partially nude were Indians, possibly blacks, boxers, and boys at the swimming hole. Nude art models were rare as late as the Eakins affair at the Pennsylvania Academy. A delightful painting by Winthrop Chandler shows that even the physician had problems. He is attending a patient who, lying in a curtained, high-post bed, is invisible except for an arm and hand pushed through the curtains. Although England was less modest than America, even there before the Regency the only part of the body bared even partially to view was the female breast. Illustrated, 18th-century versions of *Fanny Hill* (the book was imported to Salem "with cuts and without") show that even in the intimacy of the bed chamber total nudity was rare. Underclothes, it has been suggested, were worn largely to protect expensive, custom-made clothes from the dirty skin of the wearer. (I have been unable to find more than one American reference to a bathroom before the 19th century.) Portraits and surviving examples of clothes and jewelry show that although well-to-do, early Americans were seldom as richly appareled as their European contemporaries, nevertheless at least on such formal occasions as portrait sittings, they were elaborately dressed. Work clothes, as worn before well into the 19th century when documented by such genre painters as Mount, Edward Hicks, and Bingham, remain largely *terra incognita.* Information on such "special costume" as the clothes of undergraduate and teacher (English-type caps and gowns were worn at Harvard and Yale in the 18th century), the minister (thoroughly documented in New England by Peter Pelham's prints), and the soldier is easier to uncover.

One of the library's prints shows that, at least in New York City in 1839, fashions for both men and women were being set by London. Only later in the century did Paris succeed in dictating to American women.

The Veil in Action

Once clothed, polite Americans in the 18th and early 19th centuries had to use their bodies according to intricate sets of rules. The rules were frequently codified in illustrated manuals either imported or, in the 19th century, printed in the United States. I earlier mentioned the equitation manuals. Equally prescribed for in illus-

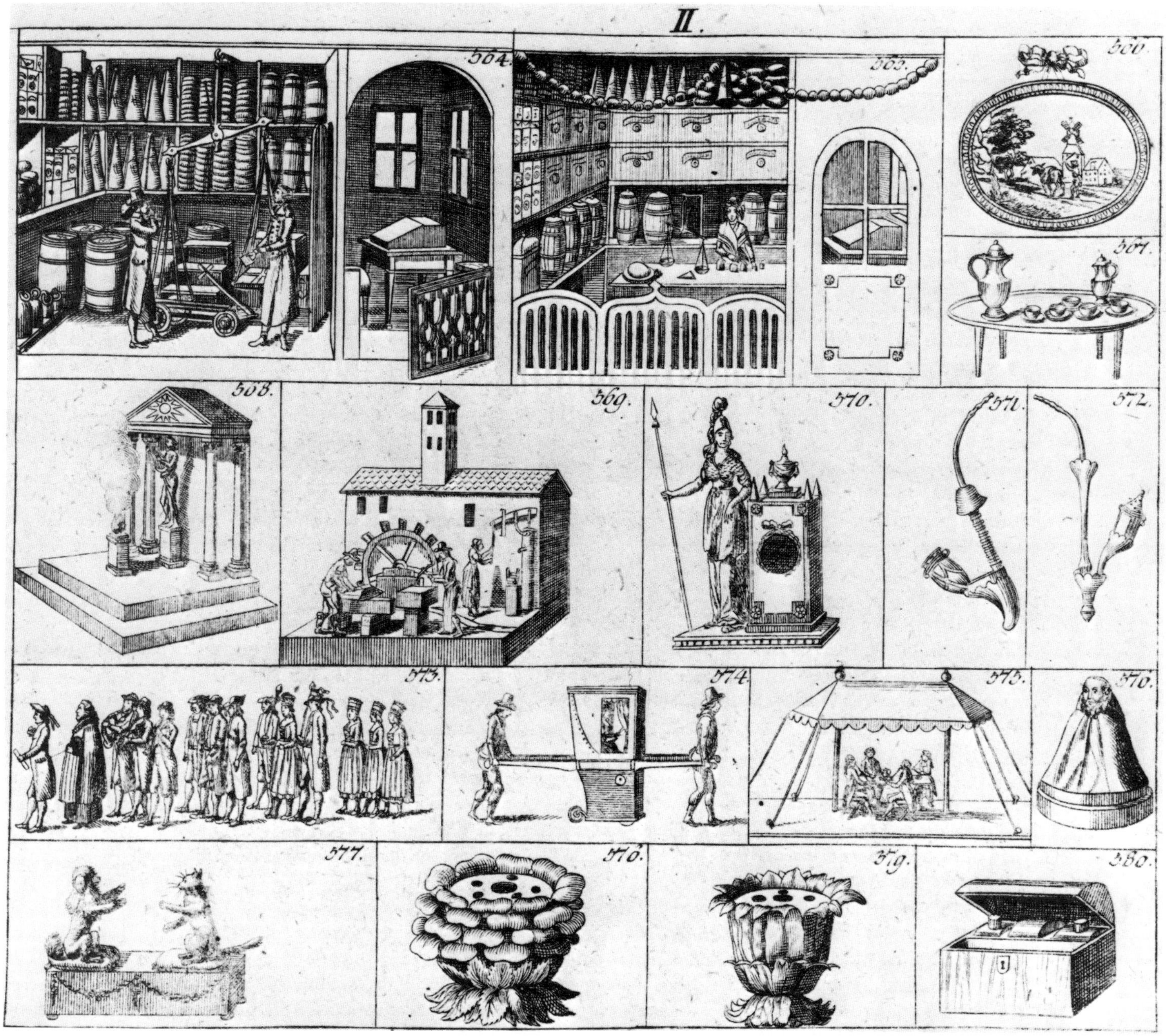

Sheet of illustrations of German toys from the catalog, *Magazin von verschiedenen Kunst-und andern nüzlichen Sachen . . .* (Nürnberg, 1812).

trated books were military drill, ballroom dancing and ballet, the gestures of the actor in drama or opera, and the gestures of the rhetoritian. At Harvard in 1831 gesture was taught by Jonathan Barber who issued an illustrated textbook showing how the undergraduates at that university were expected to behave on the lecture platform. Closer to daily life were the manuals on etiquette which provided rules for every form of polite social intercourse. An early example is F. Nivelon's *The Rudiments of Genteel Behavior* (London, 1737). A charming American book on the rules of formal social intercourse was published in Boston in 1810 by a dancing master named Francis D. Nichols. Its title in part is *A Guide to Politeness; or a System of Directions for the Acquirement of Ease, Propriety and Elegance of Manners.* The plates illustrating the code are described as representing "graceful attitudes." This book makes anyone who has ever suffered through dancing school very sympathetic to the Boston young.

The World of the Child

The world of the child is little known before the mid-19th century when the romantic notion, perhaps inspired by Rousseau, brought about their treatment not as small scale adults but as an age category with its own rights and privileges. The passage from short pants to long ones in my own youth marked the proud transition from grammar to high school, but in the 18th century the passage was from dresses to knee britches, and it took place very early in life. Winterthur owns a portrait by Joseph Badger of Boston that represents a boy who is in the process of shifting from the role of the infant to that of what Louisa May Alcott called a "little man." He is still wearing his baby dress, but he is wearing with it a curled and powdered wig.

However, even the 18th-century child was provided with at least some toys. To judge from catalogs in the collection at least the child of well-to-do parents was supplied with marvelous toys from France and Germany. The catalogs are extremely useful because so many early toys have disappeared.

The world of the early American child is illuminated, however, by children's books, many of which are elaborately illustrated with instructional plates, such as Francis Quarles' *Emblems* which was available in Boston in the 17th century or Amos Comenius' *Orbus pictus.* Other plates were merely entertaining. That the entertainment was mild can be gathered from the title of a book of 1810 in the collection illustrated by William Charles, the Scots caricaturist who worked in New York and Philadelphia. It is called *The Little Woman and the Pedlar, with the strange distraction that seized her, and the undutiful behaviour of her little dog on that occasion.* There was nothing to my knowledge that even faintly resembled the modern comic book.

The World of the Ill, the Insane, and the Criminal

Our concern in collecting is not wholly with the healthy and the normal. After all, disease, mental illness, and crime were very much a part of the early American scene. I thought we should have books on the two most famous diseases of pre-Jenner days. I therefore bought early works on gout and smallpox. The work on gout was unillustrated, but the volume on the second disease was illustrated. I have been unable to look at it since I first opened it, but it sits on our shelves waiting for a more courageous research worker. Another medical problem of the early American was to know when to bleed a patient. The Pennsylvania Germans frequently published illustrated bleeding charts in the 18th century so that the operation could be performed under the most auspicious astrological circumstances. Franklin in Philadelphia also published cuts of the "astrological man." In his almanacs, however, there was all the necessary information, but, appropriately for the rational scientist-publisher Franklin, the text made no mention of the astrological uses to which the astronomical tables accompanying the cut could be put.

The development of the hospital was important in the early American handling of disease. In the library are several views of one of America's earliest hospitals, the Pennsylvania Hospital where Dr. Benjamin Rush struggled to ameliorate the dreadful treatment of the insane. Unfortunately, we have nothing comparable to the well-known plate of Bedlam in the *Rake's Progress* series to document the interior, but there exists an engraving of Rush's invention to restrain patients. It was a chair in which the patient was fastened when he became violent. Its use was proposed in 1811 for treatment of George III, but his English physicians continued to use the "Strait-Wastecoat." Incidentally, the museum owns a portrait of Dr. John de Sequeyra who from October 1773 to 1793 was "attending physician" at what is now the Eastern State Hospital of Williamsburg, Va. During the period Dr. de Sequeyra practiced, its name was less euphemistic. It was called "The Hospital for the Reception of Idiots, Lunatics, and Persons of Insane or Disordered Minds." The doctor was one of America's first psychiatrists.

America was a world leader in prison reform. The citizens of Philadelphia developed a penological innovation which was baptized as "the Philadelphia System." Basically it involved solitary confinement. The "Walnut Street Goal" was of such importance that William Birch engraved and sold two colored views of it. Views of several other Philadelphia and Pennsylvania prisons are also in the collection.

"The New York System" was based on the plan of common labor for the convicts. Its principal early monument was Sing-Sing—a prison for which we have some of the original drawings.

American penological innovations attracted so much attention that in the early 19th century a considerable number of books were published on the prisons of the United States and their operation. Alexis de Tocqueville came here to do a report on them for the French government. It was published in 1833 and, like many of the other books on the subject, was richly illustrated.

The World of Advertising

In contrast to modern Madison Avenue "hard sell" techniques, early American advertising was more like the English. Both, for instance, used signs that informed their largely illiterate publics by visual as well as verbal means. Cut outs of shoes told where the cordwainer's wares could be found. The Old State House in Boston houses an 18th-century wooden statue of a mariner which is said to have advertised the navigational instruments in the shop near which it stood—an ancestor of the 19th-century's cigar store Indians.

In addition, illustrated advertisements were inserted in the journals of the day. Unlike those in modern newspaper and magazine illustrations, they usually were not custom made. Instead they were bought by the printer from type founders. They could be selected from trade catalogs of type specimens. We have a small collection of these at Winterthur, including a very handsome one of ornamental, colored, wooden type.

The cuts used in periodical advertisements might also be used in other forms. The same firm that published the newspaper might also do "job" printing of handbills and posters.

One of the most interesting forms of advertising was the "trade card." The "card" started as a small handbill presumably distributed in the streets or used by the proprietor as a bill form. The earliest examples usually portrayed the shop sign which was placed over the shop door or on the street in front of the tradesman's shop—a custom found in Philadelphia as late as the 1770's. A variant was a rebus. Sir Ambrose Heal in his book on trade cards illustrates one portraying a sign carved in the form of a human leg and foot. The card and sign belonged to "Robert Legg Upholsterer *at the Sign of ye Leg* in Holborn." The trade card of the mid-18th century in England also frequently portrayed the goods offered by the tradesman in his shop. This custom was also followed in Philadelphia. At Winterthur we have a very handsome trade card engraved in Philadelphia by Henry Dawkins for a coppersmith in which an exuberant rococo cartouche encloses a picture of a teakettle and the text of the tradesman's advertisement. From the cartouche hung pictures of examples of his goods and a picture of a sign representing his device of "the Golden teakettle." The print is inscribed in manuscript "Phi[l]. Nov. 13, 1776."

As signs were removed and street numbers were assigned to the houses and shops of London (Sir Ambrose says the last sign came down in 1773), the cards changed. This parallelism of culture change (to use anthropological-archeological lingo) also held in Philadelphia. We have a card of a second coppersmith who had his printer set an inscription giving the date "Oct. 31, 1796." There are no pictures, and now the sign reference has disappeared, and the address is given: "No 25 South Front St." The card was now much smaller and printed on heavy cardboard. In the 19th century the card form was retained, and the cards were engraved in the early years. As lithography developed, the cards, usually fairly small, were richly decorated, frequently in color. A very fetching, early 19th-century engraved card in our collection was issued by the painters Raphael and Rembrandt Peale. It was colored by hand. Thus were laid the origins of the cigarette card of the late 19th and early 20th century.

From an archeological point of view the above pieces of evidence at least hint at a degree of parallelism in American and British art, city planning, and administration which cries out for further investigation. In 1938 Professor B. Malinowski published an important essay called "On the anthropology of changing African cultures" in a volume of other essays titled *Methods of Study of Culture Contact in Africa.* The material available for the study of "colonialism" in North America is as equally interesting as the African and, as I have said before, well documented.

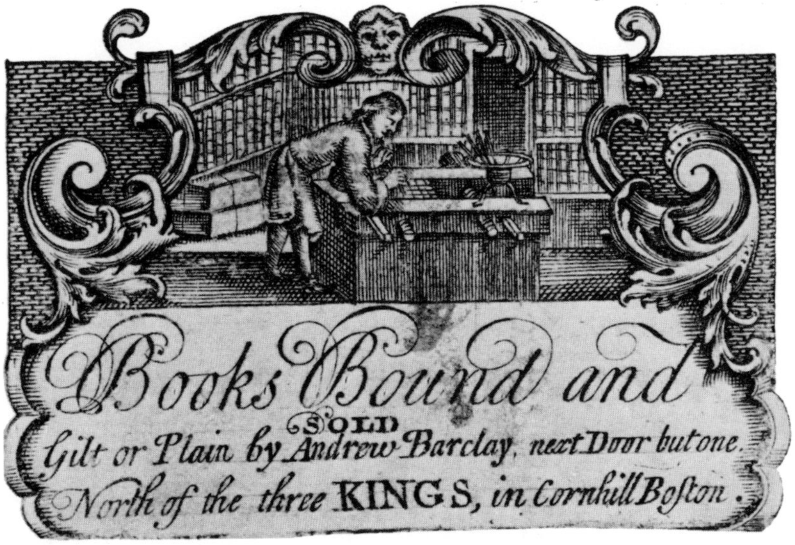

Advertising card of Andrew Barclay, bookbinder (Boston, ca. 1764).

I think that I have given enough examples to show something of the range of my collecting of prints and illustrated books. But I might add a word on the method guiding my acquisitions. As indicated earlier I am by training an archeologist and anthropologist. My major guide in collecting evidence for the study of early American culture and its European background consists of two books produced by a team of anthropologists under the leadership of Professor George P. Murdock of Yale University. They are the *Outline of Cultural Materials* and its companion volume the *Outline of World Cultures.* Together, they systematically outline the components of culture and the distribution of the cultures around the world. We have extracted from the two *Outlines* the material pertinent to our own subject of early America. We are attempting to index our pictures using the Yale method and hope to have in the future not only an important picture collection, but also one cataloged and classified in such a way that the researcher will be readily able to retrieve information on the content of each picture. Recreation and entertainment, technology, the craft products, and the food quest are a few categories in the Yale system.

We hope that in time our collections will prove fruitful material for a future in which the historian will use visible evidence and the archeologist and anthropologist will admit the interest of historic as well as prehistoric and "primitive" materials. My patron saint, Aby Warburg, long ago recognized the value of the study of "primitive" culture for the understanding of historic Western European art. I hope that my efforts in building the libraries at Winterthur for the study of pre-1913 American art and life and its European sources will bear similar fruit.

Revivalist Themes in American Prints and Folksongs 1830-50

Elizabeth Gilmore Holt

Elizabeth Gilmore Holt has taught art history at Duke University, Talladega College, American University, and Michigan State University and has lectured at numerous universities and museums. Her published works include Literary Sources of Art History *(Princeton University Press, 1947),* A Documentary History of Art, *2 vols., (Doubleday, 1957–58), and* From the Classicists to Impressionists; A Documentary History of Art and Architecture in the 19th Century *(Anchor, 1966). She is completing the documentary history series with* The Triumph of Art for the Public: Salons and Exhibitions of the 19th Century. *This paper is based on material from a forthcoming volume on religious prints and folksongs during the Jacksonian period.*

The devotional prints and religious folksongs of Jacksonian America have many themes in common, for both reflect a broad spectrum of popular taste. Six or seven dominant themes which reveal the contemporary concerns of the people appear in both prints and songs. They mirror the country's mood when Andrew Jackson, Old Hickory, the hero of the Mississippi Valley and the thinly settled Western regions, was elected President.

It was generally acknowledged that the success of the new nation and the perpetuity of free government must be sustained by the intelligence of the people. By 1840, thanks to the efforts of a national body of teachers, together with labor's agitation for free, democratic schools and the people's lively interest in public affairs, only one American in 20 could not read the laws of the land and the Holy Bible, two pillars on which it was generally maintained free government must rest.

The strength of the laws depended on a public sufficiently informed to participate in their enactment and support their enforcement. A free press of 200 newspapers existed when the 19th century opened. By 1833 there were 1,200, and in 1860 as many as 3,000. Enterprising New Yorkers opened the era of the daily newspaper. *The Sun,* the first penny newspaper, appeared in 1833.

The sturdiness of the nation's second pillar, knowledge of the Holy Scriptures, was maintained by the Protestant evangelical denominations: Baptists, Methodists, and Presbyterians. The settlers of the seaboard, the Western Reserve, men of the Western Waters, with the Bible and probably a copy of *Pilgrim's Progress* in their pockets, fought against arbitrary rule and for the doctrine of government by covenant—the free consent of the governed people. They had sprung from a soil enriched with new translations of the Bible. Knowledge of the Holy Scriptures made its possessors masters of Divine Truth. Human authority was immeasurably below Divine Truth, so the Bible, the one authoritative Word of God, was the cornerstone on which home and community rested.

The frontispiece to Brown's Self-Interpreting Bible,

published by Hodge and Campbell of New York in 1792 and drawn by William Dunlap, shows a seated figure of America holding the Constitution and reaching for the Holy Bible. John Scoles provided the wood engraving in which the Resurrected Christ and the Peaceable Kingdom are combined for the frontispiece to the 1801 New Testament, printed for William Durrell in New York.

The admonition "Search the Scripture for therein are contained Word of Eternal Life" was heeded as a civic duty. The Sacred Scriptures were the foundation of the Christian religion, "a religion which furnishes motives to the faithful performance of every patriotic civil and social duty," in words found in the preface to Isaiah Thomas' Bible of 1791. Children were started on their search of the Scriptures by a *Curious Hieroglyphick Bible* introduced into this country by Isaiah Thomas in 1788. Using a device borrowed from the ancient Egyptians, key words in selected passages, such as Isaiah 11:6, were represented by a picture to amuse and interest children. Thomas copied an English Bible published in London in 1784, derived from the prototype hieroplyphic Bible published by Mattsperger in Augsburg in 1684. Kellogg & Thayer employed the device for a lithograph to illustrate the millennial text from Isaiah 11:6.

To ensure that poor as well as rich possessed the truths of Scriptures, the American Bible Society provided Bibles free or at a modest price. Lifted from its protecting box, the family Bible was placed open on a table, as on an altar, and the family gathered around it to listen to God's Word. Pictures of the important ritual of family Bible reading and the room where it took place had wide appeal, and the popular lithographic firms offered different versions. A Currier print of 1846 depicts the rite in a tastefully furnished room. The furnishings of a genteel home could be modeled after such a print.

The Second Awakening in America duplicated the religious fervor of early Christianity and gave rise to similar pictorial images, based on themes that are rarely found after the 12th century in European art. To find representations of an open Bible enshrined on an altar, one must go back to 5th-century mosaics in the Baptistry at Ravenna or Hagios Georgios in Thessalonika.

Unison singing was an essential element of the worship service of the dissenting sects in England. The religious ballads and folk hymns of the Baptists, Methodists, and Presbyterians came with them to this country. Sunday school opened with hymn singing. Scriptural reading, recital of verses memorized at home—as Tom Sawyer did—and prayers were all interspersed with singing.

In the Western Reserve region, new strength was given to the general ground swell of song by the Second Awakening or New Light Movement. The revival began at a Kentucky camp meeting and swept over the entire country. Books of religious folksongs, *Southern Harmony, Kentucky Harmony, The Jubilee, The Sacred Harp,* and others, went from edition to edition. *Southern Harmony* sold 600,000

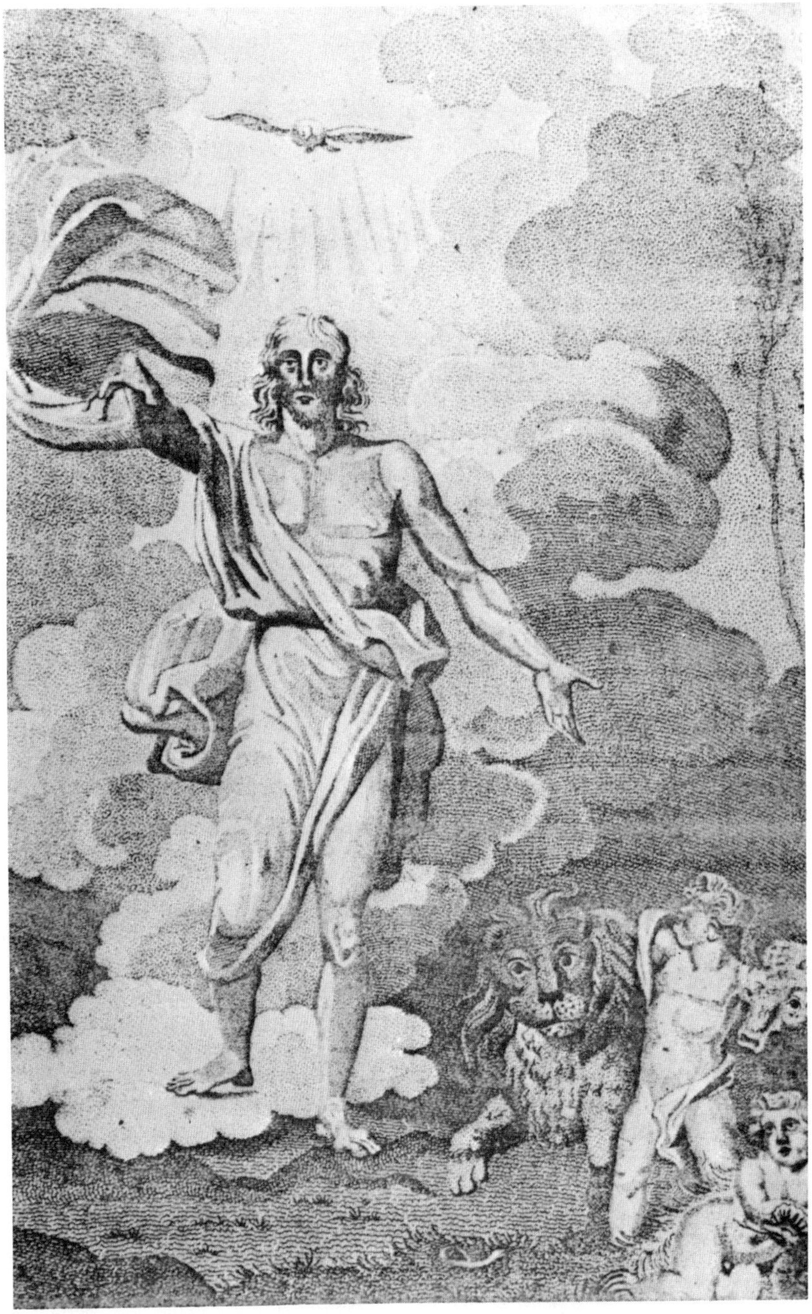

John Scoles' engraving of the Resurrected Christ and the Peaceable Kingdom. Frontispiece to an 1801 New Testament.

copies between 1835 and 1854.

The intrinsic beauty and universal appeal of the hymns, religious ballads, and revival spirituals nourished the religious spirit of the country. Stimulants to the faith of the common man, these three types of songs spread by group singing, were the predominant popular music for the first half of the century and formed a devotional expression unique to America.

People were able to buy inexpensive song books, sheet music, and pictures to embellish their homes, thanks to the invention of lithography by the Austrian printer Aloys Senefelder. Lithography appealed to Americans. It was rapid, cheap, and could meet the demands for large-scale reproduction.

Commercial lithographers enlisted self-taught, obscure artists with natural talents and paid them by the drawing. They were unencumbered by the pictorial devices that were the recognized requisites for fine art, which American art academies had adopted from their European counterparts. Confident and uninhibited, the artists felt no need to copy slavishly. They simply lifted bits and pieces from what was at hand to make a naive, patchwork-quilt kind of picture.

"Works of art to brighten the home within the reach of all" was the selling slogan of the popular lithographic firms. For many pioneers and settlers, the "work of art" represented a nostalgic memory of social stability and conveniences formerly enjoyed. Like a hymn hummed while doing daily chores, pictures brought a sense of cheer and comfort. Hung on a cottage or cabin wall, they symbolized a standard of life to be won by sober piety and labor.

The national taste in the "works of art within the reach of all" between 1830 and 1850 is illustrated by the lithographic sales catalogs. A count by subject of prints published by Nathaniel Currier in 1851 shows that 137 religious and moral titles were offered in a list of 718. He and other firms could rely on a steady, constant demand for devotional prints.

In 1828, the popular political choice for President was Andrew Jackson of Tennessee. With his election, the common folk were confident their emancipation was at hand. An earlier feeling became, between 1830 and 1850, the certain belief that here in America:

> . . . a purified people, with institutions based on the laws of Nature—identified in the words of Webster with the law of God—would, if true to their covenant, found a refuge for the world's oppressed and a model for other nations to copy. In 1848, this generation, now in its old age, believed it saw the world actually copying this model. . . . In matters of politics and economics Americans were nearly all millenarians, believing that they themselves would see the realization of human happiness; in religion the belief that this generation would with their own eyes, living, even see God, went far beyond the confines of the small sect who made that belief an article of creed. . . .[1]

America was thought of as the new Eden. After crossing the vacancy of the ocean, the colonist stepped ashore into a new Canaan, crowded with bizarre natural creation. Primeval forests, strange fruits and food, unknown birds and animals, and a new race of mankind confronted him. As a European, he had known nature in terms of hedgerows enclosing velvet meadows and woods growing in park-like hunting preserves. There nature was "in hand"; here he was faced with what might be termed the essence of the idea of nature and was forced to adjust his self-image. Instead of the Renaissance maxim, "Man the measure of all things," he was moved in humility to ask, in the words of the Psalmist, "What is man that thou art mindful of him?"

In a Currier print, *Adam Naming the Creatures,* strong emphasis is placed on the animals. Adam, withdrawn to a distant corner, is hardly noticeable beside his best friends, the horse and dog. He appears to be more than a little uncomfortable when confronted with the "swarming creatures." This is understandable when we notice the snobbish expression on the animals' faces. After all, they were here first.

Shortly after the print was drawn the episode in Genesis 2:19-20 was told in the gospel song attributed to Henry Chandler in the *Social Harp* and dated 1854.

> When Adam was created, he dwelt in Eden's shade,
> As Moses had related, before a bride was made.
> Ten thousand times ten thousand of creatures swarm'd around
> Before a bride was formed or any mate was found.[2]

Currier's lithographer had found a plausible portrayal of Paradise for his print in the frontispieces to two Bibles. Both are wood engravings by Alexander Anderson (1775-1870), who renounced the physician's scalpel for an engraver's chisel. One is in a Kimber & Sharpless Bible printed in Philadelphia in 1829. The other was printed in Brattleboro, Mass., in 1832. The *Creation* frontispiece of 1829 is ascribed to Brueghel by Anderson. He dropped the ascription from the 1832 frontispiece when he made the slight alteration of replacing the single figure of Adam with two tiny figures of Adam and Eve. Anderson's wood engravings are, as he acknowledged, fairly close copies of the Flemish artist, Jan Brueghel the Elder's paintings, especially Brueghel's *Adam and Eve in Paradise* now in the Städelsches Kunstinstitut, Frankfurt am Main. Jan is sometimes called the Paradise Brueghel because he painted, with slight variations, the heavenly region seven times. An engraving of the Frankfurt painting by J. Heath & S. Middiman, English engravers, may have been the model for American artists confronted with the task of depicting Paradise in Bibles printed in this country. Brueghel's image of Paradise conveyed a connotation of everlasting joy, release from labor, and an all prevading harmony between fauna, flora, and creatures—elements which appealed to Americans.

In Nathaniel Currier's print *Adam and Eve in the Garden of Eden,* Adam has turned back to look once more at the distant vista before accepting the apple Eve offers at the serpent's snarling insistence. The lines of Adam's

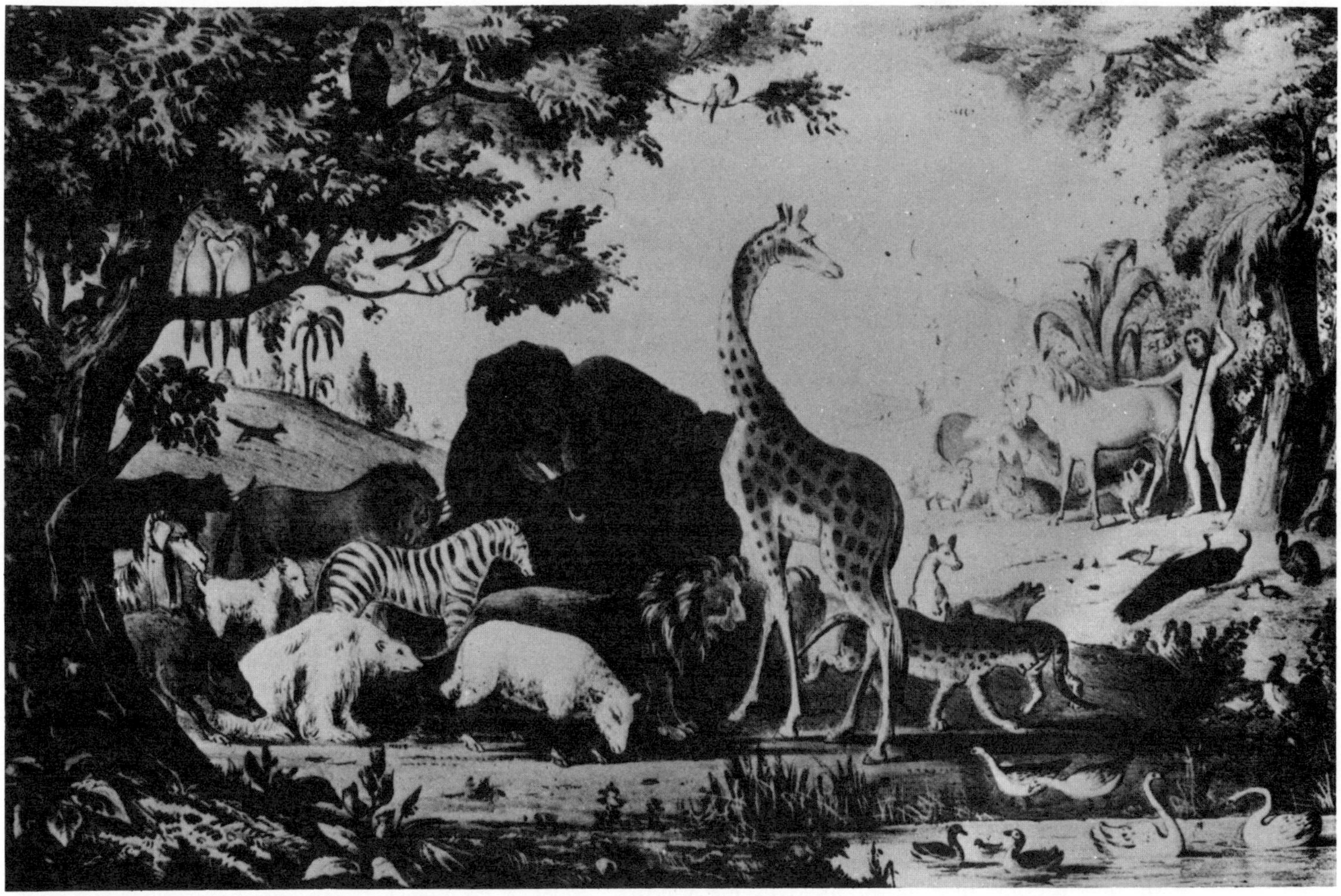

Currier, Adam Naming the Creatures.

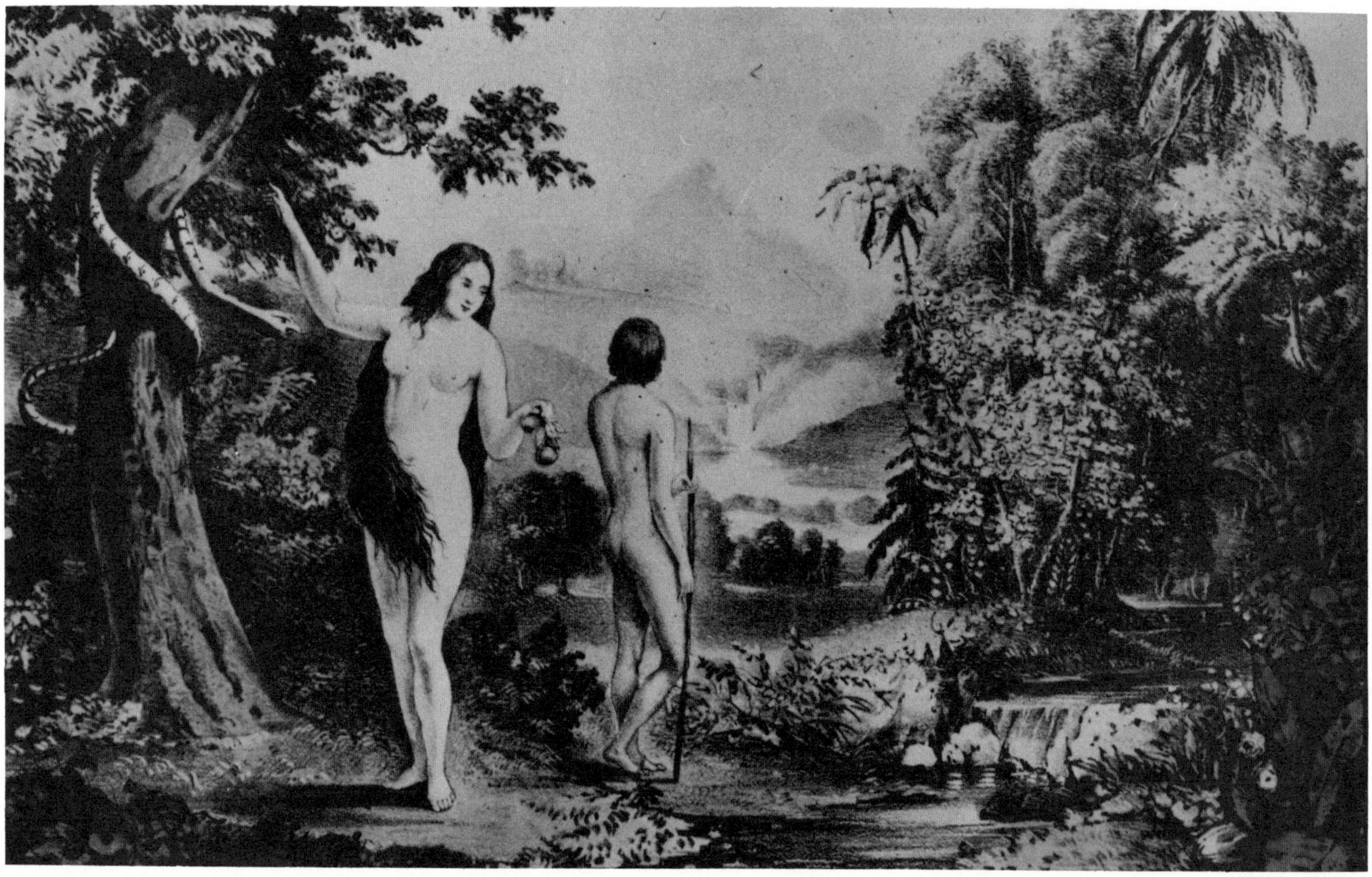

slight figure convey a nostalgic resignation. In the *Wesleyan Psalmist* (1842) is a religious ballad sung to a tune reminiscent of an old Cornish song:

Man at his first creation in Eden God did place,
The public head and father of all the human race;
But by the subtle serpent begui'd he was and fell,
And by his disobedience was doomed to death and hell.

Now at the time appointed Jesus unveiled his face,
Assumed our human nature and suffered on our place;
He suffered on Mount Calvary and ransomed all for me,
The law demands attention, to pay the penalty.

The inherent reverence for all forms of life which characterized the Quakers and Methodists was blended with a sacramental attitude toward nature, that was called forth by her majesty and, in this country, by a sense of kinship with nature in a common purpose—the establishment of a new world. Before Christ's sacrifice for man's redemption, Noah and all living creatures had been saved by God's grace. The old world was destroyed by a deluge. The Americans chose to represent Noah and the pairs of creatures when they emerged from the ark into a pure, washed-clean world. European artists painted the lush world Noah and the animals left when they entered the ark.

Americans reputedly suffer from a guilt complex and an overwhelming sense of sin. Sin and problems connected with it, European critics find, forms a major theme in American literature. Certainly a deep feeling of sin made the question "What must I do to be saved?" an all important one to the Jacksonian American. Several scriptural episodes gave the answer: "Your faith has saved you." The folksingers used these passages for spirituals, and lithographic firms illustrated them. The artists who drew the prints worked in an atmosphere and sprang from a cultural soil where an intensity of spiritual conviction caused them to parallel early Christian art, both in choice and treatment of subject. The image smashers of Cromwell and an inculcated abhorrence of the political machinations of the Roman church turned evangelical Protestant sects away from popish imagery. Their visual experience was with illustrations in *Pilgrim's Progress,* Sunday school books, chapbooks, German Lutheran picture Bibles, and the emblem books of Holland.

Baptism is the sacrament of the church which gives remission from original sin. The earliest copyrighted lithograph in the Library of Congress collections is *The Baptism of Our Savior,* drawn by John Baker and published by Justin Pierce in 1836. Ann Johnson's large watercolor copy of it hangs as an original work in the Abby Aldrich Rockefeller collection, Williamsburg, Va. An incessant debate over the efficacy of child versus adult baptism ensured a good sale of the print. A comparable rendition, rooted in similar religious conviction, is found in a 13th-century mosaic in St. Mark's, Venice. However,

Left: Currier, Adam and Eve in the Garden of Eden.

John Baker's lithograph, The Baptism of our Saviour, *published by Justin Pierce in 1836.*

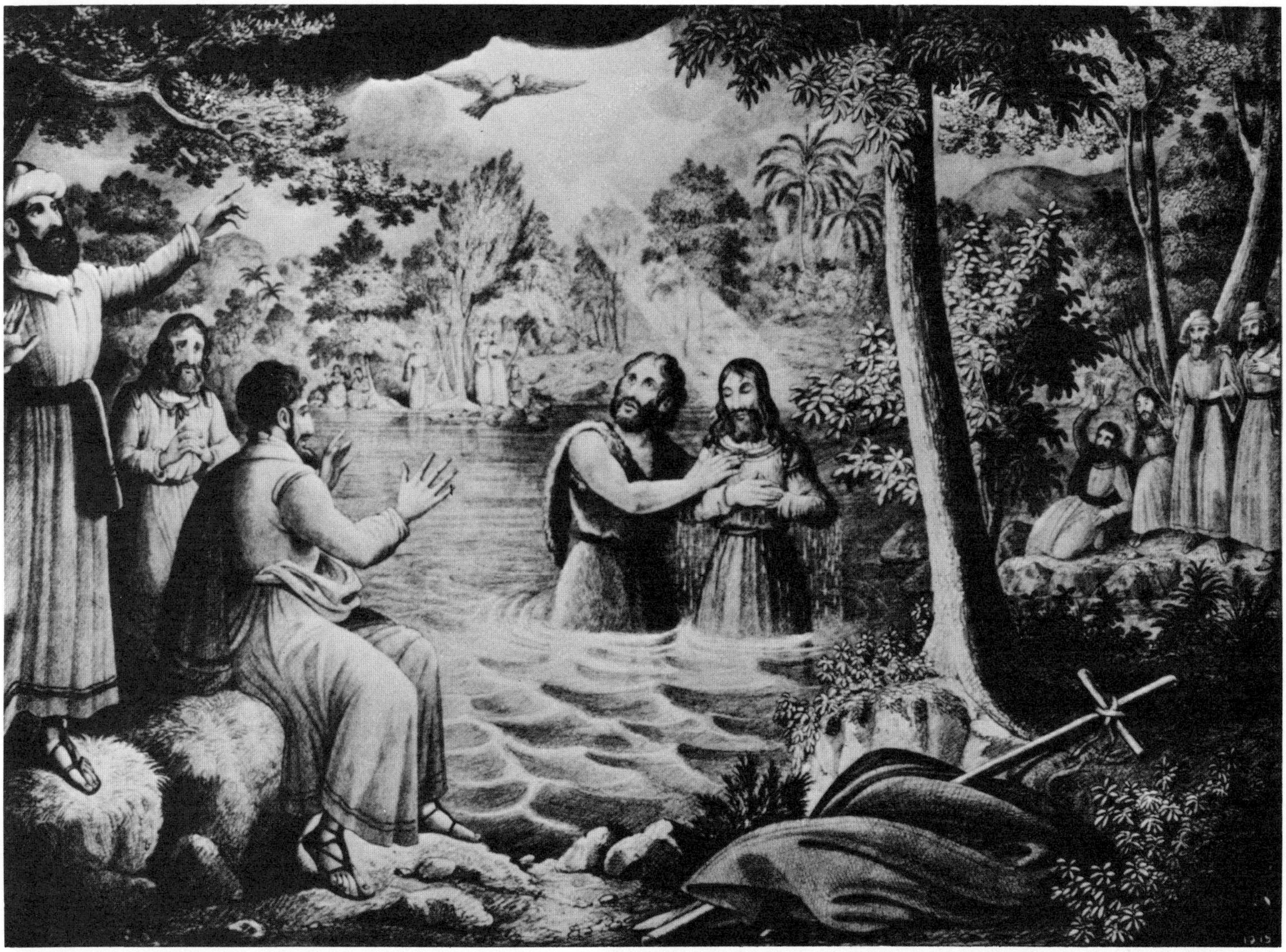

by the 15th century, focus had shifted to an intellectual interest in the nude, replacing religious belief, as evidenced by Andrea del Verrocchio's *Baptism of Christ.*

Christ walking on the sea of Galilee (Matt. 14:26-32) dramatically illustrates His power over natural elements and, equally dramatically, His power to save the frightened Peter when he began to sink. The awesome miracle was powerfully portrayed in a 12th-century mosaic at Monreale, Sicily. Subsequent generations generally ignored the episode or combined it with the miraculous draught of fishes related in Luke 5:7-9. When the first event was depicted, Christ walks serenely on the water, while Peter, bewildered and frightened, is apparently left to drown. In the early 19th century, a renewal of religious fervor in Europe and America led once more to the representation of the episode. In 1806, Philip Otto Runge was commissioned by the pastor-poet Ludwig Kosegarten to execute an altar painting for a sailors' chapel on the Baltic Sea. Runge, born in a pietistic community and a contemporary of Swedenborg and Kierkegaard, wrote Goethe of his concern to reconcile wild nature with the appearance of Christ. Goethe commented later, ". . . in all the gospels no loftier and more expressive subject exists than Christ who walks softly over the waves to the aid of sinking Peter. This scene has seldom been painted. The greatest advantage for the living artist is that Raphael has not treated it." [3]

The narrative was superbly portrayed with restrained, moving poignancy in a lithograph published by Currier, with the subtitle "Save me Lord!" Currier's artist could not have known Runge's unfinished painting. Searching for the source of the Currier print, I found a print similar in composition and spirit, in a small book in the British Museum, entitled *A Series taken from the New Testament designed as Ornaments for those Apartments in which Children receive the first Rudiments of their Education* (London, 1790). Mrs. Sarah Trimmer, a blue-eyed matron with an interest in the life of robins, whose energies were dedicated to the Sunday school movement in England and America, wrote the Scripture lessons that the 64 prints illustrated. The book had many editions—a copy is in the Library of Congress—and seeing the wood engraving in it may have stimulated Currier's artist to attempt the subject.

The often wayward pioneer was offered the possibility of a second chance in his spiritual life by the parable of the Prodigal Son. God, envisioned as a benevolent father welcoming home his lost son, demonstrated His compassionate forgiveness. The story is found early in American prints. Amos Doolittle was the first to publish four wood engravings to illustrate the parable. Other series and versions were soon available. Kellogg & Thayer's Prodigal Son left a less affluent, fashionable home than did Currier's Prodigal Son. The Prodigal Son of Kellogg & Thayer's series resembles in costume and type, Christian as he is depicted in the illustration "Christian directed by Evangelist to the Wicket-Gate" in an edition of *Pilgrim's Progress* printed in Burlington, N.J., in 1805. The story, a favorite with revival preachers, was told in a religious ballad for which Ananias Davisson, an arranger of unwritten music, claimed the tune. He included it in the *Supplement* to his popular *Kentucky Harmony* in 1820. Variant tunes are found in the *Wesleyan Psalmist* (1824) and the *Southern and Western Pocket Harmonist* (1864).

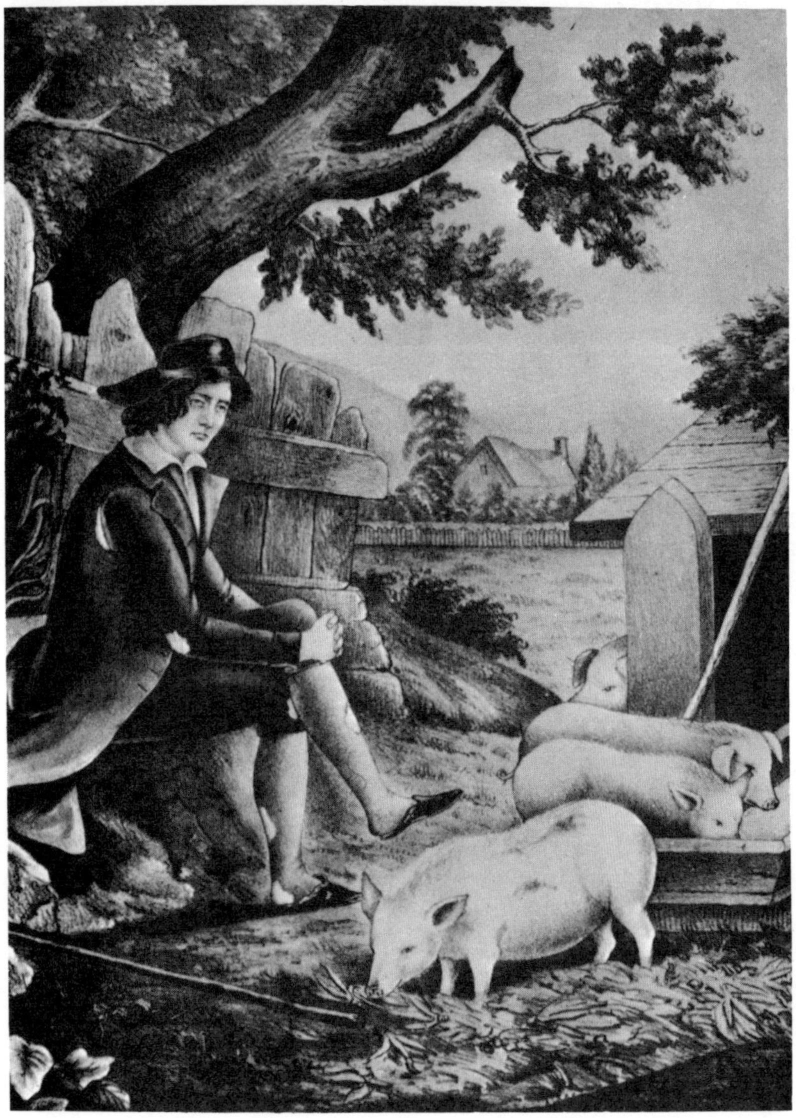

Above: Kellog & Thayer's The Prodical Son in Misery.

Far right: Christian directed by Evangelist to the Wicket-Gate *in an 1805 edition of* Pilgrim's Progress.

Afflictions, tho' they seem severe,
are oft in mercy sent;
They stopt the prodigal's career
and caused him to repent,
Altho' he no relenting felt
till he had spent his store;
His stubborn heart began to melt
when famine pinched him sore.

What have I gain'd by sin, he said,
but hunger, shame and fear;
My father's house abounds with bread,
while I am starving here.
I'll go and tell him all I've done,
fall down before his face;
Unworthy to be call'd his son,
I'll seek a servant's place.

The father saw him coming back,
he looked, he ran, he smiled;
He throws his arms around the neck
of his rebellious child.
Father, I've sinned, but O forgive;
enough; the father said.
Rejoice, my house, my son's alive
for whom I mourn'd as dead.

Now let the fatted calf be slain,
go spread the news around;
My son was dead, but lives again,
was lost now is found.
'Tis thus the Lord his love reveals,
to call poor sinners home;
More than a father's love he feels
and welcomes all that come.

A spiritual theme that is unique to this period and popular in America, centers around the 22d chapter of Revelation:

> Then he showed me the river of the water of life, bright as crystal, flowing from the throne of God and of the Lamb through the middle of the street of the city; also, on either side of the river, the tree of life with its twelve kinds of fruit, yielding its fruit each month; and the leaves of the tree were for the healing of the nations.

The imagery of this passage and of the third verse of the first Psalm caught the imagination of men and women in America with a fresh force of prophecy. The verses described a vision of Paradise and the New Jerusalem in a symbolism congenial to a people searching for the road to God among the streams, fields, woods, valleys, and hills of a new country. Rev. William McDonald used this imagery in his text that parodied a Scottish song, "Braes of Balquihidden," and was sung to its tune. It is found in *Olive Leaf* (1878).

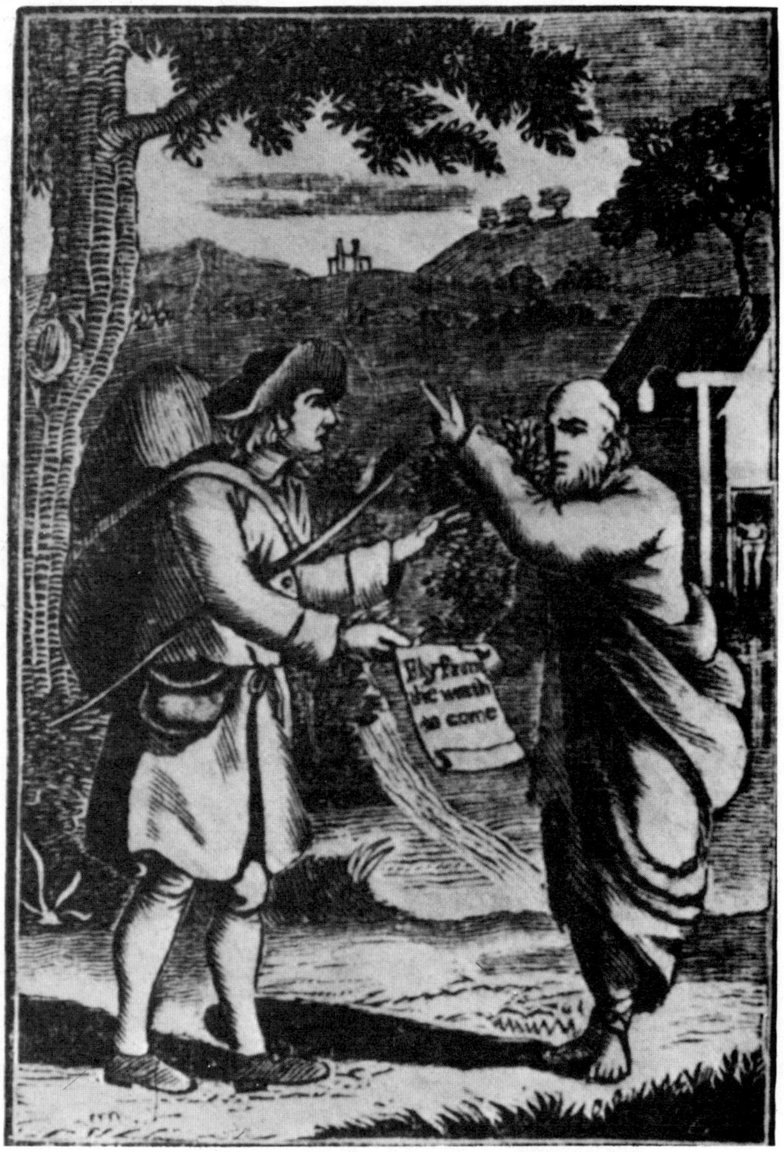

Sinner go, will you go
to the highlands of heaven.
Where the storm never blows
and long summer's given,
Where the bright blooming flow'rs
are their odors emitting
And the leaves of the Bow'rs
in the breezes are flitting.

Where the rich golden fruit
Is in bright clusters pending,
And the deep laden boughs
Of life's fair tree are bending;
And where life's crystal stream
Is unceasingly flowing,
And the verdure is green,
And eternally growing.

The biblical verses were translated into a visual literary form for the frontispiece to a *New Hieroglyphick Bible* printed in London in 1794 and offered for sale in Boston the same year. The two parts of the frontispiece are entitled "The Hieroglyphicks of a Christian" and "The Hieroglyphicks of the Natural Man." The only copy of the 1794 edition I know of is in the American Antiquarian Society's library. Subsequent editions of this rival to the *Curious Hieroglyphick Bible* of 1784, introduced here by Isaiah Thomas in 1788, have only the "Hieroglyphick of

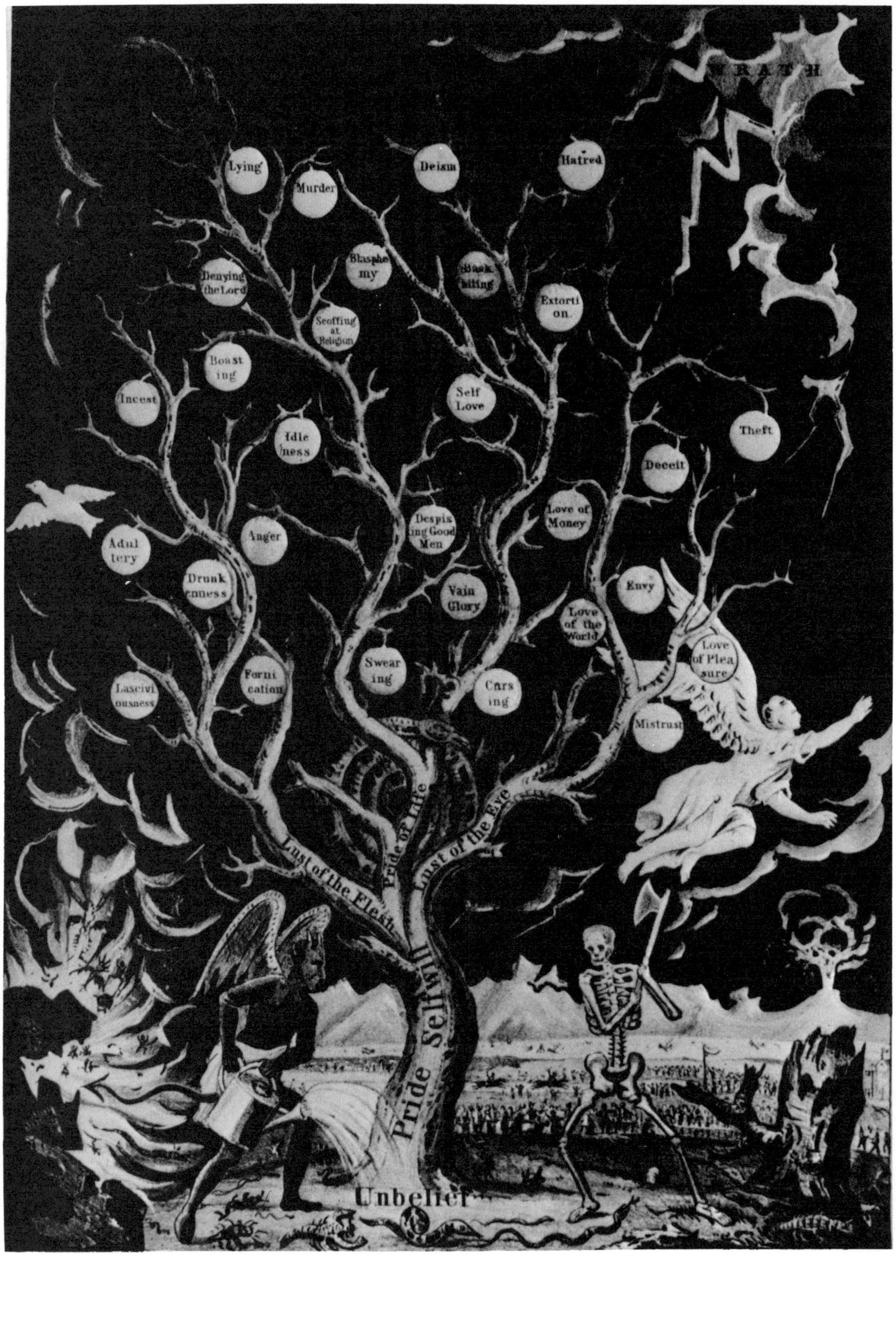
WRATH
Lying
Murder
Deism
Hatred
Blasphe my
Denying the Lord
Back biting
Extorti on
Scoffing at Religion
Boast ing
Incest
Self Love
Idle ness
Theft
Deceit
Love of Money
Despis ing Good Men
Anger
Adul tery
Drunk enness
Vain Glory
Envy
Love of the World
Love of Plea sure
Swear ing
Forni cation
Lascivi ousness
Curs ing
Mistrust
Lust of the Flesh
Pride of Life
Lust of the Eye
Pride Selfwill
Unbelief

The Tree of Death. The Sinner, by Currier.

the Christian." An American edition of 1818 restored the original frontispiece, minus the figures. Many Trees of Life and the very similar Trees of Virtues are found before the 12th century. The obscure source from which this form, based on Revelation and not on the parable of the tree in the Gospels, emerged at the end of the 18th century is a perplexing riddle. It was a disappointment not to find its form represented among the pages of the Mattsperger Bible in Stuttgart.

Nathaniel Currier, who grew up in Roxbury, near Boston, may have owned a copy of the first edition of the *New Heroglyphical Bible* of 1794. He "lifted," with only slight alterations, the frontispiece from the little book for two prints he published, one *The Tree of Death: The Sinner,* the other, *The Tree of Life: The Christian.* Other firms published Tree of Life prints taken either from Currier's print or from his source.

The imagery of the stream and tree also illustrated the reward that awaited Christian in *Pilgrim's Progress.* After he had made his way through the river, he reached the bank on which stood the Tree of Life, where two ministering spirits in white, shining raiment waited for him.

A copy of *Pilgrim's Progress,* possibly that printed in Burlington, N. J., in 1805, was at the elbow of the artist who drew the Kellogg & Thayer Tree of Life. In the foreground is the town Vanity, with its year-round fair. The Shadow of Death with the devils is on the extreme left. The Celestial City could be reached by passing wantoness and chambering. One small door was set in the wall enclosing the Celestial City, where stood the Tree of Life with its never-fading fruits. Men and women gazed hopefully over the wall of this world to a vision beyond. The stanzas of a gospel spiritual written by Samuel Stennett (1727-1795) that appeared in the *Sacred Harp* (1844) described their longing.

On Jordan's stormy bank I stand
And cast a wishful eye,
To Canaan's fair and happy land
Where my possessions lie.

O the transporting rapt'rous scene
That rises to my sight,
Sweet fields arrayed in living green
And rivers of delight.

There generous fruits that never fail
On trees immortal grow;
There rocks and hills and brooks and vales
With milk and honey flow.

All o'er those wide extended plains,
Shines one eternal day;
There God the Son forever reigns,
And scatters night away.

No chilling winds, or poisonous breath
Can reach that healthful shore;
Sickness and sorrow, pain and death,
Are felt and fear'd no more.

When shall I reach that happy place,
And be forever blest?
When shall I see my Father's face,
And in his bosom rest?

Cold water was not a popular drink with the first colonists. Beer, brandy, wine—"the good creatures of God"—were considered to be healthful, strengthening beverages and were in wide use. By and large, however, the colonists were reasonably sober folk and were encouraged by their society to remain so.

The importation of rum from the West Indies early in the 18th century changed all that. Sugar and rum came in to sweeten and sadden life in the colonies. Good money could be had from distilling rum from molasses. Soon New England rum was good enough to be exported to England. By 1823 enough distilled liquors were manufactured to raise the annual per capita consumption to seven and one-half gallons. Dr. Benjamin Rush, the Philadelphia physician and signer of the Declaration of Independence, made a first appeal for temperance. People began to form themselves into temperance societies. A real force behind the temperance movement was the Washington Total Abstinence Society, founded by six hard drinking men in Baltimore in 1840. It soon had 600,000 reformed drunkards as members, but many "backslid."

The cause of temperance was spread by the graphic and literary media. Every lithographic firm published series of four or six pictures in which the tragic story of a weak-willed person is told, and the *Drunkard's Progress,* used the step devices of the *Life and Ages of Man.* The cause was strengthened by popular ballads which described the results of intemperence as graphically as do the prints. John McCurry, the compiler of the *Social Harp* (1855), claimed the song "John Adkin's Farewell' and dated it 1851—the year the Maine Law was passed.

Poor drunkards, poor drunkards, take warning by me,
The fruits of transgression behold now I see;
My soul is tormented, my body confin'd;
My friends and my children left weeping behind.

Much intoxication my ruin has been,
And my dear companion I've barbarously slain;
In yonder cold graveyard her body doth lie,
And I am confined and must shortly die.

Farewell my dear children, wherever you be;
Though quite young and tender and dear unto me;
I leave you exposed in nature's wide field,
In which God is able poor orphans to shield.

When sorrows oppress you and sickness comes on,
You'll cry for your mother, but, oh, she is gone;
Your father, in anger, struck her on the head,
She bled, groan'd, and languish'd, and now she is dead.

My soul now His pleasure I humbly submit,
And with my last burthen fall down at His feet;
To plead for His mercy that flows from above,
That pardons poor drunkards, and crowns them above.

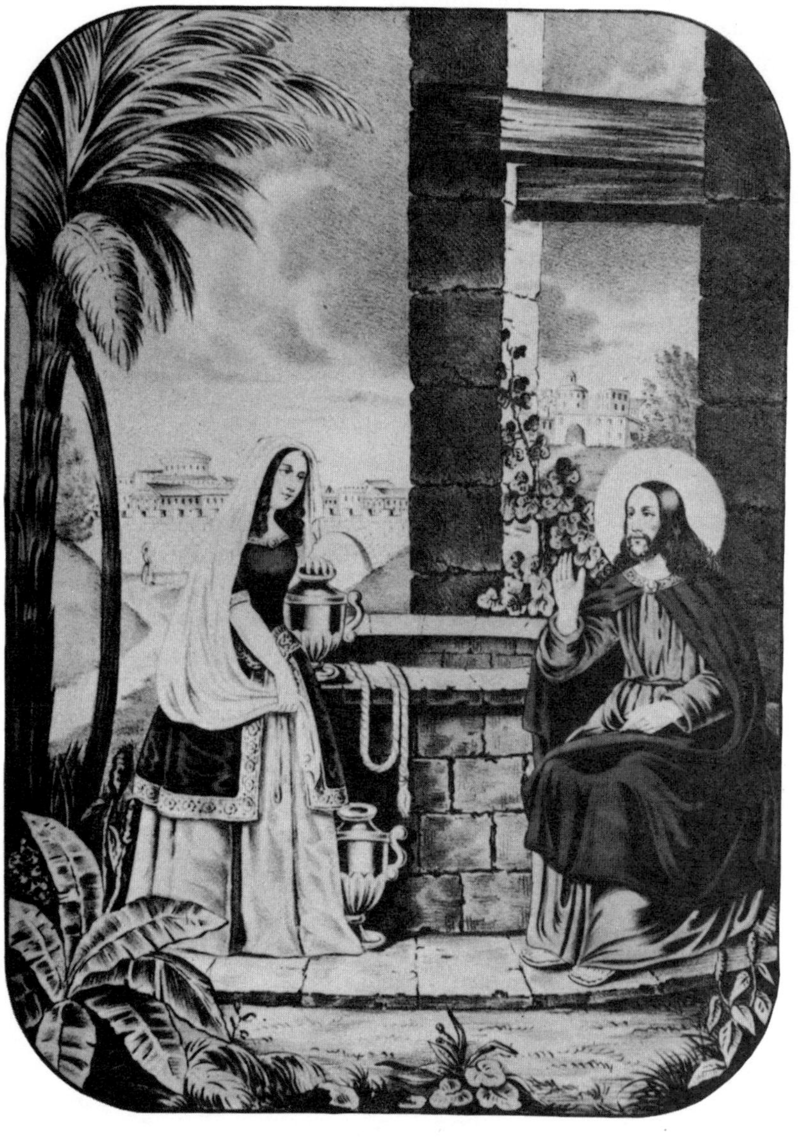

Above: Currier, Christ at the Well.

Right: One of many In Memoria pictures by Nathaniel Currier.

Temperance was greatly aided by a beneficial society, The Order of the Sons of Temperance, formed within the movement. A Currier print of 1848 portrays the virtues a Son of Temperance emulates. His clear eyes look confidently to a successful future. His narrow-waisted coat and nankeen trousers set off the order's regalia. The order increased to 232,200 members by 1850, and 46 years after its founding had 2,500,000 members and had collected and dispersed nearly nine million dollars.

Another beneficial association, the Independent Order of Good Samaritans and the Daughters of Samaria, was established in New York in 1847 to rescue those who had been fallen upon by "rummies" as they traveled life's highway. Currier's print *Christ at the Well,* with the caption "Whosoever drinks this water shall never thirst," served two markets: one which revivals created by urging people to drink the living water of faith and be saved; the other, the temperance movement and its militant Cold Water Army.

At the close of a century or when a combination of events presage profound changes, men seem to sense an epoch is ending and thoughts dwell on death and the motto "sic transit gloria mundi." Confronted with the inevitability of decay and frailty of flesh, mankind seeks consolation in religion.

At such a time in 1802, the Second Awakening swept through the American countryside. In its wake death—the gateway to Paradise for the righteous and the portal to hell for the wicked—became a preoccupation. One's daily actions determined the road one took. Today, we rarely think of death, for we have it segregated in modern hospitals. Then, when the threat of death was ever present, the walls of cabins, cottages, and city dwellings were hung with pictures and prints inscribed with the name of one the household held in sacred memory. For those who lacked the time or skill to embroider or paint In Memoria pictures, lithographic firms offered a variety of prints suitable to the bereavement. The most elegant of Currier's 15 "Memory" prints listed in his catalog of 1851 were probably drawn by Fanny Bond Palmer. The appropriate grave monument in classical style was the acme of what a family would like to place in the cemetery. The face of the monument was left blank, ready for the epitaph to be inscribed in pen and ink. Such a print enabled poor, humble folk to honor suitably the memory of loved ones, even if there was no money for a tombstone.

The preoccupation with death suddenly awakened a general concern for the place where mortal remains would rest until the trumpet call of Judgment Day. Dr. Jacob Bigelow founded Mt. Auburn Cemetery in Cambridge, Mass., the first secular, garden cemetery in America. Philadelphia's Laurel Hill and Brooklyn's Greenwood followed. A cemetery was placed in the plan of new towns. For Jacksonian Americans, who were often weary from harsh struggle against the wilderness and untamed nature,

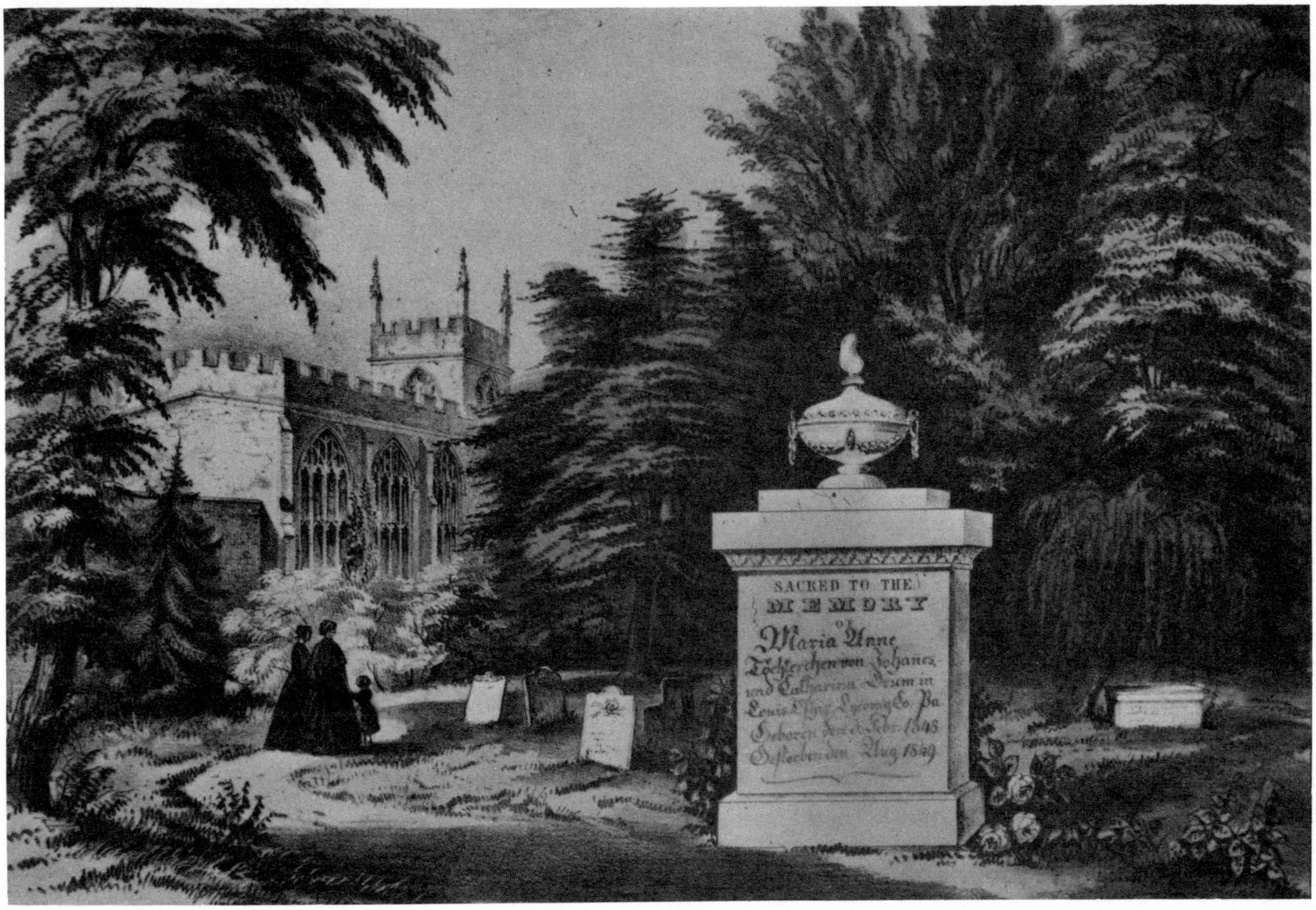

the cemetery, carefully laid out in new towns, was described as a haven in *A Guide to Mt. Auburn,* with "uncrowded quietude, glistening turf, cool sweet–winding avenues and paths. . . ." Death was the gateway to this paradise.

Appropriate words were adapted and sung to the tune "Burn's Farewell." It was published in the *Masonic Harp* (1858).

O come. Come with me to the old church yard,
I well know the path through the soft greensward;
Friends slumber there, we were wont to regard,
We'll trace out their names in the old church–yard.

For deep is their sleep, though cold and hard
Their pillows may be in the old church-yard.
O mourn not for them their grief is o'er,
Weep not for them they weep no more.

. . . were I at rest beneath yon tree,
Why should you weep, dear friends, for me?
I'm wayworn and sad, O why then retard
The rest that I seek in the old church-yard?

In quietude sweet, in the old church-yard?
We'll rest in the hope of that bright day,
When beauty shall spring from the prison of clay,
When Gabriel's voice and the trumpet of the Lord,
Shall waken the dead in the old church-yard.

O weep not for me, I am anxious to go
To that haven of rest where tears never flow;
I fear not to enter that dark lonely ward;
For soon I shall rise from the old church-yard.

Yes, soon shall I join that heavenly band
Of glorified souls at my Saviour's right hand;
Forever to dwell in bright mansions prepared
For saints, who shall rise from the old church-yard.

In 1843 and again in 1844, followers of William Miller put on white garments and gathered in cemeteries to await the second coming of Christ. The fever of that expectation cooled, but the expectation remained. Currier received a contract from the American Tract Society for two folio-size prints, one the *Crucifixion,* the other *Resurrection.* John Cameron, a hunchback, reformed drunkard, and mainstay of the firm, was assigned to design them. He gave his imagination full rein. Turbulent skies reflect the tremendous effect of the Resurrection on the world. Christ and an angel dominate the scene by their brightness, not by monumental size. Cameron was probably stimulated by the dramatic light and dark effects employed by the popular English artist, John Martin, whose illustrations of the Scriptures were copied for many American Bibles. Cameron's self-confidence was sufficient for him to reject copying any one in toto. He simply selected items he needed and arranged them in a composition to achieve his own vivid effect. His *Resurrection* is a naive, joyous representation of the event that fed the hope of every Christian. Similar tension and intensity gripped Lowell Mason, the popular hymnwriter of the period, when he composed:

Yes, the Redeemer rose, the Savior left the dead,
And o'er our hellish foes High raised his conquering head;
In wild dismay The guards around
Fall to the ground, And sink away.

Behold th'angelic bands In full assembly meet,
To wait his high commands, And worship at his feet.
Joyful they come, And wing their way,
From realms of day To Jesus' tomb.

Then back to heaven they fly The joyful news to bear,
Hark! as they soar on high, What music fills the air!
Their anthems say, . . . "Jesus, who bled, Hath left the dead,
He rose to-day."

Ye mortals! catch the sound, Redeemed by him from hell,
And send the echo round The globe on which you dwell;
Transported cry, . . . "Jesus, who bled, Hath left the dead,
No more to die."

Between 1830 and 1850, devotional lithographic prints and religious folksongs were two complementary art forms which brightened the lives and homes of the people.

NOTES

[1] Carl Russell Fish, *Rise of the Common Man* (New York: The MacMillan Co., 1927), pp. 2–4.

[2] All the hymns are quoted from George Pullen Jackson, *Spiritual Folk-Songs of Early America* (New York: J. J. Augustin, 1937) and *White Spirituals in the Southern Uplands* (Chapel Hill: University of North Carolina Press, 1933).

[3] Translated from a quotation given in Klaus Lankheit, "Vision, Wundererscheinung und Wundertat in der christlichen Kunst," *Triviale Zonen in der Religiösen Kunst des 19.Jahrhunderts* (Fritz Thyssen Stiftung, Frankfurt a/M, V. Klostermann, 1971) Studien zur Philosophie und Literatur des neunzehnten Jahrhunderts, Bd. 15, pp. 76–101.

Little Loretto, Kentucky

Edgar Breitenbach

Edgar Breitenbach, who recently retired as chief of the Prints and Photographs Division, Library of Congress, is an art historian interested in iconographic research. His publications include Speculum humanae salvationis *(Strassburg, 1930),* Santos: The Religious Folk Art of New Mexico *(Colorado Springs, 1943), and* The American Poster *(New York, 1967). This paper is published here by permission of* American Heritage.

This brief paper deals with only one print. Its title is in three languages, Flemish, French, and English. The English reads: "Little Loretto, Kentucky, United States of America." I have chosen the print because it ties in perfectly with the theme of our sessions: it is factual, and yet at the same time it is fictitious, and although it is drawn and engraved by an otherwise unknown Belgian artist named Courtois living in Malines, Belgium, its subject matter is thoroughly American. As far as I can establish—I have made inquiries in several local institutions—it is the earliest view of a Kentucky settlement that has come down to us. Yet this is a most ambiguous print; although it purports to be a view, its real purpose, as we shall see, is to encourage the recruitment of priests and to solicit donations. This may be a bold claim, but I consider this innocent-looking print to be the distant ancestor of the modern real estate advertisement and the recruiting poster. It actually seems to be saying "I want you!"

We acquired this etching about seven years ago from a collector who had picked it up in Europe. It frankly intrigued me the moment I saw it; it appeared to be so trustworthy, but at the same time it was so blatantly spurious. Quite obviously, the artist had never visited the Blue Grass State; the landscape, dotted with palm trees and including a waterfall cascading amidst exotic vegetation, is delightfully incongruous for Kentucky. To complete the fantasy, there is an alpine range in the background, drawn in the tradition of Flemish artists of the 16th century. Indeed, the historian John Gilmary Shea, writing in 1891 to one of the Loretto nuns, was moved to some gentle sarcasm:

> Many thanks . . . for the delightful old view of the Convent of Loretto. It is so quaint and odd that it deserves a place among queer pictures. They tell a story of an officer of the English army in India who, having been sent with a detachment into a new part of the country near the mountains, thought that a sketch of the new fort and its surroundings would interest friends in England. So he prepared a careful sketch and sent it to the *London Illustrated News.* He received by return mail a letter of thanks, but when the paper arrived, to his horror and the intense enjoyment of all his fellow officers, the whole picture had been filled up with palm trees, when, in fact, there was not a tree of any kind in sight from the fort. It was in vain for him to protest that his sketch had not been followed, he was the butt of all regimental jokes. When he wrote to London complaining indignantly of the liberty taken with his drawing, they replied that the English public required palm trees in pictures from India! The Belgian printmaker seems to have had the same idea.

The original print Little Loretto Kentucky United States of America, *done by Courtois in 1806 or 1807.*

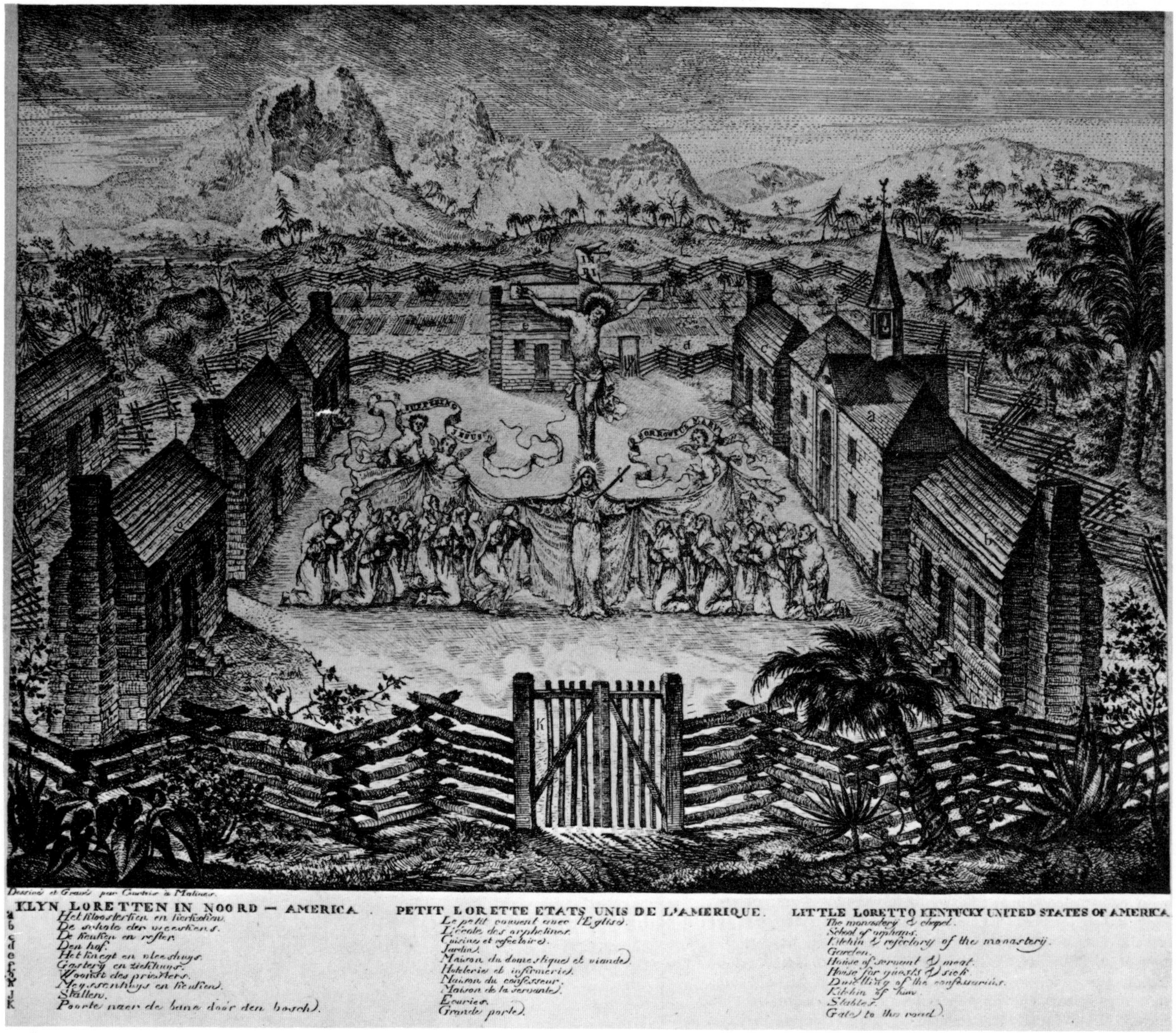

Yet in spite of all these liberties, the print cannot be put into the same category as the fictitious prospects of American cities made in Augsburg for commercial distribution. The settlement itself, even down to such details as the rail fence surrounding it, has an air of authenticity about it. One is struck by the stark simplicity of the buildings. This is how the earliest medieval monasteries which the Scot-Irish missionaries built in the wilderness of the Swiss Alps may have looked. The function of each building is carefully recorded in the explanatory notes beneath the print. Here the artist quite obviously is not letting his fantasy run wild but is following the instructions given to him by his client. It is this aspect that makes the print American.

Courtois' client was the great Father Charles Nerinckx, the founder of the Loretto Society, a teaching order of nuns that is still in existence; it was the first Catholic congregation to be founded on American soil that had no parent house abroad. Its full, somewhat cumbersome, name was "Friends of Mary at the Foot of the Cross;" hence the emblematic design in the center of the courtyard of nuns kneeling under the protective cloak of Our Lady of Sorrows, who is standing under the cross. The Madonna of the Protective Cloak as an iconographic subject was very popular during the late Middle Ages but was practically obsolete in the beginning of the 19th century when our print was made. This is one of several instances where religious motifs, nearly forgotten in Europe, reappeared in America—a phenomenon not uncommon in the religious folkart of New Mexico and the Pennsylvania Dutch.

Charles Nerinckx was exceptionally well suited for life on the frontier. He was physically strong, resourceful, an able organizer, and not one to be daunted when things didn't turn out as he had hoped they would. In secular matters he was a nonconformist, ready to make great sacrifices rather than give up his convictions. As a member of the clergy, he was naturally accustomed to receiving orders from his superiors and to giving orders to his flock. Here he showed very little flexibility. In fact, he was such a hard taskmaster that in the end it proved his undoing. What he lacked was an understanding of the principles of a democratic society. Give-and-take and compromise were concepts quite alien to him.

Nerinckx was born in 1761 in what today is Belgium but which at that time was still the Austrian Netherlands. In the 1790's he became a political dissenter, who refused to give the loyalty oath to the new government after the French conquest of Flanders. Under the threat of imprisonment, he was forced to live in hiding for several years but eventually escaped via Holland to America. He arrived in Baltimore in 1804 and offered his services to Monsignor Carroll, bishop of Baltimore. His offer was accepted, but first he had to learn English. This he did after spending some time with the Jesuits in Georgetown in the newly created District of Columbia. In the end he was assigned to St. Stephens in Marion County, Ky. To get there from Washington was not an easy matter in 1805. He started out in a wagon train organized by groups of Trappist monks. After a few days he grew tired of his silent companions and of the slow pace of the wagons. In Bedford, Pa., he bought a horse for $75.00 and continued on his own across the mountains and down the Ohio, until he finally reached his destination in mid-July. St. Stephens was the headquarters of Father Theodore Badin, a native of France and, like Father Nerinckx, a refugee from the French Revolution.

It is almost impossible for us to realize the enormous physical difficulties which the clergy had to face in those days in a sparsely populated, mountainous, and large roadless country. A settler stayed close to his homestead, but a minister had to be constantly on the move to cover his far-flung parish circuit. Between the year 1787, when the first Catholic priest arrived to care for the spiritual needs of the settlers, and 1805, when Father Nerinckx began his mission, only seven priests were active in Kentucky. Of these, four left after a short time, one was killed by a horse, another by a falling tree. That Father Badin, and later Father Nerinckx, stayed so long shows that they must have been possessed of extraordinary moral and physical stamina.

Father Nerinckx seems to have realized from the first that for his mission to succeed he must have assistants. In September, two months after his arrival, he wrote to his parents in Belgium that he intended to establish a sisterhood. When this attempt failed, he sought the advice of Father Badin, who, with 10 years of experience behind him, had succeeded in winning the confidence of his parishioners. One of them, James Dent, agreed to donate a 400-acre tract to be used to establish a church, a convent school for girls, and an orphanage. It is this projected community, I believe, that is shown in our print, which was made by Courtois in either 1806 or 1807. I realize that this interpretation may not be shared by the Loretto Sisters, who cherish the belief that it shows the convent *after* its completion several years later. Our copy, however, bears a handwritten dedication to a Belgian nobleman, Comte de Robiano, dated 1807. We must therefore assume that it is based on a sketch sent to Courtois by Father Nerinckx, who subsequently distributed copies to potential donors while soliciting funds for his convent school.

The trilingual key to the picture explains the function of each of the buildings, which are set around an oblong inner court. The turreted structure on the right, the only one to have two stories, is the convent, with the church at its center. This arrangement was probably dictated by practical considerations, since the windows in the upper walls of the nave would have permitted the nuns to join in the service without being seen by the lay worshippers. European convent churches frequently include this feature. The convent is flanked by the school and orphanage towards the entrance gate and by the cabin containing the kitchen and the refectory towards the rear. Facing the building on the opposite side are the house of the resident priest, his kitchen with living quarters for his cook (the only cabin with no windows into the courtyard), and a hut, used either for guests or for the sick. On the far side, opposite the entrance gate, is the cabin for the use of the nuns' male servant, who was also the custodian of the convent's supply of cured meat. Outside the courtyard, to the far left, are the stables. On the right, behind the church, a tall cross marks the place of the graveyard. There is a vegetable garden beyond the inner enclosure, and the entire community is surrounded by a rail fence, which supplies the authentic touch of old Kentucky.

The fact that our picture is a projection of what could be done if funds were forthcoming does not in the least diminish its documentary value. There was nothing fancy about any of the buildings, which were designed to supply just the barest necessities of civilized life. The building material was entirely native wood, except for the foundations and the chimneys; only six of the seven buildings provided a place where people could keep warm during the cold winter months—the church and the living quarters for the nuns had no such amenities. Considering the conservative character of Father Nerinckx and the stubbornness with which he stuck to his plans, we may safely assume that the Loretto convent, when it was finally built, did indeed look like the community on our print. Reconstructions of military forts in the 19th century seem to support this view: simple log cabins with stone chimneys, facing an oblong courtyard.

In February of 1808 Father Nerinckx was able to write to his parents that the foundations had been laid; by Whitsuntide he reported that the building was far enough along to receive its roof.

> It is 70 feet long, and will have a chapel about as long and wide as the house, surmounted by a turret. Some outbuildings will be added. It is situated one mile from Father Badin's house. Six or seven of our young ladies have applied to be the first religious, but it seems that there are many more who are anxiously watching how the undertaking will succeed, and who will join the community as soon as it is an accomplished fact.

It never did become a fact, however; before the first young women could move in, a disastrous fire broke out, which reduced all but the chimneys to ashes.

For several years after the disaster there is no mention of any new attempt to establish a convent school. We can be sure, however, that Father Nerinckx was only biding his time, waiting for the right opportunity to present itself. That opportunity finally came in the winter of 1811–12. In the early part of the new year, James Dent, the donor of the 400 acres, returned from a visit to Maryland, bringing back with him his young niece, Mary Rhodes, whose brother was also a settler. Mary's function was to undertake the teaching of her brother's children, and soon the children of neighboring settlers were added to her care. When the numbers grew too large for her to handle, Father Nerinckx persuaded her to take on another young woman, Christina Stuart, as her assistant. This event signaled the birth of the teaching order of the Sisters of Loretto.

The two young women, both of an extremely pious nature, shortly thereafter resolved to withdraw from the world. They found a couple of dilapidated log cabins which other settlers had abandoned and moved into them, living in one and teaching in the other. Such a step demanded great courage, not only because of the hardships involved but also because it meant a complete break with the conventions of a pioneer society. In April, together with a third recruit, Ann Havern, they received the veil from Father Nerinckx and submitted themselves to a religious life under rules drawn up by him. More young women joined in the weeks that followed, and there is a record of a second ceremony of veil-taking in the early summer. The establishment of this first little religious community was a triumph for Father Nerinckx and was a tribute both to his gift for organization and to his powers of spiritual guidance. He was capable of enormous self-denial, and the young nuns seem to have been determined to emulate him. Father Maes, in his *Life of Reverend Charles Nerinckx,* writes:

> Stockings and shoes were worn only from the 1st. of November till March 25th, the sisters going barefooted the balance of the year. This severe custom was introduced at the request of the first sisters, who begged of Father Nerinckx to let them try and go barefooted as did the holy anchorites of old. He at first refused the desired permission, but yielded at last to repeated entreaties. Some time before his death, however, he ordered the sisters to wear shoes all through the year and never to resume the former practice. During the first years, breakfast consisted of bread and vegetable soup or rye-coffee served in tin cups; supper of bread and milk or sage tea, without either meat or butter; dinner was dished up in tin plates and consisted of one kind of meat (when they could get it) and vegetables; pious reading during meals was the only dessert allowed, unless some neighbor's charity afforded them the luxury of fruit. The beds were the simplest expression that useful piece of furniture is susceptible of, viz: a shake-down of straw on the bare floor, without either sheet or pillow! The sisters were too poor to get any.

The school was welcomed by the settlers, but many of them, especially the bachelors, resented the religious order, which in a sparsely populated region could only mean a serious drain of eligible young women. At first they were content to sneer: "Let's be happy that the priest rids the State of old maids." Later, hostility to the order grew so strong that even among his own parishioners there were those who accused him of misappropriating funds. In October 1812 Father Nerinckx vindicated himself with great forcefulness in a pamphlet directed to his critics, which effectively silenced them.

Some time between 1812 and the fall of 1815, when he left for a visit to Europe, Father Nerinckx replaced the poor huts which had been the earliest home of the order with larger and sturdier buildings. In the end, the community may well have resembled the master plan of 1807.

On his visit to Europe, Father Nerinckx first spent some

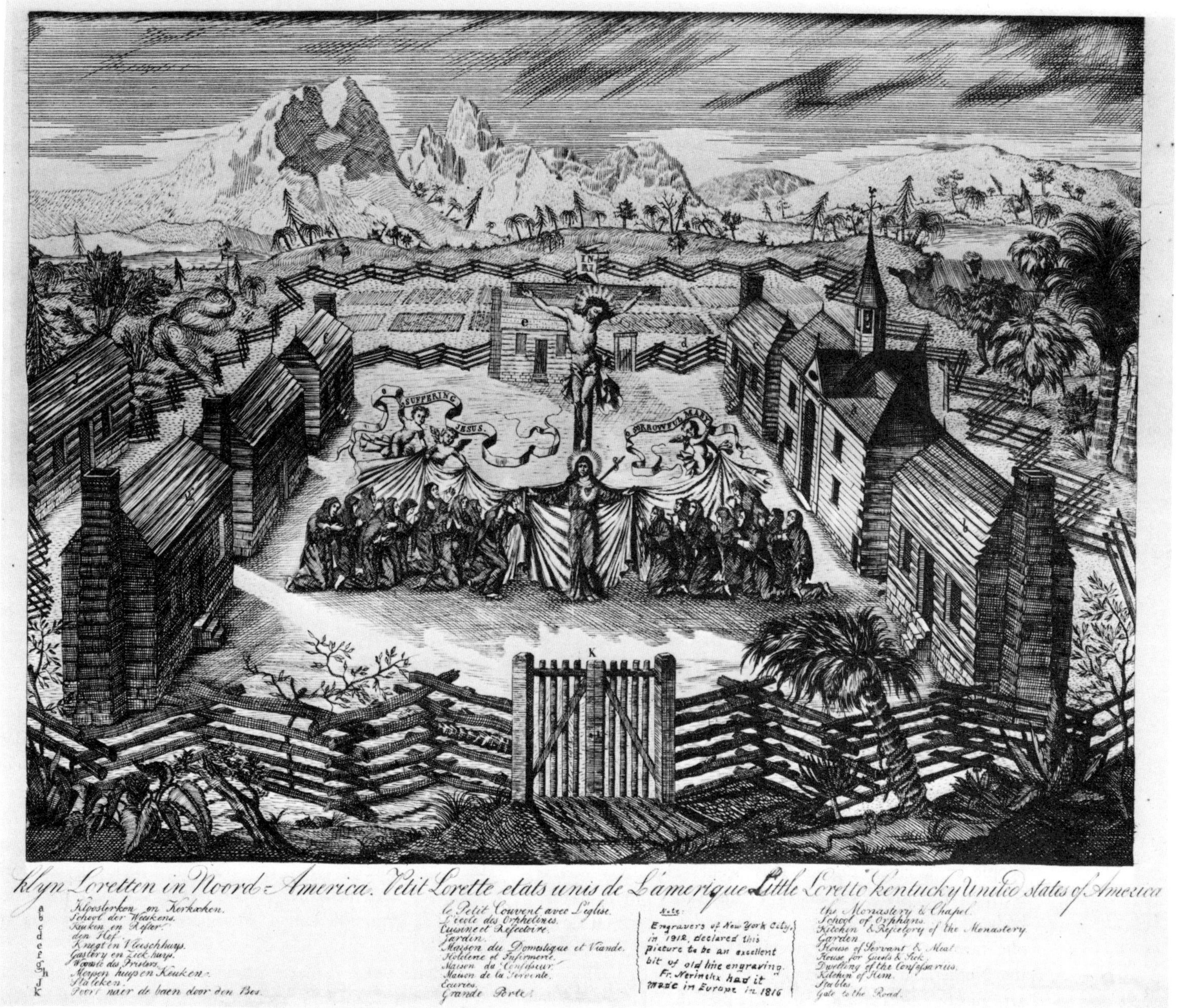

The later version of the print, done in 1816. Courtois' name was omitted, and a note added later by one of the Loretto sisters reads, "Engravers of New York City, in 1912, declared this picture to be an excellent bit of old line engraving. Fr. Nerinckx had it made in Europe in 1816."

time in his native Belgium and then went on to Rome, arriving there in April 1816. The rules of his order were confirmed by the Pope soon after. Before returning to America he once more visited Belgium to solicit funds, books, and church furnishings to help him carry on the work of his mission. Again, he made use of his print in support of his campaign. As the original edition was evidently exhausted, a new plate had to be made. The new version, though much coarser than the first one, repeats every detail, palm trees and all. Courtois' name, however, has been deleted, tactfully, it would seem, though a handwritten note by one of the Loretto sisters informs us: "Engravers of New York City, in 1912, declared this picture to be an excellent bit of old time engraving. Fr. Nerinckx had it made in Europe in 1816."

The journey of 1816 turned out to be successful, in terms of fund raising. He was even able to persuade nine volunteers to accompany him back to America, but of these, eight got no farther than Georgetown, where they became Jesuits, and the ninth, who had gone on ahead with part of the baggage to New Orleans, died of yellow fever en route.

The story of this baggage throws some interesting light on the kind of religious art brought to the United States in the early 19th century and underlines the enormous difficulties involved in getting it to its destination. Nerinckx's baggage, weighing some 8,000 pounds, contained a great variety of church vestments, chalices, monstrances, ciboriums, an antependium, a tabernacle, 100 paintings, and even church bells. In a letter of 1818 addressed to his benefactors in Belgium, Nerinckx gave an account of his expenses, saying that on arrival every passenger had to fill out a declaration giving a description of the articles imported, as well as their value, and swear to the correctness of the declaration. In 1817 this procedure applied to all American ports except New Orleans, which between 1815 and 1820 had free port privileges. Nerinckx therefore decided to separate his baggage into two parts—one for the southern sea route, the other for the overland haul. The ocean voyage to New Orleans would have been cheaper had there been no doctor's bills and burial costs for his unfortunate companion. Because there was no one to arrange for the trip between New Orleans and Loretto, this part of the baggage still had not arrived a year and a half later when he wrote this report, although it may have reached its destination in the end. It would be interesting to find out how many of these Belgian objects are still to be found in Kentucky churches. One seemingly important painting, depicting the life of St. Bernard, hung over the altar of St. Joseph in the cathedral of Louisville in about 1880.

Nerinckx was hopeful that these art treasures might be used as models for local craftsmen. If they were, I am not aware of it. Unlike the Spanish settlers of New Mexico, the Catholics of Kentucky created no religious folkart. Poverty cannot be the reason, as both groups were equally poor. I rather suspect that the emergence of a religious folkart depends on such factors as: 1) a population of similar ethnic stock, sharing a common tradition, 2) a religious belief that is accepted by the majority of the people in a given region. This would explain why the German Protestant settlers of Pennsylvania left a sizable body of religious imagery, and the widely scattered Catholic farmers of Kentucky, coming from France, Germany, the Netherlands, and Ireland, relied on imported religious art, mostly discards, to be sure, like the things people give to a charity rummage sale.

After his return to Loretto in the summer of 1817 Father Nerinckx had less than seven years to live, and these years were full of difficulties and tribulations. He had established Loretto only after overcoming great obstacles; even then, the saintly young Mary Rhodes who became the first mother superior was destined to die at the end of the first year, in December 1812. During his lifetime, seven new convents were established in Kentucky. Although he remained their nominal head, he granted them a large measure of independence. In 1812 a Father Chabrat, the parish priest of Bardstown, was appointed as supervisor of the Bethania Convent, one of the sister convents to Loretto. This convent had an unusually high mortality rate among the nuns, so much so that it had to close after only six years. Father Chabrat, a younger man, in view of this sad experience, questioned the practicality of the strict rules drawn up by Father Nerinckx, even though they had been approved by Rome. This eventually led to a conflict, in which Father Chabrat had the support of the bishop of Kentucky in nearby Bardstown. Father Nerinckx, who by this time was getting old and had no heart for a fight, preferred to leave Kentucky in 1824 and retire to Missouri, where he had established a school the previous year (the Convent of Bethlehem at the Barrens in Perry County). He died the same year at the age of 62.

Father Chabrat had in the meantime become acting superior of all the Kentucky convents and was particularly concerned with Loretto. On the death of Father Nerinckx, he seems to have deliberately set out to erase everything that might contribute to his memory. A few months after Father Nerinckx' decease, Father Chabrat, with the approval of his bishop, decreed that the nuns of Loretto should abandon their buildings and move to new quarters at St. Mary's, known as Father Badin's Farm. The extraordinary thing is that the nuns, apparently acting on their own initiative, set fire to the buildings of Loretto before they left, sparing only the cabin of Father Nerinckx. They afterwards claimed that this was done to prevent the buildings falling into the wrong hands and being used for secular purposes. Father Chabrat, for his part, ordered all of Father Nerinckx' books and papers destroyed. In this connection, one touching little incident has been recorded, in which one of the sisters snatched from the flames a copy of Father Nerinckx' farewell address to them.

In later years Father Nerinckx came to be regarded as something of a saint, and during the second half of the 19th century he inspired several tributes in verse. These poems, displaying more religious zeal than poetic merit, sang his praises unstintingly, while not sparing his enemies. The story of Loretto, first glimpsed as a visionary undertaking among the wilds of Kentucky and destined to vanish mysteriously only a score of years later, remains to haunt us. What Father Nerinckx achieved, however, was of lasting worth, and his life work is being continued to this day by the teaching sisters of the Loretto Order.

Illustrated News in Early American Prints

Peter C. Marzio

Peter C. Marzio is Associate Curator of Prints at the Museum of History and Technology of the Smithsonian Institution, where he has worked on exhibitions on Rube Goldberg, Timothy Cole, Pop Hart, and Louis Prang, in addition to setting up the permanent Henry R. Luce Hall of News Reporting. He has written articles and exhibit catalogs on early American prints, and his books include Rube Goldberg: His Life and Work *(New York, Harper & Row, 1973).*

The Utility of Colonial Prints

On January 28, 1779, colonial engraver Thomas Coram advertised in the *South Carolina and American General Gazette* that he was willing to engrave "coats of arms, names, cyphers, notices and ornaments on plate or seals, &c. bills of parcels, names and ornaments engraved on copper plates, for tradesmen and others; a few packs of visiting cards in the present taste, and neatly printed in purple and other colours." He promised to "cut his work expertly" and to fill his orders promptly. Like a contemporary engraver from New York, John Hutt, Coram went so far as to offer "Stamps cut for the news paper on the shortest notice." Neither Coram nor Hutt nor most other colonial engravers advertised his works as aspiring solely to fine art. Repeatedly their advertisements were aimed at specific utilitarian needs. They made it clear that American graphic art, although varying in artistic quality, performed specific social functions.[1]

In the terms of the late William Ivins, colonial graphics were "exactly repeatable pictures" conveying specific kinds of information in simple, economical form. An overwhelming number were published not as single sheets but as illustrations in newspapers, books, magazines, and broadsides. These pictures were printed in conjunction with words and were designed to function in a literal manner, harmonizing so completely with written texts that the words and the pictures became inseparable.[2]

Many of these early American prints were embryonic forms of illustrated journalism. Produced as visual reports of the recent past, they often aspired to the qualities of timeliness and specificity which characterize present day news reporting. The desire for accurate pictures of current events was not unique to American colonists; European artists and printmakers also wished for such prints, produced with speed and economy. They too understood that a bonanza awaited any man who could produce illustrated news. In A. Hyatt Mayor's latest tour de force, it is demonstrated how several schools of printmakers during the 17th and 18th centuries searched for technological remedies to solve the tedium and the slowness of known printmaking processes. The big breakthrough, of course, came with the invention of lithography in the 1790's. For America, in particular, this discovery was revolutionary. Now all could see, as well as read, the news.[3]

Every major printmaker, including Nathaniel Currier,

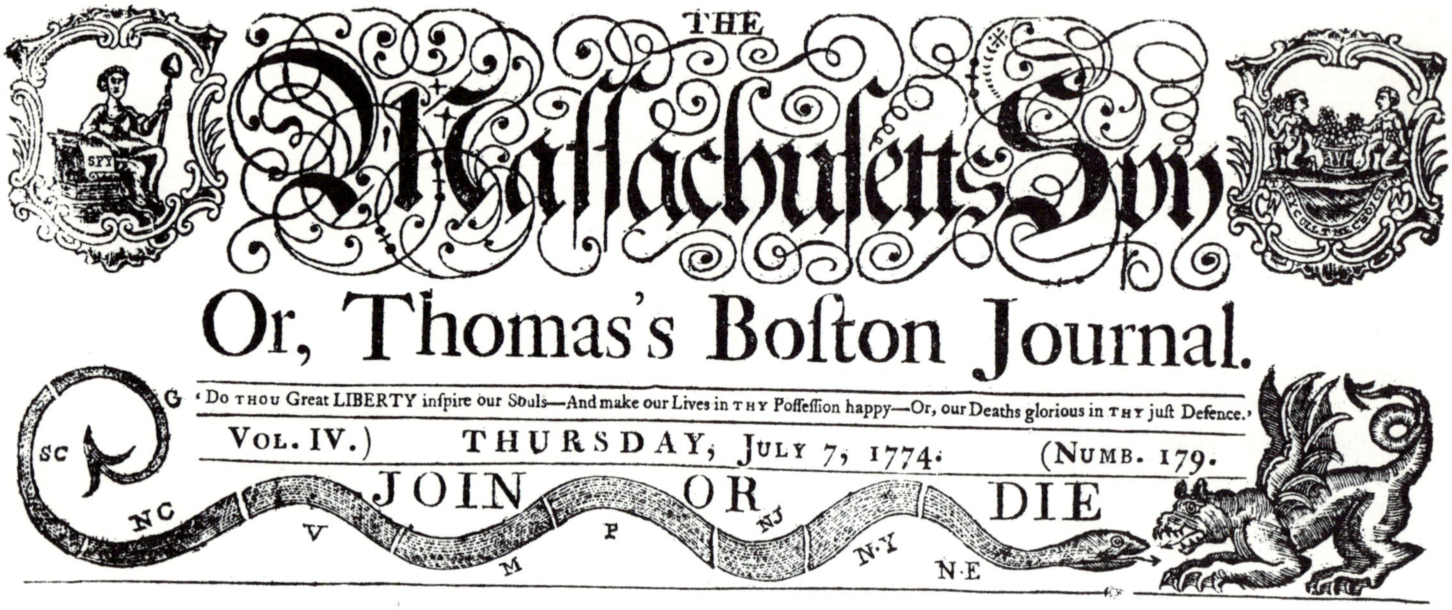
THE Maſſachuſetts Spy
Or, Thomas's Boſton Journal.
'DO THOU Great LIBERTY inſpire our Souls—And make our Lives in THY Poſſeſſion happy—Or, our Deaths glorious in THY juſt Defence.'
VOL. IV.) THURSDAY, JULY 7, 1774. (NUMB. 179.
JOIN OR DIE

Louis Prang, and the Pendleton family, peddled picture news during the first three-quarters of the 19th century. For most of these artist-businessmen, illustrated news was an important financial pillar, and they competed feverishly to "scoop" their rivals.

Before the days of news photography and the halftone screen, all that an objective newsman could report was the eyewitness account of an honest draftsman. But even this was open to question. It was physically impossible for any artist to draw any more than a very select part of all the things he saw. When working with a deadline—as in the golden years of *Harper's Illustrated*—the artist seldom had the opportunity to add corrective touches. Yet it is the artist, not the photographer, who has been responsible for recording most of our visual history.

Strangely enough, most historians tend to ignore the artist as a news reporter. Since we do not know what is real and what is imaginary, they claim, we should look elsewhere for truth. This myth has been exploded by Dr. Ronald Tyler in his study of prints relating to the Mexican War. Moreover, it seems that "historical" prints tell us more about the past and the people of the past than about the subject matter they depict. When the editors of D. Appleton and Co. published Carl Nebel's lithographs in George Wilkins Kendall's *The War Between the United States and Mexico* in 1851, for example, they felt compelled to caution any gullible reader against accepting the truthfulness of the color lithographs.

> Every reader must be aware of the impossibility, in painting a battle scene, of giving more than one feature or principal incident of the strife. . . . The artist has . . . chosen what he deemed the more interesting as well as exciting points of each combat, and trusts that the public may excuse any errors which may be discovered. Something the painter is always compelled to sacrifice for effect, but in the present series of illustrations the greatest care has been taken to avoid inaccuracies. . . .[4]

This introduction by the publishing company did not arise from a social concern for truthfulness, I suspect, but from a hardheaded appraisal of the popular American attitude toward specific facts. The artist of the American Revolution, John Trumbull, ran up against this attitude when he commissioned engravings of his flamboyant recreation of scenes from America's war for independence. Hoping to cash in on the idolization of the war heroes, he sought to elevate Washington and his followers above the "vulgarism of ordinary life" (to use Sir Joshua Reynold's phrase), to transform the sloppiness and the confusion of the recent past into a grand style of cleanliness and order.[5]

Trumbull, like Nebel 50 years later, worked from facts, personal observations, and official reports, but his engravings were commercial failures, in part because they compromised historical truth for artistic generality. They lacked the specificity which a journalist or historian brings to the reporting of an event. One contemporary asked "what is the point of time?", and another artist-chronicler, William Dunlap, lectured in 1834:

> When a man becomes a 'graphic historiographer' he has a duty to fulfill that cannot be dispensed with. If the historian or the 'graphic historiographer' cannot tell the whole truth, he must not at least violate the known truth.[6]

Historical inaccuracies were troublesome enough as unique expressions of Trumbull's paintings, but they were intolerable when engraved, printed, and distributed by the thousands.[7]

Newspapers and Printmakers

The popular faith and demand for visual accuracy, which D. Appleton & Co. so clearly perceived and which John Trumbull stubbornly resisted, was rooted in the colonial period. Printmakers, particularly engravers, were closely associated with newspapers and other news media. When

Left: Masthead by Paul Revere for The Massachusetts Spy, *July 7, 1774.*

Right: Woodcut of the British flag in the January 26, 1707, edition of The Boston News-Letter.

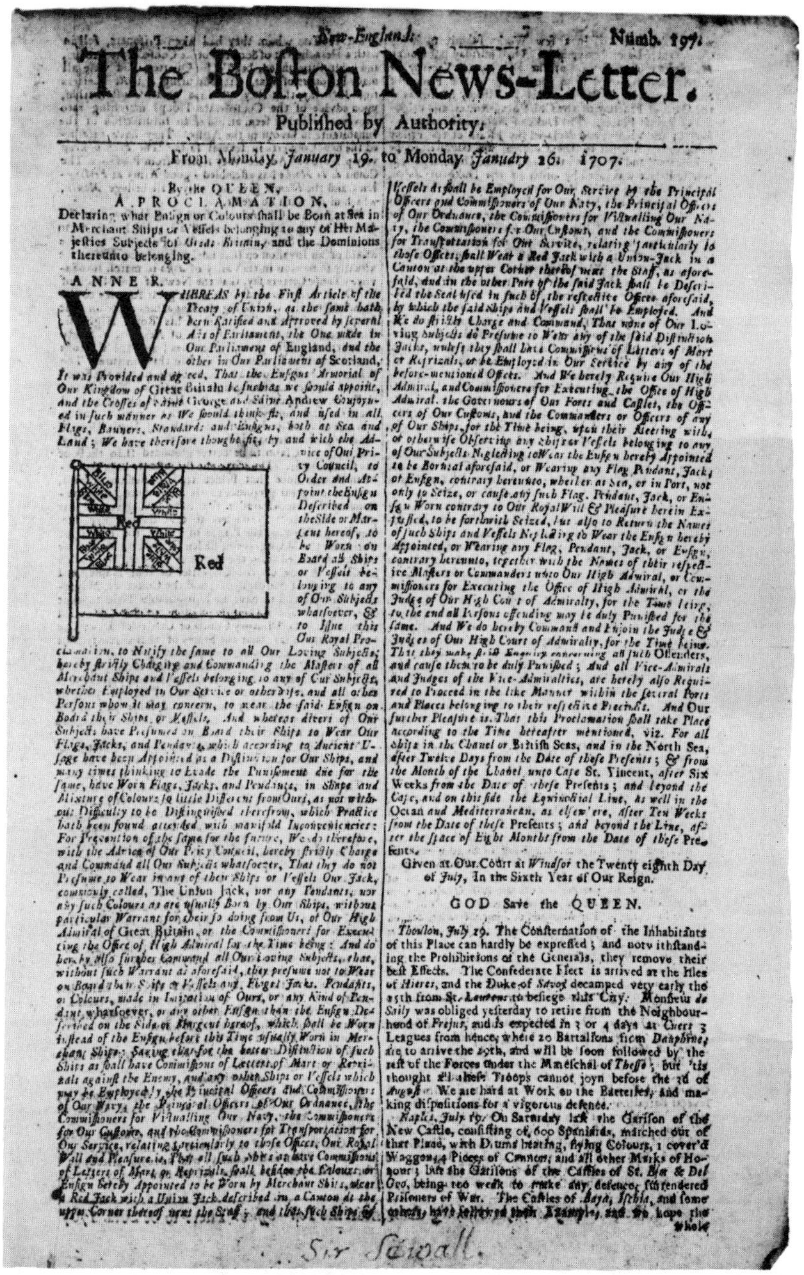

New-England. Numb. 197.

The Boston News-Letter.

Published by Authority.

From Monday *January* 19. to Monday *January* 26. 1707.

By the QUEEN,
A PROCLAMATION,
Declaring what Ensign or Colours shall be Born at Sea in Merchant Ships or Vessels belonging to any of Her Majesties Subjects of *Great Britain*, and the Dominions thereunto belonging.

ANNE R.

WHEREAS by the First Article of the Treaty of Union, as the same hath been Ratified and Approved by several Acts of Parliament, the One made in Our Parliament of England, and the other in Our Parliament of Scotland, It was Provided and agreed, That the Ensigns Armorial of Our Kingdom of Great Britain be such as we should appoint, And the Crosses of Saint George and Saint Andrew Conjoyned in such manner as We should think fit, and used in all Flags, Banners, Standards and Ensigns, both at Sea and Land; We have therefore thought fit, by and with the Advice of Our Privy Council, to Order and Appoint the Ensign Described on the Side or Margent hereof, to be Worn on Board all Ships or Vessels belonging to any of Our Subjects whatsoever, & to Issue this Our Royal Proclamation, to Notify the same to all Our Loving Subjects; hereby strictly Charging and Commanding the Masters of all Merchant Ships and Vessels belonging to any of Our Subjects, whether Employed in Our Service or otherwise, and all other Persons whom it may concern, to wear the said Ensign on Board their Ships or Vessels. And whereas divers of Our Subjects have Presumed on Board their Ships to Wear Our Flags, Jacks, and Pendants, which according to Ancient Usage have been Appointed as a Distinction for Our Ships, and many times thinking to Evade the Punishment due for the same, have Worn Flags, Jacks, and Pendants, in Shape and Mixture of Colours so little Different from Ours, as not without Difficulty to be Distinguished therefrom, which Practice hath been found attended with manifold Inconveniencies: For Prevention of the same for the future, We do therefore, with the Advice of Our Privy Council, hereby strictly Charge and Command all Our Subjects whatsoever, That they do not Presume to Wear in any of their Ships or Vessels Our Jack, commonly called, The Union Jack, nor any Pendants, nor any such Colours as are usually Born by Our Ships, without particular Warrant for their so doing from Us, or Our High Admiral of Great Britain, or the Commissioners for Executing the Office of High Admiral for the Time being: And do hereby also further Command all Our Loving Subjects, that, without such Warrant as aforesaid, they presume not to Wear on Board their Ships or Vessels any Flags, Jacks, Pendants, or Colours, made in Imitation of Ours, or any Kind of Pendant whatsoever, or any other Ensign than the Ensign Described on the Side or Margent hereof, which shall be Worn instead of the Ensign before this Time usually Worn in Merchant Ships: Saving that for the better Distinction of such Ships as shall have Commissions of Letters of Mart or Reprizals against the Enemy, and any other Ships or Vessels which may be Employed by the Principal Officers and Commissioners of Our Navy, the Principal Officers of Our Ordnance, the Commissioners for Victualling Our Navy, the Commissioners for Our Customs, and the Commissioners for Transportation for Our Service, relating particularly to those Officers, Our Royal Will and Pleasure is, That all such Ships as have Commissions of Letters of Mart or Reprizals, shall besides the Colours or Ensign hereby Appointed to be Worn by Merchant Ships, wear a Red Jack with a Union Jack described in a Canton at the upper Corner thereof next the Staff; and that such Ships or Vessels as shall be Employed for Our Service by the Principal Officers and Commissioners of Our Navy, the Principal Officers of Our Ordnance, the Commissioners for Victualling Our Navy, the Commissioners for Our Customs, and the Commissioners for Transportation for Our Service, relating particularly to those Officers, shall Wear a Red Jack with a Union-Jack in a Canton at the upper Corner thereof next the Staff, as aforesaid, and in the other Part of the said Jack shall be Described the Seal used in such of the respective Offices aforesaid, by which the said Ships and Vessels shall be Employed. And We do strictly Charge and Command, That none of Our Loving Subjects do Presume to Wear any of the said Distinction Jacks, unless they shall have Commissions of Letters of Mart or Reprizals, or be Employed in Our Service by any of the before-mentioned Offices. And We hereby Require Our High Admiral, and Commissioners for Executing the Office of High Admiral, the Governours of Our Forts and Castles, the Officers of Our Customs, and the Commanders or Officers of any of Our Ships, for the Time being, upon their Meeting with, or otherwise Observing any Ships or Vessels belonging to any of Our Subjects Neglecting to Wear the Ensign hereby Appointed to be Born as aforesaid, or Wearing any Flag, Pendant, Jack, or Ensign, contrary hereunto, whether at Sea, or in Port, not only to Seize, or cause any such Flag, Pendant, Jack, or Ensign Worn contrary to Our Royal Will & Pleasure herein Expressed, to be forthwith Seized, but also to Return the Names of such Ships and Vessels Neglecting to Wear the Ensign hereby Appointed, or Wearing any Flag, Pendant, Jack, or Ensign, contrary hereunto, together with the Names of their respective Masters or Commanders unto Our High Admiral, or Commissioners for Executing the Office of High Admiral, or the Judge of Our High Court of Admiralty, for the Time being, to the end all Persons offending may be duly Punished for the same. And We do hereby Command and Enjoin the Judge & Judges of Our High Court of Admiralty, for the Time being, That they make strict Enquiry concerning all such Offenders, and cause them to be duly Punished; And all Vice-Admirals and Judges of the Vice-Admiralties, are hereby also Required to Proceed in the like Manner within the several Ports and Places belonging to their respective Precincts. And Our further Pleasure is, That this Proclamation shall take Place according to the Time hereafter mentioned, viz. For all Ships in the Chanel or British Seas, and in the North Sea, after Twelve Days from the Date of these Presents; & from the Mouth of the Chanel unto Cape St. Vincent, after Six Weeks from the Date of these Presents; and beyond the Cape, and on this side the Equinoctial Line, as well in the Ocean and Mediterranean, as elsewhere, after Ten Weeks from the Date of these Presents; and beyond the Line, after the space of Eight Months from the Date of these Presents.

Given at Our Court at *Windsor* the Twenty eighth Day of *July*, In the Sixth Year of Our Reign.

GOD Save the QUEEN.

Thoulon, July 29. The Consternation of the Inhabitants of this Place can hardly be expressed; and notwithstanding the Prohibitions of the Generals, they remove their best Effects. The Confederate Fleet is arrived at the Isles of *Hieres*, and the Duke of *Savoy* decamped very early the 25th from St. [illegible] to besiege this City. Monsieur de *Saily* was obliged yesterday to retire from the Neighbourhood of *Frejus*, and is expected in 3 or 4 days at [illegible] 3 Leagues from hence, where 20 Battalions from *Dauphine*, are to arrive the 29th, and will be soon followed by the rest of the Forces under the Mareschal of *Thesse*; but 'tis thought all these Troops cannot joyn before the 3d of *August*. We are hard at Work on the Batteries, and making dispositions for a vigorous defence.

Naples, July 19. On Saturday last the Garison of the New Castle, consisting of 600 Spaniards, marched out of that Place, with Drums beating, flying Colours, 1 cover'd Waggon, 4 Pieces of Cannon, and all other Marks of Honour; but the Garisons of the Castles of St. *Elm* & Del *Ovo*, being too weak to make any defence, surrendered Prisoners of War. The Castles of *Baya*, *Ischia*, and some others, have followed their Example, and we hope the whole

engraver John Norman of Philadelphia advertised in the *Pennsylvania Journal,* July 16, 1777, he emphasized the timeliness of his subject matter and the accuracy of his facts. His ad read:

> Just published, and now selling . . . (price Three Dollars) The Theatre of War, in North America, with a polymetric table shewing the distances and roads of the principal places, towns, forts, rivers, &c. Being a complete map of the Thirteen United States, divided by different colours, and of all that hath been heretofore comprehended under the name of the British colonies in North-America.[8]

Earlier, when the Stamp Act threatened to double the price of newspapers, a number of engravers had been commissioned to incise the notorious skull and crossbones with the legend: "This is the Place to affix the STAMP." In addition to individual prints, good cuts for mastheads and special illustrations for newspaper advertisements were in continual demand. The ledgers of Paul Revere reveal entries for cuts in lead commissioned by news publishers. His elaborate mastheads for Isaiah Thomas' *Massachusetts Spy,* which incorporate Benjamin Franklin's "Join or Die," and his cuts of coffins mourning the victims of the Boston Massacre suggest the range of his technical and artistic skills. Other engravers, of course, also used the divided snake for mastheads. Revere was too much of a rebel to be a news reporter, but his print of the Boston Massacre, as well as those by Henry Pelham and Jonathan Mulliken, were reprinted in various news media particularly broadsides and pamphlets, during the 1770's. Cartoons satirizing contemporary problems also appeared, keeping the engraver of unique prints busy in the production of news.[9]

The first news illustration in an American newspaper was the new design for the British flag, which appeared on January 26, 1707, less than three years after the *Boston News-Letter* rose as the first continuously published newspaper in English America. This simple cut contains two principal elements of most colonial news illustrations. First, although it was printed nearly five and one-half months earlier in Europe, it was as fresh as most transatlantic news in any colonial journal. It was not unusual to read European news which was one or even two years old in the early issues of the *Boston Gazette.* This delay was partially a result of the tenuous and slow communications technologies, but it also resulted from the common practice of printing news in chronological order, paying no attention to timeliness or immediacy. In some cases "fresh news" remained in the printer's desk drawers for nearly a year waiting to find its way into print. It was a bold move to discontinue "the method of carrying on a Thread of occurrences," as Bartholomew Green of the *Boston News-Letter* did in 1726, but by midcentury most printers followed his lead. This change in procedure—the publishing of the newest news—could not alter the slowness of communications systems, however, so "immediacy," although becoming more and more desirable, was usually absent from any form of news reporting.[10]

This means that "news," in 18th-century terminology, could very well be defined in today's terms as "recent history," or at least the reporting of previously unknown events of the not too distant past. Many colonial prints which have been classified as historical pieces might better be labeled as news, for in many cases prints and illustrations carried unique information about specific recent events which the written word had failed to convey.

The picture of the British flag contained a second

feature which became typical of colonial news prints: simply put, it was meant to be read. Every age learns to see in a specific way, and in most cases this style of vision is not purely a function of esthetic preference but of the level of technology. The colonial picture of the English flag was a product of a precise, literal vision which demands that the viewer grasp the pieces before he can understand the whole. In order to "see" the flag successfully, the viewer first had to "read" the colors.

Almanacs and Illustrated News

The illustrations in other publications, particularly the American almanacs, functioned in a timely and literal manner. During the Revolution when many colonial newspapers were forced to shut down, the almanacs substituted as a popular news medium. "A VIEW of the Present Seat of WAR at and near New York" appeared in Nathaniel Low's Almanac for 1777 and provided the first visual report of the newest war zone. I do not know of a single newspaper that carried this picture or any picture which visualized the New York campaigns.[11]

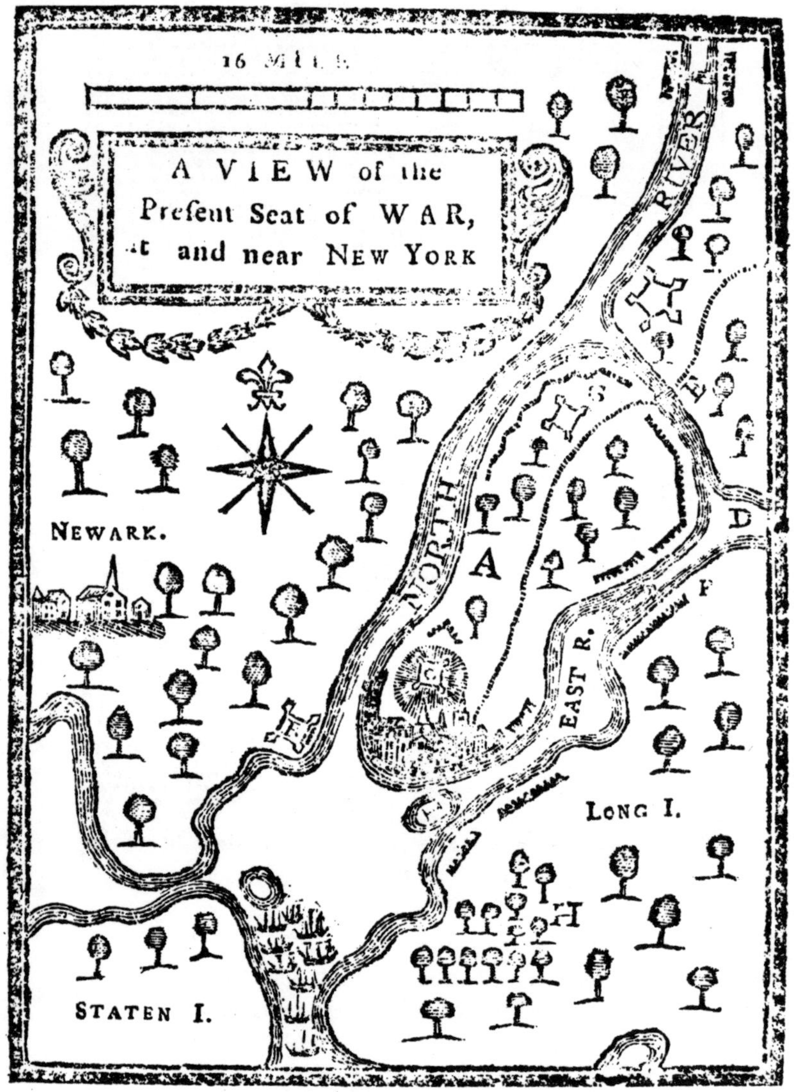

Woodcut, A View of the Present Seat of War at and near New York, *from Nathaniel Low's* An Astronomical Diary . . . 1777 (*Boston, Printed by J. Gill, 1776*).

Colonial almanacs also incorporated many other subjects commonly carried in today's newspapers. On June 18, 1749, when the planet Mars reached its orbital position closest to the earth, the moon passed between the two planets presenting a rare and certainly newsworthy event. Several newspapers made passing mention of the occurrence, but Nathaniel Ames' almanac, issued in December 1749, transformed it into an illustrated news story. After a rather obtuse description of the event, Ames resorted to a graphic report. "But that my Reader may see with his Eyes the remarkable Situation of our Earth, and her Attendant Moon, and the Planet Mars on that Day, I shall here insert the following Diagram." The diagram, of course, was keyed so that the reader simply followed the event A, B, C, D, E, F, G, H, recreating in a literal or chronological fashion exactly what happened.[12]

Graphic reports of "Neues from the Stars"—as one European chronicler labeled his almanac—were common astrological reports throughout the colonial period. The anatomical man was a general kind of news illustration. Like the English flag and the diagram of the eclipse, which were literal pictures, the anatomical man was keyed to statistical tables and charts, all explaining the relationship of heart and mind to personal conduct. Today one may laugh at colonial astrology, but the anatomical man, who appeared in innumerable visages, was actually among the most common of the nongovernmental images in colonial America. The significance lies not in the pseudoscience but in the visual implication—a linear, precise, and intricate map to an "enlightened" destination.[13]

Among the more objective news pictures were the commemorative portraits of recently deceased persons of note—a kind of illustrated obituary page. There was a forerunner tabloid journalism as well, complete with graphic sensationalism. The *Almanack, For The Year of*

OUR Lord Christ, 1787, by Isaac Bickerstaff, included a gruesome woodcut of "A most Surprising Account of Sawney Beane, a Man Eater, and his Family, who lived in a Cave who had Murdered upwards of a Thousand People and eat of them." Bickerstaff's vivid graphic treatment of colonial cannibalism would have warmed the heart of the present-day editor of the *National Enquirer,* but it was not out of step with colonial taste. The normally decorum-minded Isaiah Thomas reported in his *New-England Almanack* for 1775 the latest information on the exploits of

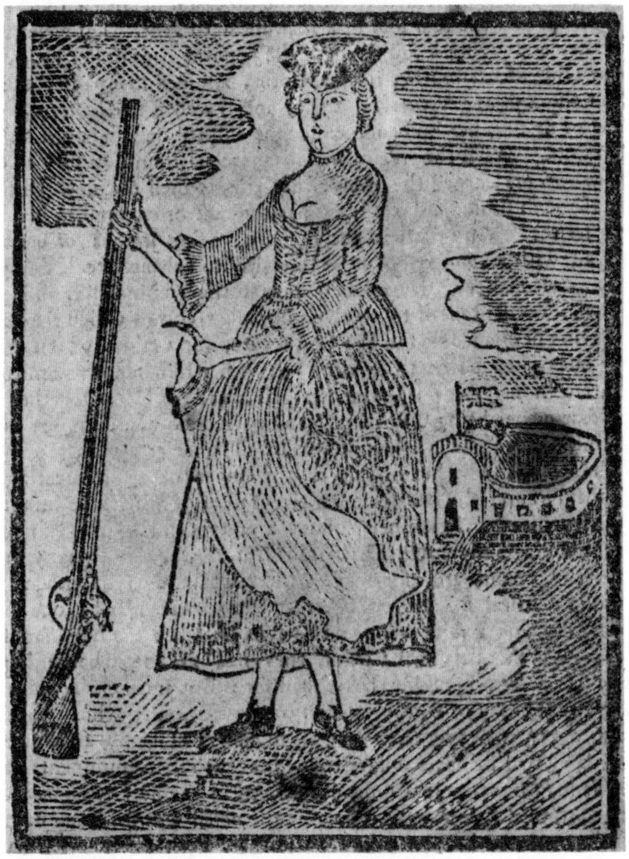

Hannah Snell, an Englishwoman who, after being deserted by her husband, disguised herself as a man and was inducted into the English navy. She braved hurricanes, war, and injury in searching for her errant spouse—at one point removing a ball of shot from her own groin to avoid detection.

And again, on the cover of Nathaniel Ames' *Astronomical Diary; or Almanac For . . . 1772* appeared a wood engraving, possibly made by Paul Revere, of a dwarf who appeared in Boston shortly before Ames went to press. Each part of the dwarf's anatomy is described in detail, but Ames felt compelled to apologize for a lack of specificity in the illustration:

> The . . . Description of the extraordinary Person who lately made her appearance in this town, may not be disagreeable to our Readers, although it may not be so particular, as the curious would desire, as she would not admit of an accurate examination.[14]

Left: Hannah Snell depicted in Isaiah Thomas' New-England Almanack . . . 1775.

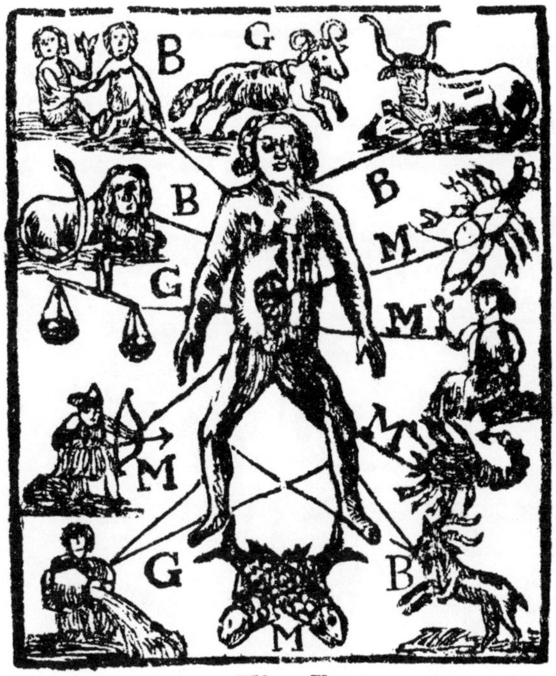

The ANATOMY of Man's Body, as governed by the Twelve CONSTELLATIONS.

♈ The Head and Face.

♓ The Feet.

To know where the Sign is

Firſt Find the Day of the Month, and againſt the Day you have the Sign or place of the Moon in the 6th Column. Then finding the Sign here, it ſhews the part of the Body it governs.

The Names and Characters of the Seven Planets

☉ Sol, ♄ Saturn, ♃ Jupiter, ♂ Mars, ♀ Venus, ☿ Mercury, ☽ Luna, ☊ Dragon's head, and ☋ tail.

The Five Aſpects.

☌ Conjunction, ☍ Oppoſition, ✱ Sextile, △ Trine, □ Quartile.

Above: Thomas More's The American Country Almanack *(Philadelphia, 1751) carried this woodcut of an anatomical man.*

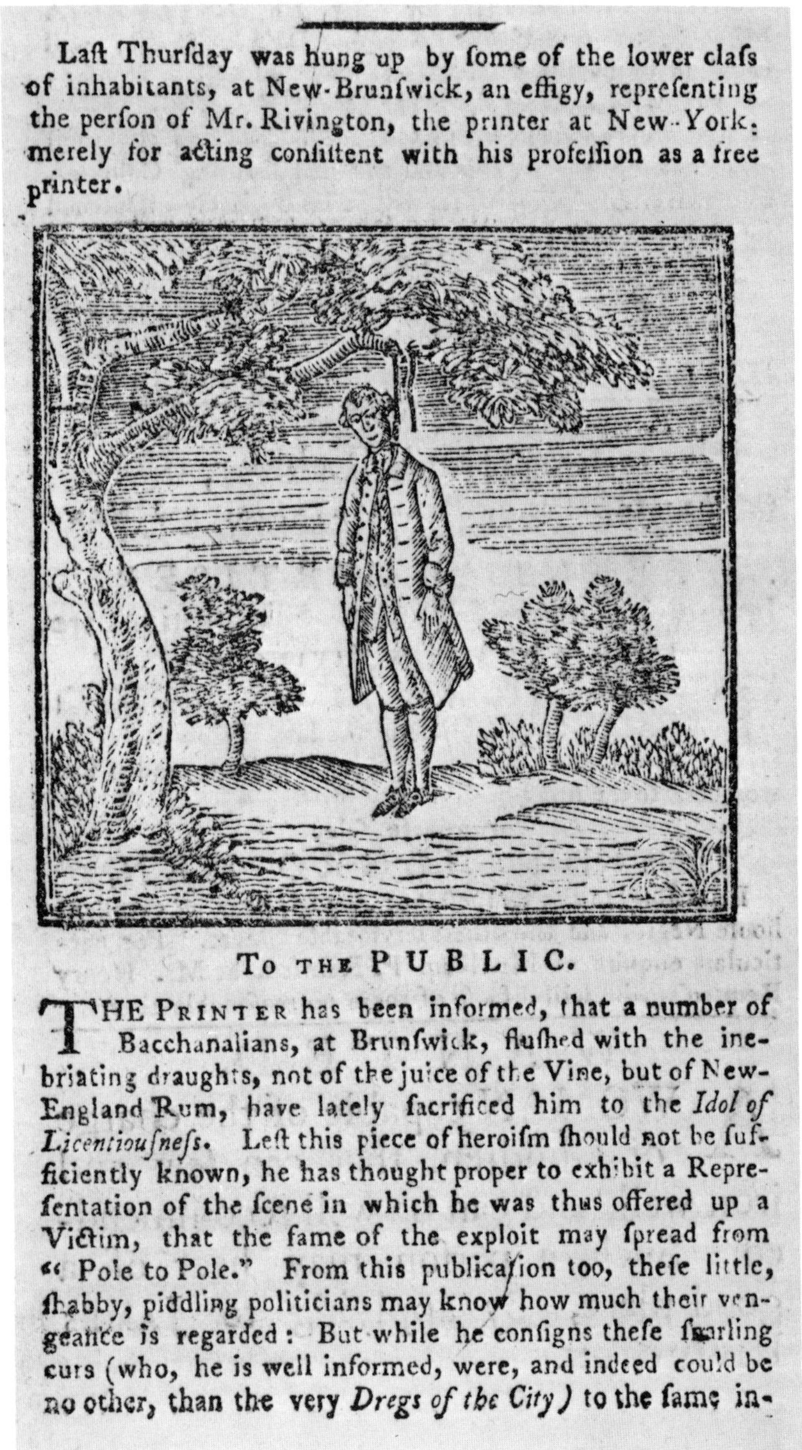

Laſt Thurſday was hung up by ſome of the lower claſs of inhabitants, at New-Brunſwick, an effigy, repreſenting the perſon of Mr. Rivington, the printer at New-York; merely for acting conſiſtent with his profeſſion as a free printer.

To the PUBLIC.

THE PRINTER has been informed, that a number of Bacchanalians, at Brunſwick, fluſhed with the inebriating draughts, not of the juice of the Vine, but of New-England Rum, have lately ſacrificed him to the *Idol of Licentiouſneſs*. Leſt this piece of heroiſm ſhould not be ſufficiently known, he has thought proper to exhibit a Repreſentation of the ſcene in which he was thus offered up a Victim, that the fame of the exploit may ſpread from "Pole to Pole." From this publication too, theſe little, ſhabby, piddling politicians may know how much their vengeance is regarded: But while he conſigns theſe ſnarling curs (who, he is well informed, were, and indeed could be no other, than the very *Dregs of the City*) to the ſame in-

Woodcut of James Rivington hanging in effigy, published in Rivington's New-York Gazetteer, *April 20, 1775.*

The almanacs' visual news service survived on into the second decade of the 19th century. Nathaniel Low's almanac of 1820 carried both a picture and a story on the "Melancholy Fate of Madame Blanchard, The Celebrated Aeronaute." With a dateline of Paris, July 6, 1819, the story was five months old when printed by Low:

> The extraordinary fete which had been for some time announced to take place this evening at the Tivoli gardens, has been signalized by a shocking catastrophe. Among the numerous spectacles, which had been announced to the public, was the ascension of Madame Blanchard in a luminous balloon furnished with fireworks. Accordingly, at half-past 10 at night, this intrepid aeronaute clothed in white, with a hat and plumes of the same colour, mounted her car. At a given signal, the balloon rose, but so slowly that part of the fireworks came in contact with the surrounding trees. However, by throwing out some ballast, Madame Blanchard soon rose rapidly. The ascension was illuminated by Bengal lights; the aeronaute waved her flag, and the air resounded with acclamations. On a sudden the balloon entered a slight cloud, which completely obscured the Bengal lights. Madame Blanchard then set the match to the fireworks, in order that they might produce the expected effect; when it was perceived that some rockets took a perpendicular direction to the balloon and set fire to it. Immediately a dreadful blaze struck terror into the hearts of the spectators, leaving them in but little doubt as to the deplorable fate of the unfortunate aeronaute. It is impossible to describe the scene which Tivoli now presented. Cries of lamentation burst from all sides; numbers of females fell into convulsions, consternation was depicted in every face! Some spectators rode at full gallop towards where it was supposed the fall might take place; and in about a quarter of an hour returned with the lifeless body of Madame Blanchard. She fell in the Street de Provence; she was in her car, enveloped in the network that had attached it to the balloon. This unfortunate lady was about 45.[15]

This sensationalistic, tabloid-style journalism, which seems so native to the 19th and 20th centuries, inspired the first picture of a news event to appear in an American newspaper. On April 20, 1775, *Rivington's New-York Gazetteer* published a woodcut of its printer James Rivington being hung in effigy by the irrate citizens of New Brunswick, N.J. Rivington was a Tory with a Hearstian approach to journalism. High sales figures—not accurate reports—were his goals, and he described the hanging himself:

> Last Thursday was hung by some of the lower class of inhabitants, at New-Brunswick, an effigy, representing the person of Mr. Rivington, the printer at New-York: merely for acting consistent with his profession as a free printer. . . .
>
> Lest this piece of heroism should not be sufficiently known, he has thought proper to exhibit a Representation of the scene in which he was thus offered up a Victim, that the fame of the exploit may spread from "Pole to Pole". . . .

The simple woodcut is as much a part of the text as any sentence. In fact, the polite and proper dress of Rivington, when juxtaposed to his charge that the culprits were "the very Dregs of the City," vindicates him, at least symbolically, from any selfish motivations.

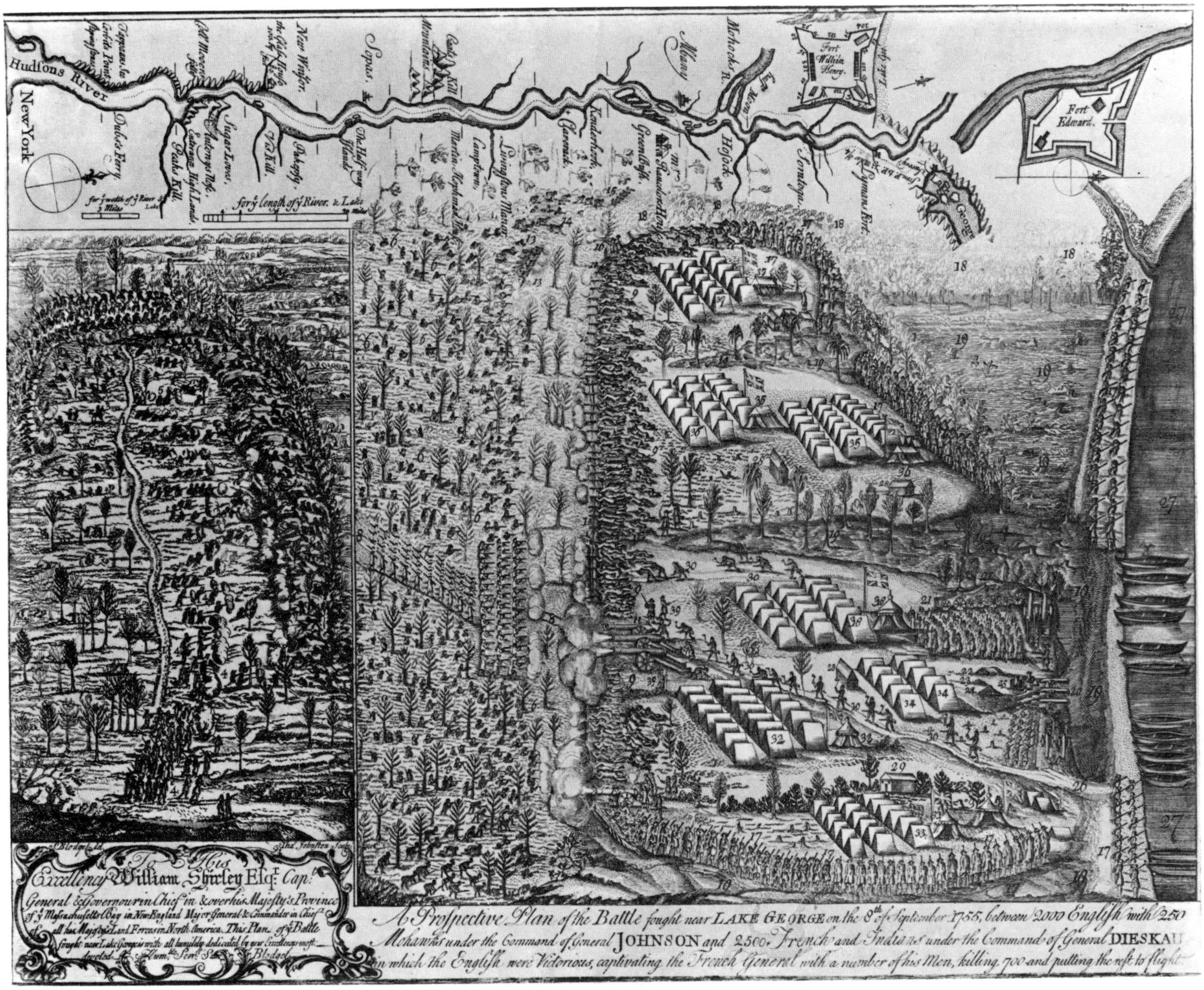

Line engraving by Thomas Johnston, A Prospective Plan of the Battle fought near Lake George, *drawn by Samuel Blodgett, 1755.*

News Prints

But the literal news illustrations were not confined to printed texts. Single sheet news prints appeared after 1750. Illustrated broadsides which, according to newspaper ads, were common, are all but extinct today. Typically, single-sheet prints were engraved by multitalented men who worked at numerous trades. Samuel Blodget (1724-1807) exemplified this occupational pluralism by working as a judge, a merchant, an early day canal planner, a sutler, and an artist. His *Battle Fought Near Lake George* is a rather strange composition—a map-and-view, as historian Lynn Glaser calls it—of four distinct parts. At the bottom left he depicts a broken column of New England militia being overwhelmed by the French. To the right is a view of the assault on "Johnson's camp." The top right is a map of part of the Hudson River and, finally, at top left are plans of Fort William Henry (built immediately after the battle) and of Fort Edward. Blodget, as noted emphatically at the bottom of the print, was an eyewitness. As Francis Parkman, in his historical account of the war, observed:

> On the adjacent hill stood one Blodget, who seems to have been a sutler, watching, as well as bushes, trees, and smoke would let him, the progress of the fight, of which he soon after made and published a curious bird's-eye view.[16]

Blodget hired a local "japanner, painter, and engraver," Thomas Johnston (1708–67), who had won some fame for engraving the first view of Yale College. The late scholar I. N. Phelps Stokes noted that Blodget's picture was the "first historical print engraved in America," yet Blodget apparently saw his work as news, not history, and he had it ready for sale on December 22, 1755, a little more than three months after the event itself and one month before many distant newspapers reported that a battle had occurred. Moreover, as in the case of other prints, Blodget's work, which came complete with a five-page quarto pamphlet, was meant to be read, and it was presented as a statement of facts—not an artistic whole—a one-frame news story complete with narration and historical background.

The same role may be attributed to Amos Doolittle's Lexington and Concord series. These four prints, which have been reproduced many times, were painted by Ralph Earl immediately after the trauma of April 19, 1775, and were translated by Doolittle into the most extraordinary works of graphic art produced in America during the 18th century. Doolittle followed the lead of Blodget by emphasizing in his advertisements the highly desirable qualities of timeliness, accuracy, and specific labelings.[17]

Other prints which fit this description are Robert Aitken's *A Correct View of the Late Battle of Charlestown,* which appeared in the *Pennsylvania Magazine* in September 1775, and Bernard Romans' larger eyewitness version, *An Exact View of the Late Battle of Charlestown*—both being advertised on September 20, 1775, three months after the event.[18]

Summary

Individual prints, as well as those which appeared in periodicals, project a journalistic vision: a preoccupation with facts, a desire for timeliness, and an impatience with the subtleties of high style. Colonial prints were practical pictures designed to fill a specific role and to transmit a specific body of information. They become historical prints only with the passage of time and the loss of a specific way of looking at things. To interpret them as social tools one must drop the question of historical truth and pursue the more realistic, the more answerable question of purpose. When looked at in this manner, colonial prints become valuable tools for analyzing the unique assumptions of popular taste. They aid us in seeing with a colonial eye.

NOTES

[1] *South Carolina . . . Gazette* (January 28, 1779) as cited in Alfred Coxe Prime, ed., *The Arts and Crafts in Philadelphia, Maryland and South Carolina 1721–1785* (Phila.: The Walpole Society, 1929), p. 17; see also pp. 16–36. *The New-York Journal or the General Advertiser* (September 15, 1774), as cited in *The Arts and Crafts in New York 1726–1776* (New York: New York Historical Society, 1938), p. 13; see also pp. 8–27.

[2] William M. Ivins, Jr., *Prints And Visual Communication* (New York: Da Capo Press, 1969), pp. 1–20.

[3] A. Hyatt Mayor, *Prints and People: A Social History of Printed Pictures* (New York: Metropolitan Museum of Art, 1971).

[4] George Wilkins Kendall, *The War Between the United States and Mexico* (New York: D. Appleton and Co., 1851), foreword.

[5] See John Trumbull, *Autobiography, Reminiscences and Letters from 1756 to 1841* (New York: Wiley and Putnam, 1841) and Theodore Sizer, *The Works of Colonel John Trumbull, Artist of the American Revolution* (New Haven: Yale University Press, 1950).

[6] William Dunlap, *A History of the Rise and Progress of the Arts of Design in the United States,* 2 vols. (Boston: C. E. Goodspeed and Co., 1918) 2:35.

[7] See William Kelby, *Notes on American Artists, 1754–1820* (New York: New-York Historical Society, 1922), pp. 52–54.

[8] Prime, p. 23.

[9] Clarence S. Brigham, *Paul Revere's Engravings* (New York: Atheneum, 1969), pp. 10–12, 52–78; Wendy J. Shadwell, *American Printmaking: The First 150 Years* (Washington, D.C.: The Museum of Graphic Art, 1969), pp. 27–29, plates 33–37; Lynn Glaser, *Engraved America* (Philadelphia: Ancient Orb Press, 1970), p. 64.

[10] Isaiah Thomas, *The History of Printing in America,* 2 vols. (Albany, N.Y.: Joel Munsell, 1874) 2:15–17.

[11] Nathaniel Low, *An Astronomical Diary; or, Almanack, For the Year of Christian Aera, 1777 . . .* (Boston: J. Gill, 1776).

[12] Nathaniel Ames, *An Astronomical Diary . . . 1750* (Boston: J. Draper, 1750), pages not numbered.

[13] See illustrations in Robb Sagendorph, *America and Her Almanacs* (Boston: Little, Brown and Co., et. al., 1970), pp. 46–47.

[14] Nathaniel Ames, *Astronomical Diary . . . 1772* (Boston: Nathaniel Ames, 1771), cover.

[15] See Sagendorph, pp. 190–191.

[16] Glaser, pp. 54, 64–65; Shadwell, p. 22; *The Arts And Crafts In New York 1726–1776,* pp. 22–23.

[17] Reproduced in Shadwell, plates 49–52.

[18] Glaser, pp. 64–65; Shadwell, plate 54 for the Aitken line engraving.

Prints of the Mexican War as Historical Sources

Ronnie C. Tyler

Ronnie C. Tyler is curator of history at the Amon Carter Museum of Western Art, Fort Worth, Texas. In addition to Santiago Vidaurri and the Southern Confederacy *(Texas State Historical Association, 1973)*, The Slave Narratives of Texas, *co-editor with Lawrence R. Murphy, (The Encino Press, 1973)*, Joseph Wade Hampton: Editor and Individualist *(Texas Western Press, 1969), and* Vision, Destiny—War! Manifest Destiny and the Mexican War *(Steck-Vaughn, 1970) he has published articles in* The American West, Southwestern Historical Quarterly, The Journal of Negro History, Arizona and the West, The Chronicles of Oklahoma, The American, *and the* Southeastern Latin Americanist.

It is ironic that the conflict known through this country as the Mexican War is, in reality, more nearly the American War. In many ways it is the most American war. It confirmed what had already become a trend in the Revolution and the War of 1812: success on the battlefield led to the presidency. It was the vehicle by which that widespread American yearning—Manifest Destiny—achieved its greatest single triumph in the annexation of the Southwest. It also was the embodiment of many characteristics that have long borne an American or frontier stamp: idealistically inclined chauvinism, aggressiveness, ingenuity, and common sense. "The very fact that the war was limited to one small part of this hemisphere, . . . that it was relatively unconfused by world issues," says Daniel Boorstin, "makes it a particularly vivid illustration of our domestic shortcomings." [1]

But the Mexican War also inspired brighter results. It provided material for numerous artists and lithographers who were just becoming commercial successes, and if the war is to be considered "American," perhaps it is appropriate that at least one of the lithographers later styled himself the printmaker for the American people.[2] The technology had been developed for several years.[3] Artists stood ready to provide scenes for the stones. The only ingredient lacking was a subject to capture the public's imagination, as the *Lexington* disaster of a few years before had intrigued the people of New York.[4] The Mexican War, coupled with entrepreneurs who possessed the energy and foresight of newspapermen, combined to render true Nathaniel Currier's later claim to his distributors: "Pictures are now a necessity." [5]

The lithographers produced literally hundreds of prints on the Mexican War, with at least 60 coming from Currier himself.[6] Perhaps the best known are the dozen by George Wilkins Kendall, the first modern war correspondent, and Carl Nebel.[7] Henry Walke,[8] Daniel P. Whiting,[9] and John Phillips [10] also witnessed parts of the conflict, but most of the artists and lithographers probably never visited Mexico. Nathaniel Currier occasionally had a sketch by a participant to work from, but more often he authorized one of his shop artists to draw a scene—probably designed from various European battle prints or newspaper accounts of the fight—or bought a sketch from one of the "job" artists who worked for the lithographers. Napoleon Sarony and Henry B. Major, James S. Baillie, and David W. Kellogg, Currier's competitors, probably used the same sources.[11]

There are some Mexican prints of the war, a few of them probably made at the insistence of Americans while the capital was occupied. Most of them are of poor quality, indicating more likely the woes of an occupied country than the poor state of Mexican lithography.[12] The Mexican prints, for the most part, are poorly preserved and virtually unknown. One alert historian observed when asked about them, "This is not one of our favorite eras." [13]

Several generalizations can be readily agreed on. From a sociological viewpoint the prints are valuable. Some of them provide good examples of costume, although John Porter Bloom, in his study of the American army in Mexico, concluded that the troops dressed very individualistically, and some wore no uniforms at all.[14] All the prints depict the troops in splendid uniforms. Other prints might be useful for a view of social life in the United States, as well as for a warped and prejudiced view of Mexico. Still others are studies in national character and popular mood that would delight anyone interested in intellectual history. They are all obviously a challenge to the art historian. But what about the historian of the Mexican War? An even more applicable generalization is that the lithographs have been virtually ignored by generations studying these fields.

The standard history of the war is still Justin H. Smith, *The War with Mexico* (1919), 2 volumes. Smith has lately been under attack not only for writing racist history but also for purposely misleading the reader in the well-known case of President Polk's intention in the matter of the boundary and in declaring war.[15] Now I must indict him for failing to pay any attention—even as illustrations—to the prints.

One of the more popular works is Otis A. Singletary, *The Mexican War* (1960), published in the University of Chicago American Civilization Series. Singletary used only a few prints as illustrations, without placing them properly in relation to the text. (Of course, some of these problems are forced upon the author by the printer and are not his fault; the fact remains that the prints are not properly used.) He makes no effort to analyze the prints or use them as sources of research material. They are poorly identified—no artist is listed, nor are there any credits.

Other single-volume treatments fare no better. Alfred H. Bill, *Rehearsal for Conflict* (1947), used only a few prints as illustrations, making no effort to incorporate them into the text. One might have expected more from Bernard De Voto, the writer who later produced the magnificently illustrated *Across the Wide Missouri* (1947), but his *Year of Decision* (1942) does not even have illustrations. Robert S. Henry, *Story of the Mexican War* (1950) and Nathaniel W. Stephenson, *Texas and the Mexican War* (1921) use no lithographs; in fact Stephenson has no illustrations at all.

Recent publications seem to be no improvement. George W. Smith and Charles Judah, editors of *Chronicles of the Gringos* (1968), use a number of illustrations but make no effort to treat them as historical sources or subjects for serious consideration. Since they used primary sources as the text for their book, they missed a fine opportunity to use some other primary sources—the prints. Seymour V. Connor and Odie B. Faulk, *North America Divided: The Mexican War, 1846–1848* (1971) use no illustrations. There is a detail from what appears to be a print on the cover, but no identification or credit is given.

Mexican historians, unsurprisingly, have done no better. Ramón Alcaraz, editor of *Apuntes para la historia de la guerra entre México y los Estados Unidos* (1948) uses maps and battle plans but no prints. José María Roa Barcena's *Recuerdos de la invasión norteamericano* (1883), long a classic on the war, uses no illustrations. The same is true of José C. Valades', *Breve historia de la guerra con los Estados Unidos* (1947).

There are some exceptions. American Heritage publications have long included illustrations, testifying to their belief in the integrity of visual materials. Fairfax Downey, *Texas and the War with Mexico* (1961) and Wilbur Cross, *Naval Battle and Heroes* (1960) both use prints but still make no attempt at analysis. Only Samuel Eliot Morison, *"Old Bruin," Commodore Matthew Calbraith Perry* (1967) has done a thorough job of investigating the prints he uses—several of the Walke set. But Morison does not use others that might have enhanced his work. For the Walke set he visited the site and photographed scenes that appear in the lithographs, enabling him to comment on the print and the reader to follow along via the photograph. His verdict is that the Walke prints are reasonably correct as well as "spirited." [16]

The question then is are the prints of the Mexican War useful to historians studying the war in addition to those studying American society or art history. Are they accurate representations of the scenes they purport to depict, or are they so carelessly done as to be useless? Are they so laced with fiction that fact is hopelessly interwoven and forever unrecognizable? Professor Walter Rundell, Jr., a few years ago accused historians of making inadequate use of nonliterary documentation.[17] Is his observation substantially correct in the case of the Mexican War historians, or are they justified in ignoring them?

Several battles serve as good points of comparison for the prints. The engagement at Veracruz was an important battle that attracted the attention of all the lithographers. The city is located on the eastern coast of Mexico, with several islands, including the one occupied by the Castle of San Juan de Ulloa, in the harbor. It was a strongly fortified city. After several days of shelling, the

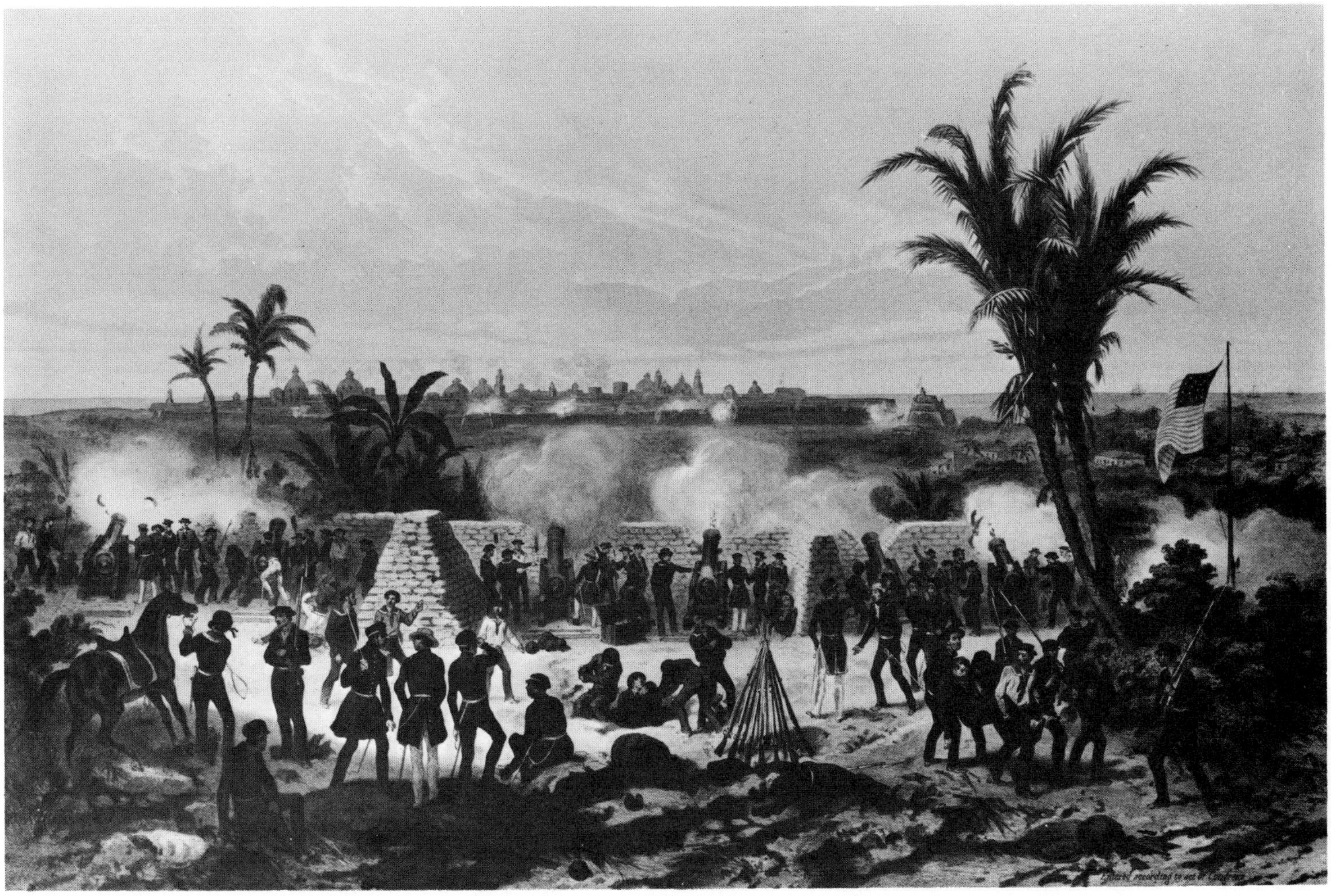

Carl Nebel, Bombardment of Vera Cruz. *The illustrations in this article are courtesy of Amon Carter Museum, Fort Worth, Tex.*

navy landed troops, who moved inland and surrounded the city, intent upon starving it out if necessary.

Several of the lithographs of the battle of Veracruz are accurate. Of all the Mexican War prints, perhaps the dozen by Kendall and Nebel are the most popular—and the most accurate. Kendall knew Mexico because he had been there several years before as a prisoner with the Texans captured in the Santa Fé expedition. He was with Gen. Zachary Taylor at the battle of Monterrey, perhaps as one writer suggested to gain some measure of revenge for his treatment at the hands of the Mexicans. Kendall was also with Gen. Winfield Scott during the southern campaign. Not only did Kendall agree with Nebel to do the folio of prints on the war, but his stories, first printed in the New Orleans *Picayune* and then circulated in other newspapers throughout the nation, probably inspired dozens of artists to create their own heroic scenes of the battles he described. Kendall thus might be responsible for more than the dozen issued under his and Nebel's names.[18]

Nebel, too, had been in Mexico for several years. He had produced one of the most beautiful and rare of all Mexican print sets: *Viago pintoresco y arqueolójico sobre la parte mas interesante de la República Mejicana* (1839). He was on the scene for most of the battles of the war, according to Kendall, who claims that Nebel made "on the spot" sketches. Justino Fernández, of the Institute of Aesthetic Investigations of the Universidad Nacional Autónoma de México, believes, however, that Nebel was in Europe at the time of the war and probably used Kendall's notes and his memory to reconstruct the scenes.[19]

In his print of the battle of Veracruz, Nebel shows battery number five of the siege forces. Ensconced behind a parapet of sandbags, they are firing cannon that came off the ships and which are still mounted on the ship-carriages. Each one weighs 6,300 pounds. The battery was located on a sandy hill that afforded a good view of the city, but it was not high enough to see the castle of San Juan in the harbor. The southern road out of Veracruz can be seen between the two palm trees and the American flag on the right of the print.[20]

Another view of the siege of Veracruz was done by Lt. Henry Walke, an executive officer of the U.S.S. *Vesuvius.* Born in Princess Anne County, Va., in 1808, Walke was appointed midshipman in February 1827. He served in both the Mexican War and the Civil War and retired at his own request in 1871. He died in Brooklyn, N.Y., in 1896.[21]

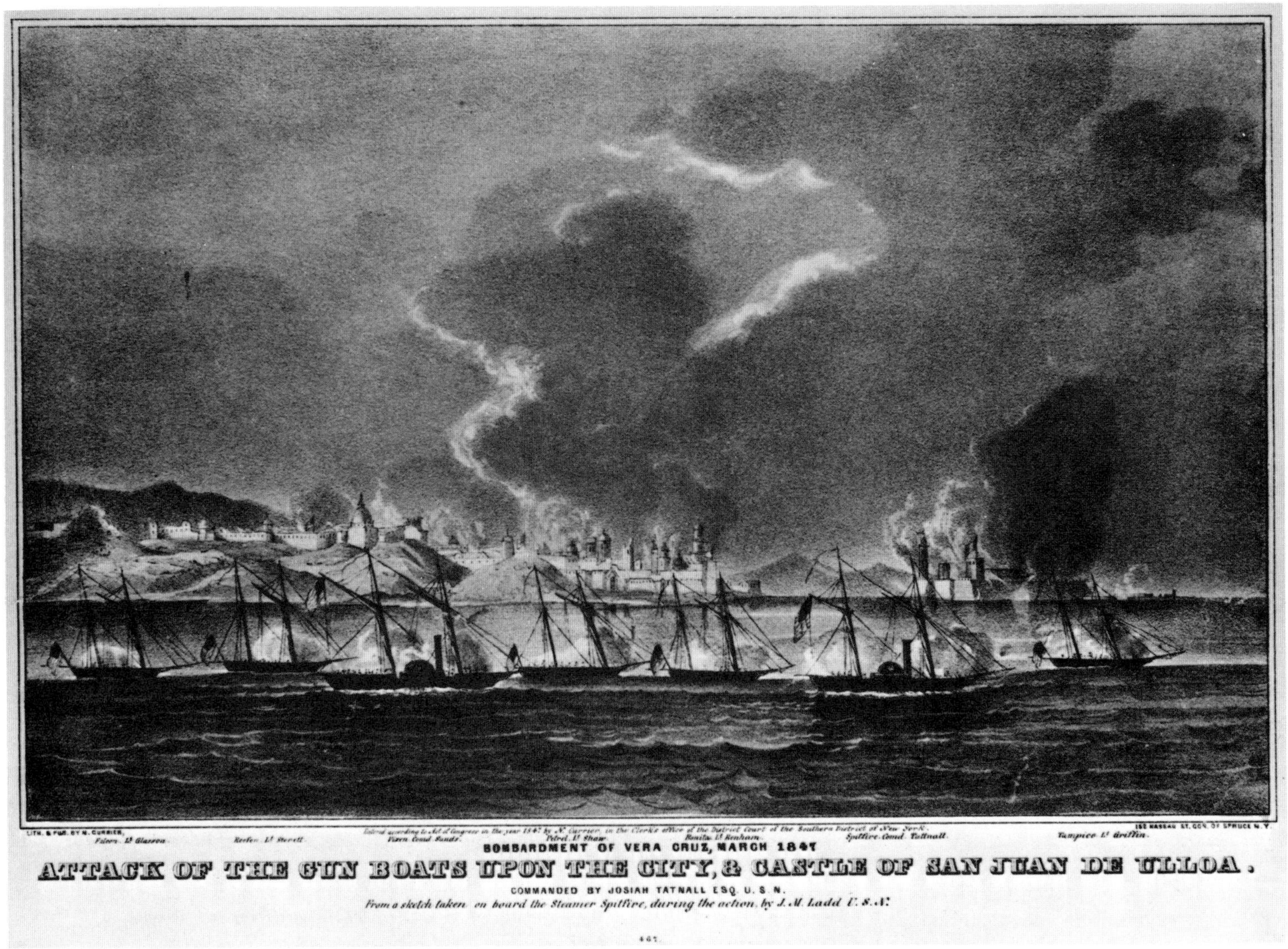

The Walke print agrees with the Nebel picture in most particulars. The sailors are more evident in Walke's picture, and Walke seems to have a higher perspective than Nebel, which is characteristic of the lieutenant's pictures.

Nathaniel Currier did at least two prints of the bombardment of Veracruz. Obvious errors contrast with the Nebel and Walke prints. All the troops are soldiers instead of sailors. Gen. Winfield Scott is too prominent, no sandbags are in view, and the perspective seems too low. The troops were on a slight hill. Another Currier view is more accurate, probably because it was taken from an eyewitness sketch by J. M. Ladd. Ladd shows Josiah Tattnall's fleet in the correct position below the city. The ships are (right to left) the schooner *Tampico,* the steam gunboat *Spitfire* (the flagship), the schooners *Bonita* and *Petrel,* the steam gunboat *Vixen,* and the schooners *Reefer* and *Falcon.* Tattnall's fleet was in close for the bombardment—closer than Perry wanted it. The fleet anchored off Point Hornos (as seen in the left center of the print, the hills before Veracruz) and drew fire from the shore. Gen. William Jenkins Worth was thankful because the fleet drew fire from a concealed gun position that he had not known about. The scene pictured by Ladd probably took place on March 22 because the Mexican gunners found Tattnall's range on March 23 and dropped shells around him. The water near the American ships seems to be quiet in this picture.[22]

Baillie offers another view of Veracruz that is obviously inaccurate. Scott is too obvious, and there are too many soldiers lined up on the wrong side of the city, using rifles instead of cannon (it was the cannonfire that brought about the surrender of the city). San Juan de Ulloa could not be seen from the American position. The ships are out of position.

Sarony & Major did a version of the battle that depicts action at the height of the encounter on March 25. There are obvious errors. The ships are the wrong kind. Such ships could hardly get into Veracruz harbor under favorable conditions because of the reefs and surely would find the entry much more difficult under such hostile conditions. The ships did not approach that close to the castle. The close-range gunfire, of course, was from Tattnall's gunboats.[23]

Walke did a print of another scene that occurred dur-

Left: Nathaniel Currier, Attack of the Gun Boats Upon the City, & Castle of San Juan de Ulloa.

Below: Carl Nebel, Battle of Cerro Gordo.

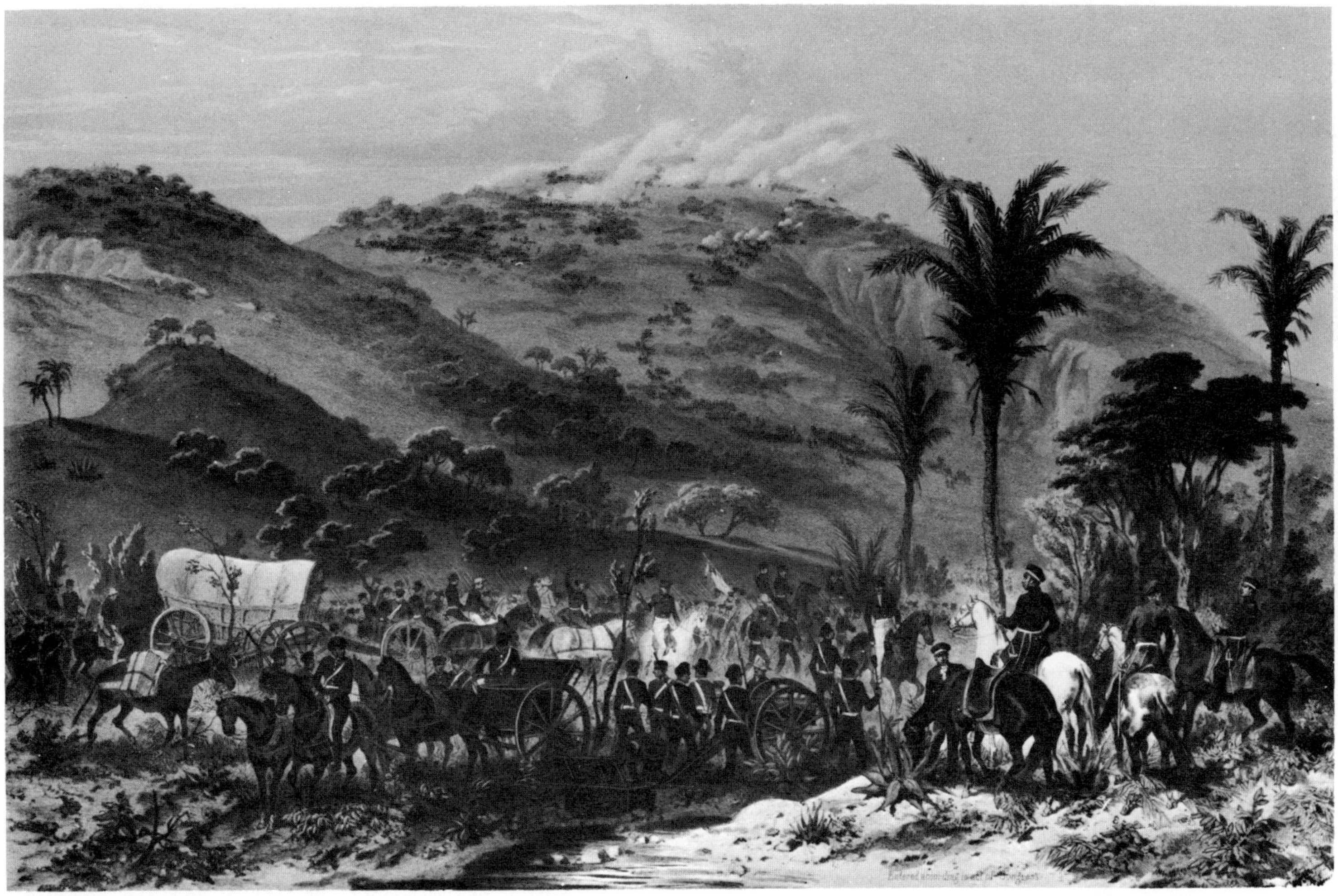

ing the seige of Veracruz. He shows the U.S.S. *Mississippi* rescuing men from the ships—the U.S.S. *Hunter,* its prize (a French blockade runner), and the pilot boat—that had run aground. Captain Isaac Mayo, four officers, and several men volunteered to rescue the stranded men. A norther was blowing while the action took place, which was probably why the boats ran aground in the first place. Morison substantiates Walke's version of the event.

The battle of Cerro Gordo offers another opportunity for evaluation and comparison of the prints.[24] The mountain pass at Cerro Gordo lies between Veracruz and Jalapa, on the route to Mexico City. Santa Anna, less than a month after his clash at the battle of Buena Vista, had regrouped his army and picked a good defensive position. He had set his troops in the pass, with two hills, El Telégrafo and La Atalaya, on his left and the Río del Plan on his right. He wanted to force Scott to attack his strong center. The story of the battle and how Capt. Robert E. Lee and the West Point engineers found a bypass on the enemy's flank are well known. Gen. David Twiggs was sent to conduct the advance.

Again, Nebel's print is the most accurate. He pictures the attack on the Mexican batteries on El Telégrafo Hill on April 18, 1847. The large hill in the background is El Telégrafo, where Santa Anna had placed four four-pounders. There was a small tower on top of the hill, which is not pictured in the Nebel print because it is obscured by cannon and musket smoke. The smaller hill on the left side of the picture is La Atalaya. The columns of men ascending El Telégrafo on the right are Col. Bennet Riley's company attacking. They have already bypassed La Atalaya. Gen. Twigg's battery that has just bombarded the Mexican artillery on El Telégrafo to start the attack can be seen on La Atalaya. The soldiers in the foreground are part of

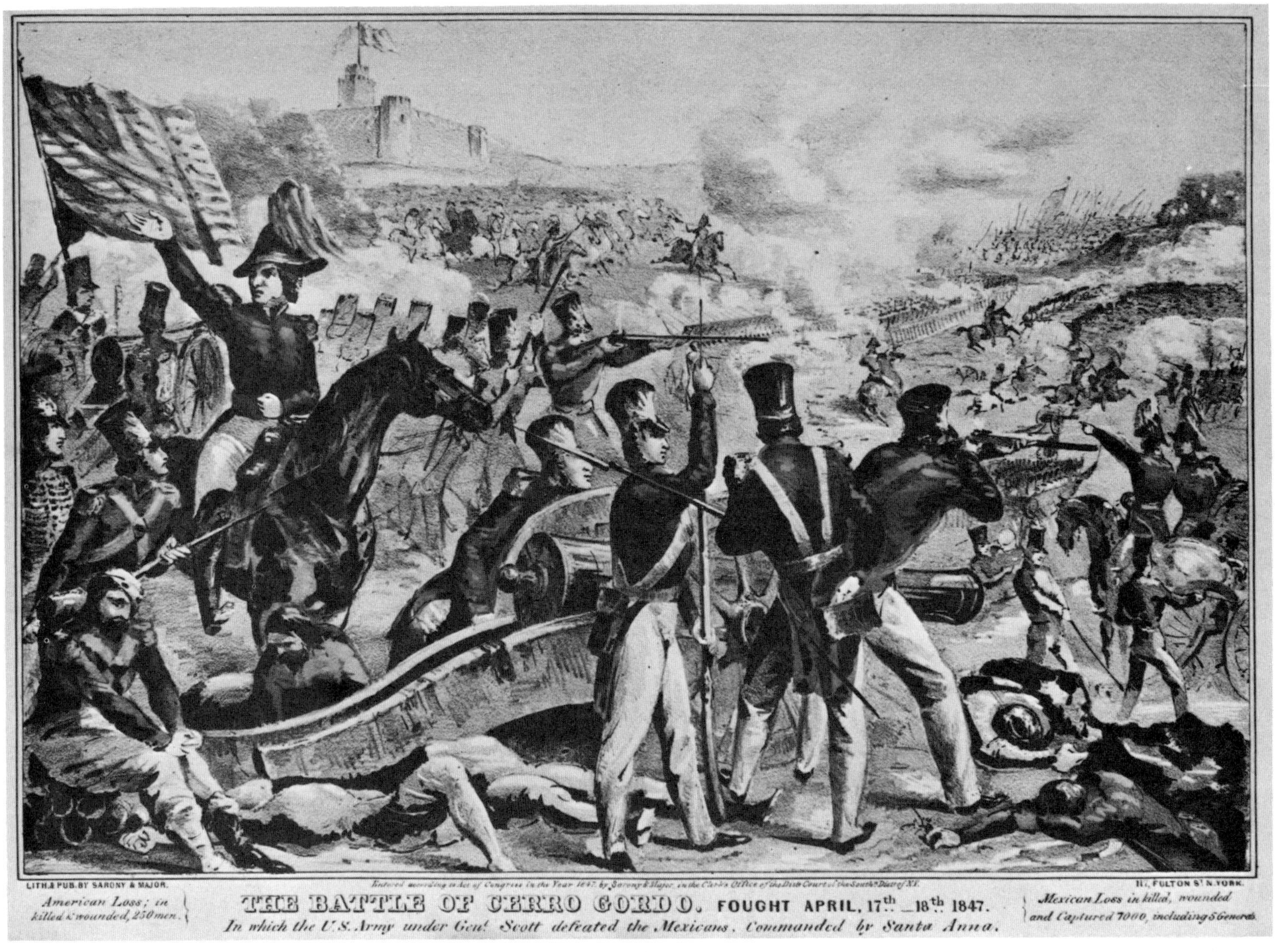

Gen. Worth's division that was to support Riley and followed him through. The Nebel print is apparently correct in all particulars. The attack began at 7 a.m., and the lithograph appears to be shaded correctly to indicate an early morning scene.

Nebel's work is quite a contrast to the work of other printmakers. Sarony & Major apparently knew that the battle took place on a hill but did not realize that Santa Anna's defenses were much more primitive. There was no such fortress on the location as is pictured in the Sarony & Major print. Baillie errs in that he has the Americans attacking from the wrong side of the hill. The Mexican camp was between the river and the hill. That is probably where Santa Anna was—not in the location that Baillie shows him. Baillie does capture the probable good humor with which Americans reflected upon this battle; the victory was such a surprise to Santa Anna that he lost his carriage, cash, papers, dinner, and wooden leg. Currier depicts what could have been true—close-in fighting on the hill—but little can be learned from this print, which could have been a copy of any number of European battle prints.

Sarony & Major, The Battle of Cerro Gordo. Fought April 17th—18th 1847.

Mexican prints of the war are rare, but there is one of the battle of Cerro Gordo, probably made at the insistence of an American, since it shows the American troops. This print, by H. Mendez, shows General Twiggs' division storming the heights of La Atalaya on April 18, 1847. It is reasonably correct, and one can get his bearings by looking at the Nebel picture.

Nebel's prints of the remainder of Scott's march to Mexico City are equally reliable. His battle of Churubusco shows Gen. Gideon J. Pillow's attack from the south-southeast.[25] Although the details are apparently correct, Pillow played little part in the battle. Had he been interested in selling prints, Nebel could have pictured a more significant aspect of the conflict, but he chose to draw what he saw. The New York lithographers who saw none of the battles were under no such handicap. In the battle of Contreras, Nebel shows Col. Bennet Riley and Col. Persifor F. Smith along with Gen. George Cadwalader's men reaching the positions of Mexican general Gabriel Valencia.

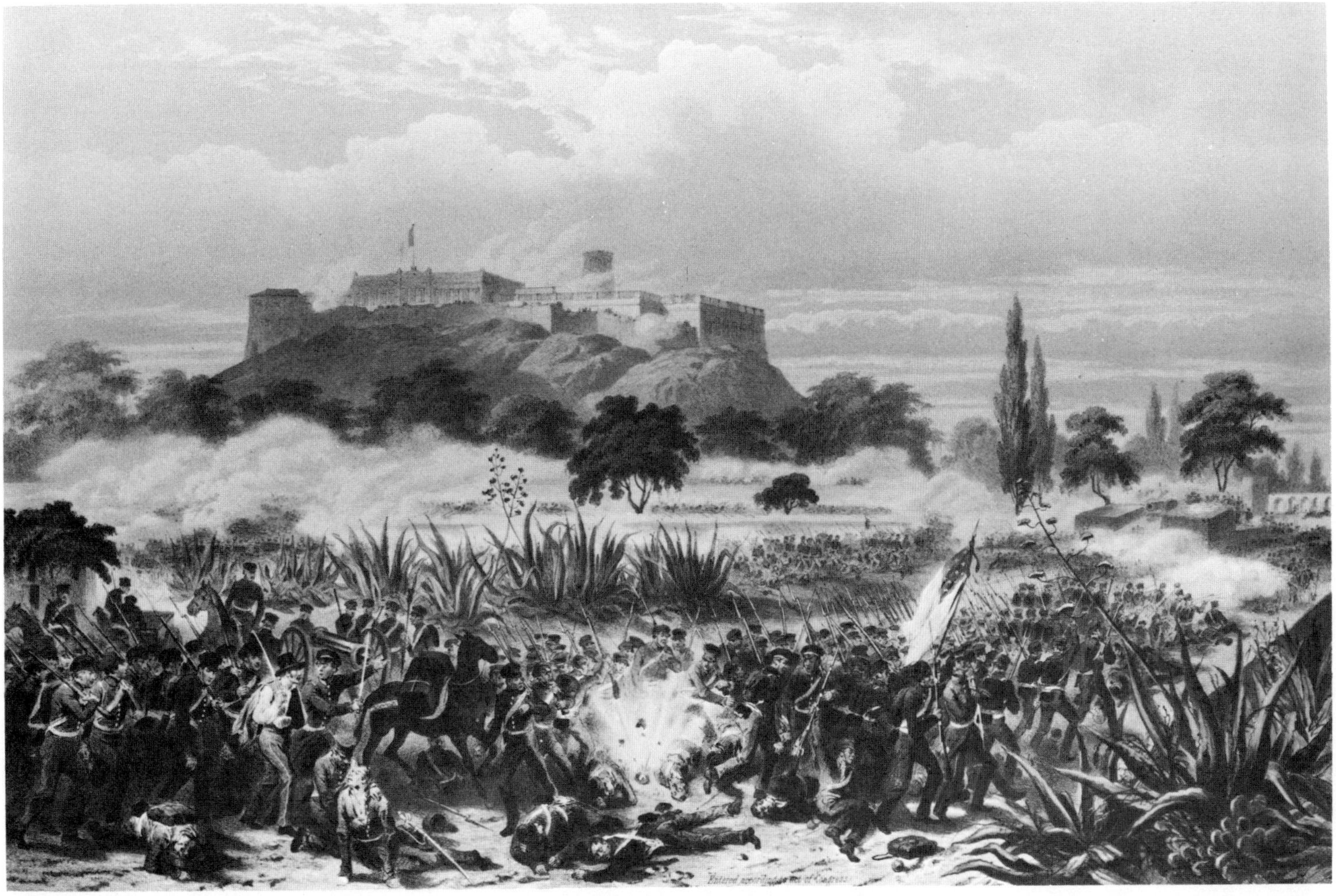

Carl Nebel, Storming of Chapultepec—Quitman's Attack.

There is a slight conflict between this print and the literary sources, for Justin Smith says that there were only two six-pounders facing Riley's men, and Nebel has pictured five.[26]

In the attack on the Casa Mata, Nebel shows Col. James S. McIntosh's men advancing on Mexican general Francisco Pérez. Pérez was without artillery in this encounter, and Nebel again resists what could have been a strong temptation to add additional hardware and drama to ensure commercial success for his portfolio. The American cannon are masked for McIntosh's assault. Mexico City is in the background, and the fortress on the right is Chapúltepec, although it is either shown at a peculiar angle or is incorrectly drawn. A confusing aspect of the picture is the small explosion behind the American lines, since the Mexicans had no artillery.[27] Nebel's print of the battle of Molino del Rey shows action on September 8, 1847. The castle of Chapúltepec is more recognizable in the distance at the left. The advancing American troops are so carefully placed that they can be identified by reference to maps and plans of the battle. Maj. George Wright's storming party is in the foreground; farther down the line are the men of Colonel Smith's light battalion. At right center are Capt. Benjamin Huger's two 24-pound seige guns.[28]

In Quitman's attack on Chapúltepec, Sept. 12, 1847, Nebel shows the southern and eastern approaches to the castle. The artist depicts Gen. P. F. Smith's force moving north. The forces under Capt. S. H. Drum and Lt. Calvin Benjamin are in possession of the cannon in the print.[29] Gen. John A. Quitman's troops are in the center of the picture. General Pillow attacked Chapúltepec from the east. The scene Nebel drew again portrays only a minute portion of the battle, and little has been written about it. But Nebel correctly shows the last few Mexican troops being driven into the fortress (right center), and General Quitman's and Col. Samuel McKenzie's troops advancing. The Mexicans had cleared the field of any ground cover.[30]

Two of Nebel's prints show action in General Taylor's northern campaign. The battle of Palo Alto is an instance in which Nebel apparently has added something to the picture to complete the composition. No hills can be seen from the site, yet Nebel has included them in the background. Nebel has correctly drawn thickets behind the Mexican position. The battle itself took place on a large, open plain. Apparently Sarony & Major did not know

Nathaniel Currier did two lithographs of Capt. C. A. May capturing the Mexican general R. Díaz de la Vega. In one May is shown with a beard, in the other without.

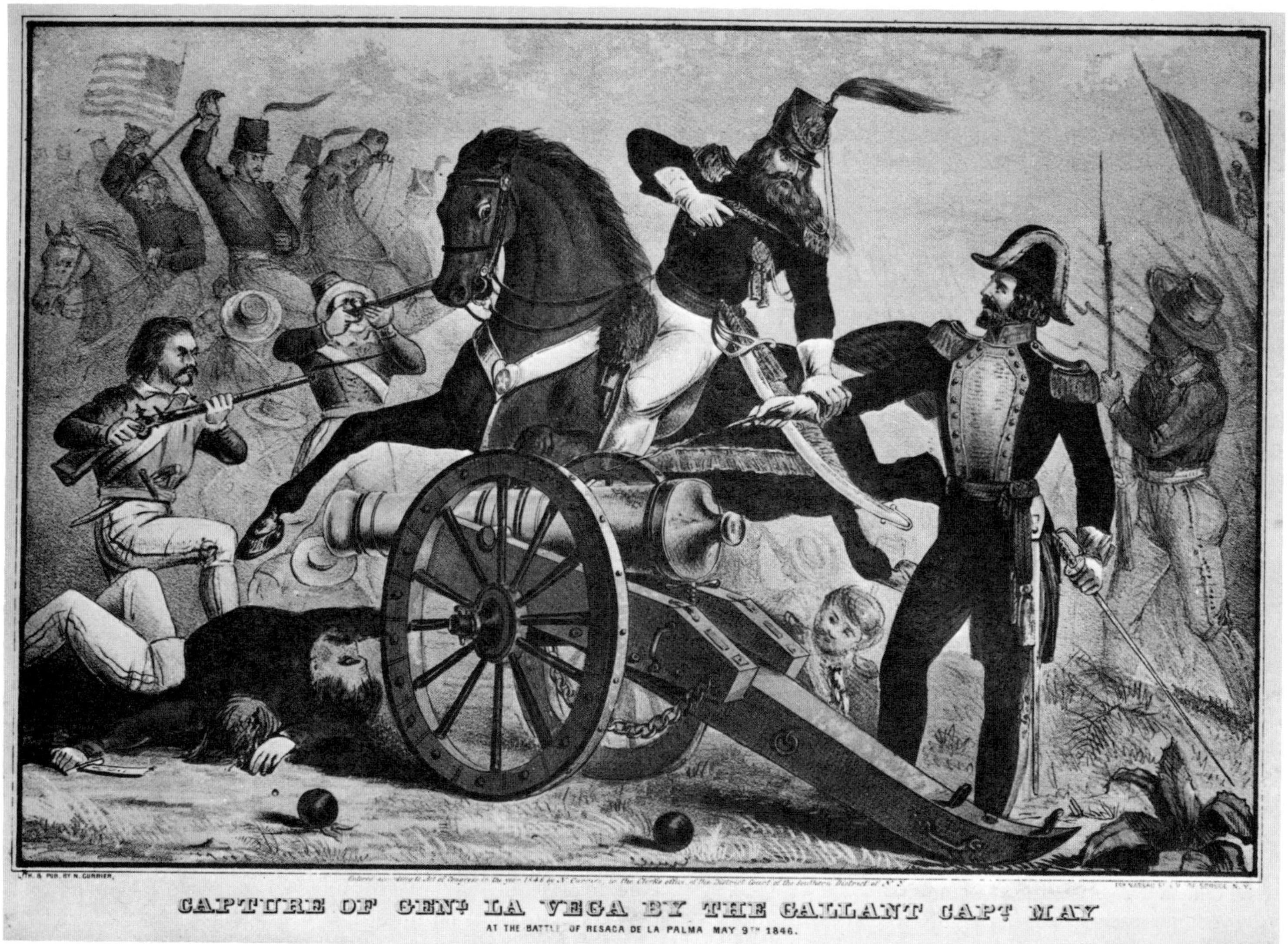

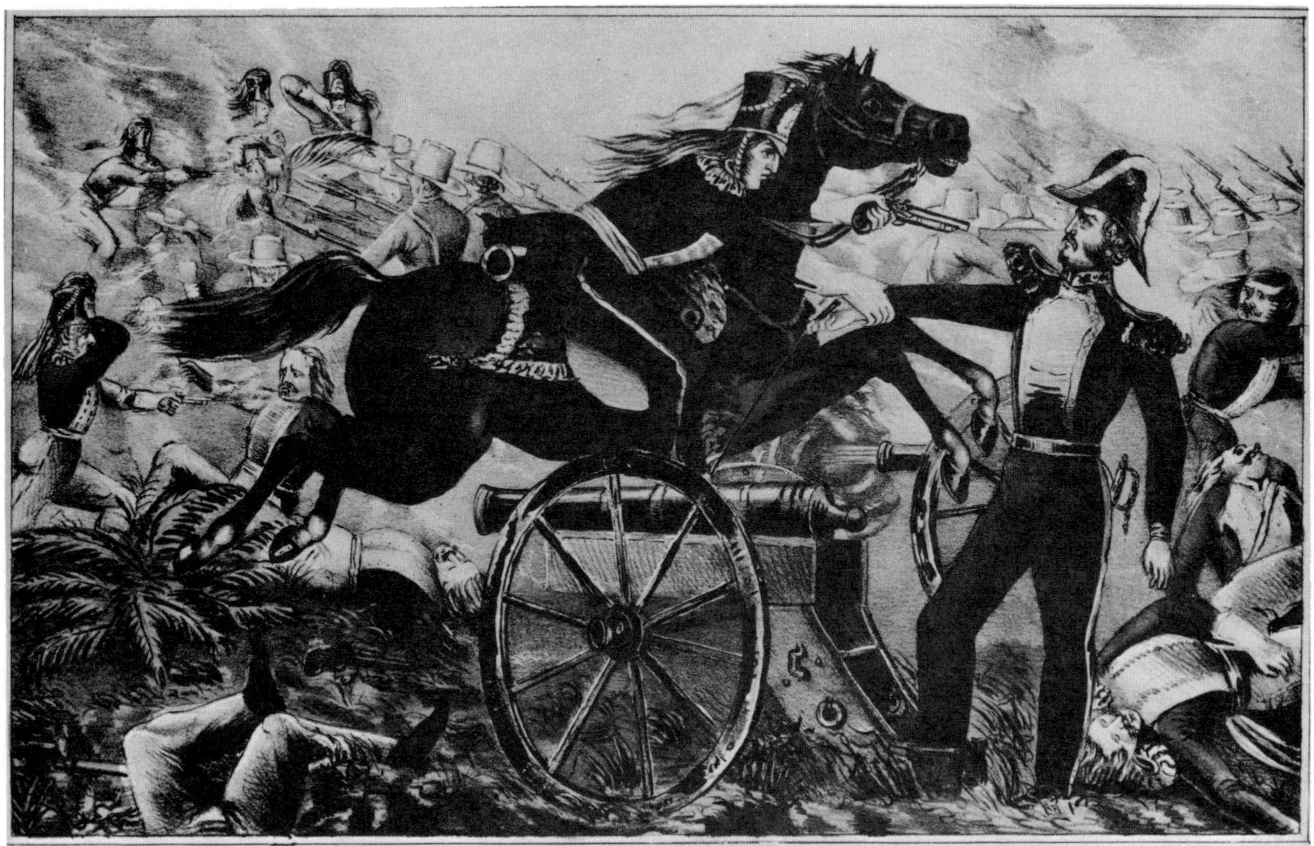

BATTLE OF RESACA DE LA PALMA MAY 9TH 1846.
Capture of Genl. VEGA by the gallant Capt. MAY.

this when they produced their view of the battle, which makes it appear that the conflict occurred in a tropical jungle.[31] The battle of Monterrey is another occasion on which the lithographers disagree. Nebel's scene is correct, with the Americans approaching the Ciudadela from the north. On the far right is the smoke of battle as General Worth attacks the Obispado. Daniel P. Whiting shows that the Obispado was indeed a bishop's palace rather than a fortress, but Currier has given the structure all the characteristics of a fort, although he has added a cross.[32]

Perhaps the prints of the battle of Monterrey also suggest another source of information for the lithographers. Monterrey was beseiged for several days and taken in house-to-house fighting. Both Sarony & Major and Currier show the fighting on the third day. Their prints are similar to some of the work of Eugene Delacroix, the French artist who did several such scenes in his illustrations of the 1830 uprising in Paris.[33]

Other meaningful comparisons can be made with the prints of the capture of Mexican general R. Díaz de la Vega by Capt. C. A. May. Currier shows May with long hair and beard, then with long hair and no beard. Sarony & Major shows the same scene but with some notable differences. May looks more like a Roman centurion. Justin Smith in his book offers yet another perspective as he wrote: "May, very tall and straight, with long black hair and a black beard that reached to his waist, became a newspaper hero, and for reasons that are rather hard to understand, was promoted several times during the war; but he seems clearly to have been essentially a cowardly sham." Smith continues, "In this fight he seized a cannon, but only the infantry prevented the enemy from recapturing it. He claimed the credit of making General Vega his prisoner, but the real captor was a bugler." [34]

Smith might have unwittingly provided the source for many of the Currier, Sarony & Major, Kellogg, and Baillie lithographs by judging that May was a "newspaper hero." It would be logical to assume that all three prints of Captain May were made from newspaper accounts of the incident—the first accounts to reach New York—which would explain why they all seem to credit May with the capture. If newspaper stories were the sources for many prints, that would also explain the many differences between eyewitness prints and the work of the New York firms.

Walke's views of the naval actions in the war are just as accurate as Nebel's prints of the ground action. As a part of Commodore Matthew C. Perry's command, Walke was at the battles of Tuxpán and Tabasco. On April 10, 1847, every important Mexican port on the Gulf of Mexico was under American control except Tuxpán, so Perry set out to conquer it. Too many supplies were coming through the port; it was the center of guerrilla activity. The city was well defended. The Mexicans had taken guns from the captured U.S.S. *Truxton.* The city was eight miles up the precarious Río Tuxpán, which narrowed from 300 yards wide at the mouth to 150 yards wide just two miles from the city. At that point a 40-foot cliff jutted into the river. The Mexicans had placed a battery on top of the cliff. Other batteries were located farther upriver.

As the ships neared the town, the *Spitfire* dashed ahead and received fire, with Tattnall and three other officers being wounded. In Walke's print the *Spitfire* is returning the fire. Most of the details in the print are correct. La Peña hill, seen at left, had already been captured by the Americans, as illustrated by the flag. Perry had ordered barges dropped for the attack; they can be seen in the river. The three schooner gunboats are correctly shown under sail. The *Vixen* and *Spitfire* are correctly shown unmasted, but Walke made some changes, as Morison points out in *"Old Bruin."* He has exaggerated the heights and telescoped two points—far apart—to make them appear to be in the same scene, much as the artists of the bird's-eye views of cities did. Hospital Hill, a mile and one-half upstream, is invisible from La Peña, since it is around a bend, but Walke shows it up close and triples its size. Tuxpán is correctly placed, but there is no mountain in the background.

Walke did several views of Tabasco. Perry wanted to capture the city of Villahermosa, up the Río Tabasco. On June 14, 1847, the U.S.S. steamers *Scorpion, Spitfire, Vixen,* and *Scourge,* with 40 barges in tow, entered the mouth of the river. Perry ordered the two bigger steamers to remove their masts to lighten their loads. There may be some distortions in the print, but the waves probably are relatively accurate. They were so bad that the Mexicans later dug a canal from the bay to the river to allow for the safe passage. Perry can be seen on the left paddlewheel box of the *Spitfire,* the first ship.

The *Scorpion* was attacked on June 15 as it moved up the river. It came abreast of the small village of Santa Teresa, which Morison could not locate, even after visiting the site, and received fire from the right bank. The *Scorpion* and *Washington* returned the fire, according to the literary documents of the engagement; the *Vesuvius* did not. But Walke, an executive officer on board the *Vesuvius,* shows the ship returning the fire. Who is correct? Perhaps the truth of the situation can be determined by a close examination of the documents, but Walke, an eyewitness to the battle, should be as reliable a source on the battle as any officer who submitted a written account.

Perhaps small details of geography are the most inaccurate aspects of Walke's lithographs. There should be no hills along the shore on the left in the print of the attack of the Mexicans from the chaparral. In the print *Naval Expedition Under Perry Ascending the Tabasco River,* the land should be rather flat, with no hills in the foreground. Similarly, in the picture of the landing of the naval expedition, there is no hill of that height on the location now. Perhaps Walke exaggerated; perhaps there has been a considerable amount of erosion since the war. But other details of this print are correct. Perry, who can be seen on top of the hill with his sword drawn, did lead the force ashore. The men can be seen landing the seven field pieces from the ships.

The capture of the city of Tabasco was a relatively easy matter after that. By the time the ships arrived, the fighting was over, for Perry had taken the city by land. In the print the *Scorpion* and the *Spitfire* are seen under fire from Fort Iturbide, and both ships are returning the fire.

What conclusions can be drawn? Were a division to be forced upon the lithographs, there would be two natural categories: eyewitness and noneyewitness. In the first category would fall Nebel, Whiting, Walke, Phillips, and, at times, Currier, when he was following a sketch provided by an eyewitness. In the second group would come most of Currier's work, Sarony & Major (although they also lithographed Walke's prints), Kellogg, and Baillie.

Historians must, of course, be cautious in their use of prints as historical sources, for if this paper proves anything, it is that some prints are as inaccurate as others are correct. But is this caution more than the same historians demand in the use of manuscripts? What historian would take the unverified description of a New Yorker who had never been to Mexico over the carefully chosen words of an eyewitness? What historian would not be led to the reasonable conclusion that a letterwriter might exaggerate—the same as an artist might—by adding an extra cannonball explosion or an extra foot to the waves in the enthusiasm of the moment? And what historian will discard the literary sources he has so carefully collected—not use them at all—rather than recognize their shortcomings as well as their truths and use them to fill in the piece in the puzzle that has been missing for so long?

NOTES

[1] Otis A. Singletary, *The Mexican War* (Chicago and London: University of Chicago Press, 1960), p. viii.

[2] Currier used several slogans during his career. His lithographs, for example, were billed as "Colored Engravings for the People." See Harry T. Peters, *Currier & Ives, Printmakers to the American People* (Garden City, N.Y.: Doubleday, Doran & Co., 1942).

[3] Peter C. Marzio, "American Lithographic Technology Before the Civil War," in John D. Morse, ed., *Prints in and of America to 1850* (Charlottesville: University of Virginia Press, 1970), pp. 215–256.

[4] When the steamboat *Lexington* caught fire and sank in Long Island Sound, more than 100 lives were lost. Three days after the disaster, with conflicting accounts circulating throughout New York, Currier produced a lithograph which the *New York Sun* carried in an illustrated story on the tragedy. The print of the *Lexington* disaster became the first of many "bestsellers" for Currier because it portrayed an incident that caught the popular imagination. See Peters, pp. 1–2.

[5] Martica Sawin, "The Backgrounds of American Printmaking," *Arts Magazine,* 30 (Sept. 1956): 37.

[6] At least 59 Currier prints of the Mexican War are cataloged in Frederic A. Conningham, *Currier & Ives: An Illustrated Check-list* (New York: Crown, 1970). The Amon Carter Museum of Western Art has in its collection one uncataloged print. Since the Currier prints are of such an ephemeral nature, other museums probably have uncataloged prints too.

[7] George Wilkins Kendall, *War Between the United States and Mexico* (New York: D. Appleton & Co., 1851).

[8] Henry Walke, *Naval Portfolio No. 1.* Lithographed in New York by Sarony & Major, the Walke portfolio of eight prints of the naval battles of the Mexican War is extremely rare.

[9] Daniel P. Whiting, *Army Portfolio* (New York: G. & W. Endicott, 1847).

[10] John Phillips, *Mexico Illustrated* (London: E. Atchley, 1848).

[11] Harry T. Peters, *America on Stone* (New York: Doubleday, Doran & Co., 1931), pp. 84–85, 242–243, 270, 350–357.

[12] Printmaking in Mexico began early. See Richard E. Ahlborn, "American Beginnings: Prints in Sixteenth-Century Mexico," in Morse, ed., *Prints in and of America,* pp. 1–22.

[13] Interview with the author in 1971.

[14] John Porter Bloom, "With the American Army into Mexico, 1846–1848" (Unpublished Ph.D. Dissertation, Emory University, 1956), pp. 17, 198.

[15] Many students of the Mexican War take Justin H. Smith's note 5 in *War with Mexico,* 2 vols., (New York: The Macmillan Co., 1919) 1:449–450, as an admission that his history is biased.

[16] Samuel Eliot Morison, *"Old Bruin," Commodore Matthew Calbraith Perry 1794-1858* (Boston: Little, Brown & Co., 1967).

[17] Walter Rundell, Jr., *In Pursuit of American History: Research and Training in the United States* (Norman: University of Oklahoma Press, 1970), pp. 155–156.

[18] Fayette Copeland, *Kendall of The Picayune* (Norman: University of Oklahoma Press, 1943), pp. 148–238.

[19] Kendall, preface, p. [1]; John James Peck, *The Sign of the Eagle: A View of Mexico, 1830–1855* (San Diego: The Copley Press, 1970), p. 165.

[20] Kendall, pp. 17–22.

[21] Walke file in ZB File, Naval Department, Naval History Division, National Archives, Washington, D.C.

[22] Smith, 2:27–32, 338–339.

[23] Eugene Maissin, *The French in Mexico and Texas (1838–1839),* trans. and intro. by James L. Shepherd III (Salado, Tex.: Anson Jones Press, 1961), pp. 74–75.

[24] Smith, 2:49–54, 349–352; Kendall, pp. 23–25.

[25] Kendall, pp. 31–33; Smith, 2: 110–118, 381–385.

[26] Smith 2: 105–109, 377–380; Kendall, pp. 27–30.

[27] Kendall, pp. 35–36; Smith, 2: 140–145, 400–403.

[28] Kellogg's print is in the Library of Congress collection.

[29] Kendall, pp. 40–41; Smith, 2: 151–153, 404–407.

[30] Kendall, pp. 39–41; Smith, 2: 154–157, 406–410.

[31] Smith, 1: 165–169, 465–466; Kendall, pp. 1–4.

[32] Smith, 1: 239–261; Kendall, pp. 5–10.

[33] Tom Prideaux, *The World of Delacroix, 1798-1863* (New York: Time Incorporated, 1966), p. 102.

[34] Smith, 1: 467.

Amiable Frauds

Frederick S. Hicks

As a consultant in American graphic arts, Frederick S. Hicks has undertaken projects for the U.S. Naval Institute, the National Geographic Society, the National Archives, and the American Heritage Publishing Co. He was the chief pictorial consultant for the U.S. Naval History Division's Naval Documents of the American Revolution *and has contributed articles to* Portfolio *and* Panorama, *catalogs of the Old Print Shop of New York. Selections from his personal collection of American historical prints have been exhibited at the Metropolitan Museum of Art in New York and at Mystic Seaport, Mystic, Conn., among other comparable institutions.*

In the course of forming my collection of early American historical—primarily naval—prints over a period of many years, I have frequently been struck, sometimes with amusement and on other occasions with a less charitable reaction, by the many examples of duplicity (quite literally) to be found in the graphic arts of a bygone era. Thus, a considerable number of views purporting to be of the celebrated engagement between the U.S. frigate *Constitution* and H.M.S. *Guerrière* on August 19, 1812, have bobbed up subsequently and, without the slightest alteration in their plates, are captioned as being of the action involving U.S.S. *United States* and H.M.S. *Macedonian* on October 25, 1812, or of that between *Constitution* and H.M.S. *Java* on December 29 of the same year.

The purpose of this paper, which in more expanded form I originally wrote at the request of *American Heritage* magazine some years ago, will be an attempt to explore with you some of my more disconcerting discoveries in the area of what, for lack of a better description, I have termed "amiable frauds," as practiced upon the picture-buying public of the past. Whatever relevance it may have in today's quest by publishers and art editors for supposedly authentic pictorial documentation lies in the regrettable fact that, in many instances, a bogus picture—unknowingly, it is to be hoped, but nevertheless deplorably in terms of accuracy—has been presented as being of a person or event wholly different from its actuality. The original chicanery is consequently perpetuated, to the detriment of modern scholarship.

My sampling of iconographic legerdemain is not set forth as being exhaustive in its field but rather as a selective survey. Most of the examples hereafter commented upon are accompanied by photographic reproductions of them. I should like to begin by bringing to your notice the existence of "identical twins," of which transparencies were done by *American Heritage* but which unfortunately are not available to me at present. They appear as transfer prints on a pair of Battersea mirror knobs bearing disparate captions, executed at what I judge to have been roughly the turn of the 19th century. One purports to show a renowned admiral of the Royal Navy, Horatio Lord Viscount Nelson, and the other is supposedly of Thomas Truxtun, the most junior of six captains appointed to the command of the same number of frigates in the fledgling United States Navy. To my knowledge, the two officers bore little if any resemblance to one another, Nelson being slight of face to the point of emaciation and Truxtun of a hearty and robust visage, in the more traditional conception of a sailor's mien. Both are absolutely indistinguishable, the point being that were the knob captioned as being a portrait of Truxtun to be selected as, for example, an illustration in a biography of him, the ordinary viewer would remain in total ignorance of his actual appearance, for it is altogether clear to me that it was in fact Nelson who was meant to be depicted, however primitively; among other things, his uniform is instructive in the matter.

To get to a more conventional print form of the graphic arts, we might next consider a stipple engraving of Maj. Gen. Horatio Gates of the Continental Army. It was executed by the well-known Cornelius Tiebout in 1798, after an original by Gilbert Stuart. In 1816 the general's portrait became that of our fifth president, James Monroe, with no changes whatever made in the plate as issued by a discreetly unidentified purloiner. That Gates' and Monroe's physical attributes are not known to have been shared in any degree was obviously a consideration that did not perturb the latter publisher.

Not to be overlooked in such an examination of remarkable transformations are several others of the same ilk. Tapping Reeve, who for almost 50 years conducted one of this country's first law schools at Litchfield, Conn., had his portrait engraved by Peter Maverick in 1829, after George Catlin's original painting. Not long afterward, Professor Reeve was presented to a credulous public as being Benjamin Franklin, in the latter of which guises he appears on plate page 43 of Charles Coleman Sellers' *Benjamin Franklin in Portraiture.*

Asher Brown Durand, one of the guiding spirits in the establishment of the "Hudson River School" of American landscape painting, in 1820 was the subject of a portrait in stipple by his one-time apprentice, one Michele Pekenino. Some three years later Pekenino produced from the same unaltered plate an alleged likeness of Simón Bolívar, doubtless to capitalize upon this country's sympathetic interest in the Great Liberator's efforts in freeing Spain's South American colonies from their motherland.

The American commanders at two very significant naval engagements on our inland waters during the War of 1812 would not readily be confused in their separate identities unless we note the following. Oliver Hazard Perry, the victor at the Battle of Lake Erie on September 10, 1813, had a boyish and somewhat rounded face. Thomas Macdonough, who won perhaps the single most important fight of our "Second War of Independence" at Plattsburg Bay on Lake Champlain exactly a year and a day later, had a slim and rather austere countenance. In two prints, however, they appear as one and the same. Macdonough's spirited stance in personally sighting a gun on board his flagship *Saratoga* was an illustration in volume 2 of *Battles*

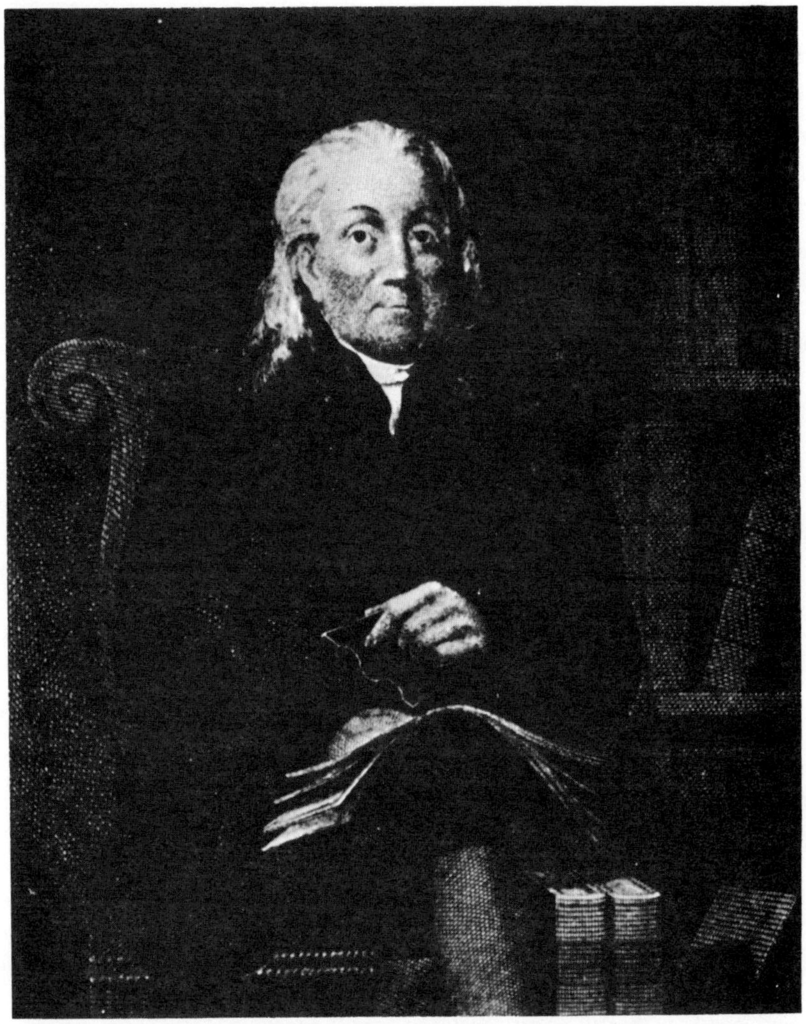

Charles Coleman Sellers' Benjamin Franklin in Portraiture *carries this picture, which is actually a portrait of Tapping Reeve.*

of America by Sea and Land, compiled by a doctor with what might be considered an apt name, Robert Tomes. The work was published in 1861 and again in 1878 by Virtue, Emmins & Company of New York. Another publisher, still unknown to me, for some reason best if not entirely known to himself, later adopted the true Macdonough and fobbed him off as Perry in an unidentified book. Any rationality in such a proceeding is beyond my powers of comprehension, since Dr. Tomes' same volume 2 included a perfectly adequate and, perhaps needless to relate, an utterly different view of the real Perry, which presumably might just as easily have been embezzled by the unknown publisher for his misleading purposes. Instead we here have Perry masquerading as Macdonough, whose flagship did in fact have on board a cock, as shown, and who is reputed to have acquired the name "Oscar." It is not recorded that Perry was encumbered by any such feathered supernumerary in his ship *Lawrence.*

The preceding is not the only example of Perry's proclivity for being found in unaccustomed surroundings. John R. Spears, a well-known American historian of the late 19th century, wrote *The History of Our Navy,* published at New York in several editions. In his volume 2 appears a small wood engraving, and the author informs his unwary readers that they are contemplating a picture of "Perry and his Officers." However, in examining early issues of *The Illustrated London News* as the possible source of a print on a wholly different subject, I came across the alleged "Perry" in his original form. In its publication of August 24, 1844, the London periodical included an article concerning the French naval bombardment of Tangier, Morocco, earlier in the same month. The piece's accompanying illustration is explicit in its caption; the central figure is that of Rear Admiral François, Prince de Joinville, third son of Louis Philippe, the "citizen king of the French," who commanded the forces involved on the occasion. Why Dr. Spears concluded that such a wildly inappropriate scene was in any way fitting to depict the hero of Lake Erie and his entourage I cannot guess, yet here they are. A pictorial history of the United States Navy of some years ago adopted Spears' hoax, presenting it as a "rare woodcut portraying Perry with a beard." That species of hirsute adornment was never a part of Perry's facial characteristics, perhaps unnecessary to recount. Moreover, it evidently does not seem to have occurred to the author that French naval officers' uniforms of the mid-19th century by no means resembled those of American officers of a generation earlier.

Let us now turn to pictured events and ships of our early naval history. In 1775 a former merchant vessel named *Black Prince* was purchased by the Continental Congress and converted into a makeshift warship under the name of *Alfred,* in honor of the legendary founder of the Royal Navy. The almost equally legendary founder of our Navy, the Scottish-born John Paul Jones, was the first to raise the flag of his adopted country from *Alfred*'s quarterdeck early in December of the same year. Jones commanded her on a not particularly eventful Atlantic cruise in the autumn of 1776. In a picture from an unidentified history book she is captioned as being on that foray. An anachronism immediately arises, in that the flag shown is of a design not authorized by the Congress until 1795.

The most stubbornly contested and bloodiest of any encounter between single men-of-war during the War of 1812 occurred 36 years following *Alfred*'s minor depredations. It brought together the U.S. sloop *Wasp* and H.M.S. *Reindeer* and took place on June 28, 1814, off the approaches to the English Channel. A certain Dr. John Frost, styling himself as a "Professor of Belles Lettres," commissioned a picture of the engagement for his *Pictorial Book of the Commodores,* published at New York in 1845. Painted by James Hamilton and engraved on wood by Charles N. Parmelee, the view will frustrate anyone's attempt to differentiate it from that of *Alfred*'s sortie, for both came from the same block. Because of the error in the national colors, previously noted in *Alfred*'s case, it is apparent to me that the Continental vessel is the imposter in this instance; her appearance in design and rig also belies her being a ship of the Revolutionary period. It is much more suggestive of the War of 1812 and of *Wasp*'s construction.

While yet a Master of Arts, Frost had put together *The Book Of The Navy,* issued in 1842 and 1843, also at New York. In it is to be found an atrociously done wood engraving of John Paul Jones' epic struggle in the Continental frigate *Bon Homme Richard* against H.M.S. *Serapis,* off the east coast of England on the evening of September 23, 1779. *Bon Homme Richard*'s flag suffers from the same anachronistic deficiency as did *Alfred*'s in the foregoing comment, but at least it is shown flying from a Continental warship. That basic detail was overlooked, as were the British colors displayed from *Serapis,* the presence of but three vessels in the scene, and its obvious intention to show a disputative meeting rather than one between friendly units of the same naval service, when the identical engraving became a rendering of the "French Fleet," contained as an illustration in an unidentified book of more or less the same period as Frost's.

Flags lend interest to the next three prints to be discussed. Thus, on the rear cover of *The Life and Adventures of James R. Durand,* credited as having been "Written By Himself" and issued at Rochester, N.Y., in 1820, is an uncaptioned and anonymously engraved picture, supposedly showing "The United States Frigate Constitution." It actually depicts a ship-of-the-line with two gundecks and at least 64 guns, which "Old Ironsides," armed with 44 guns on a single gundeck, could not have been. Nevertheless, her character as a U.S. naval vessel is unmistakably indicated by the conspicuous presence of two national ensigns, an American commodore's distinguishing flag and a commission pennant.

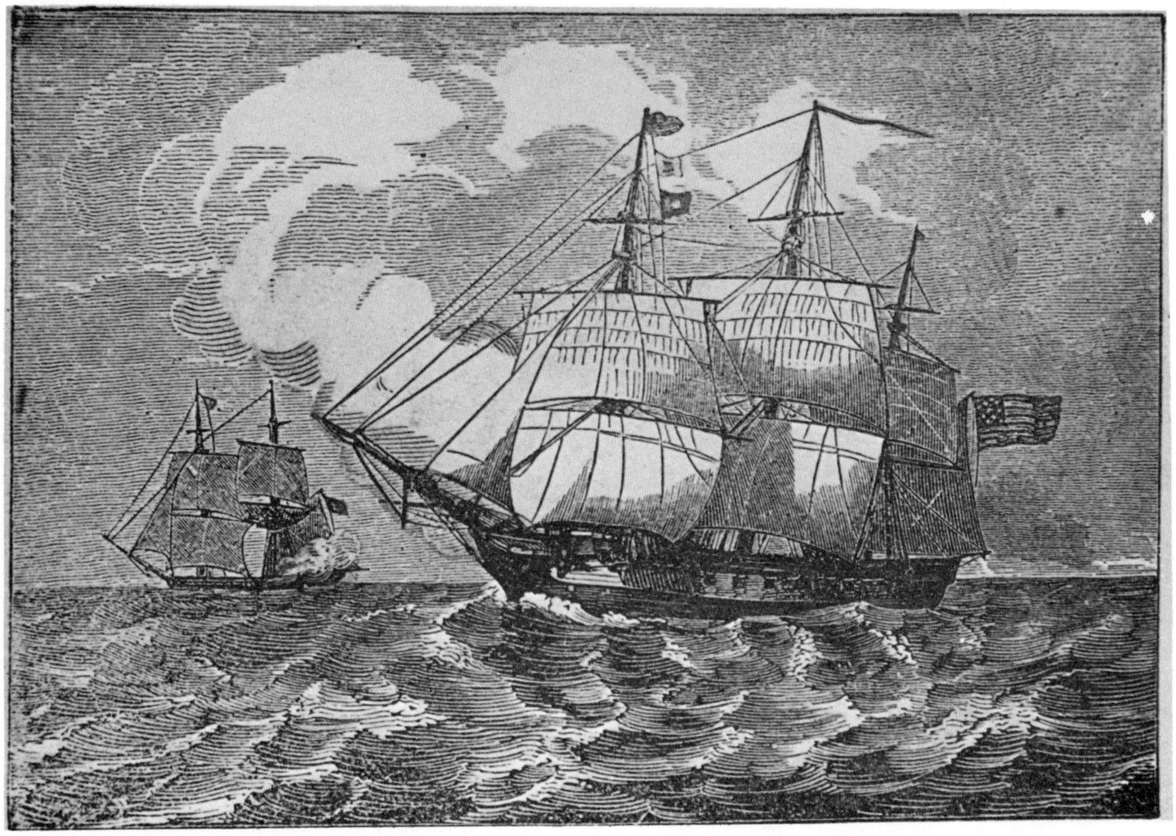

Above: The Alfred *portrayed on its cruise of the Atlantic in 1776. The flag depicted, however, is a later design. Below: The print is here identified as a depiction of the battle between the U.S. sloop* Wasp *and H.M.S.* Reindeer *during the War of 1812.*

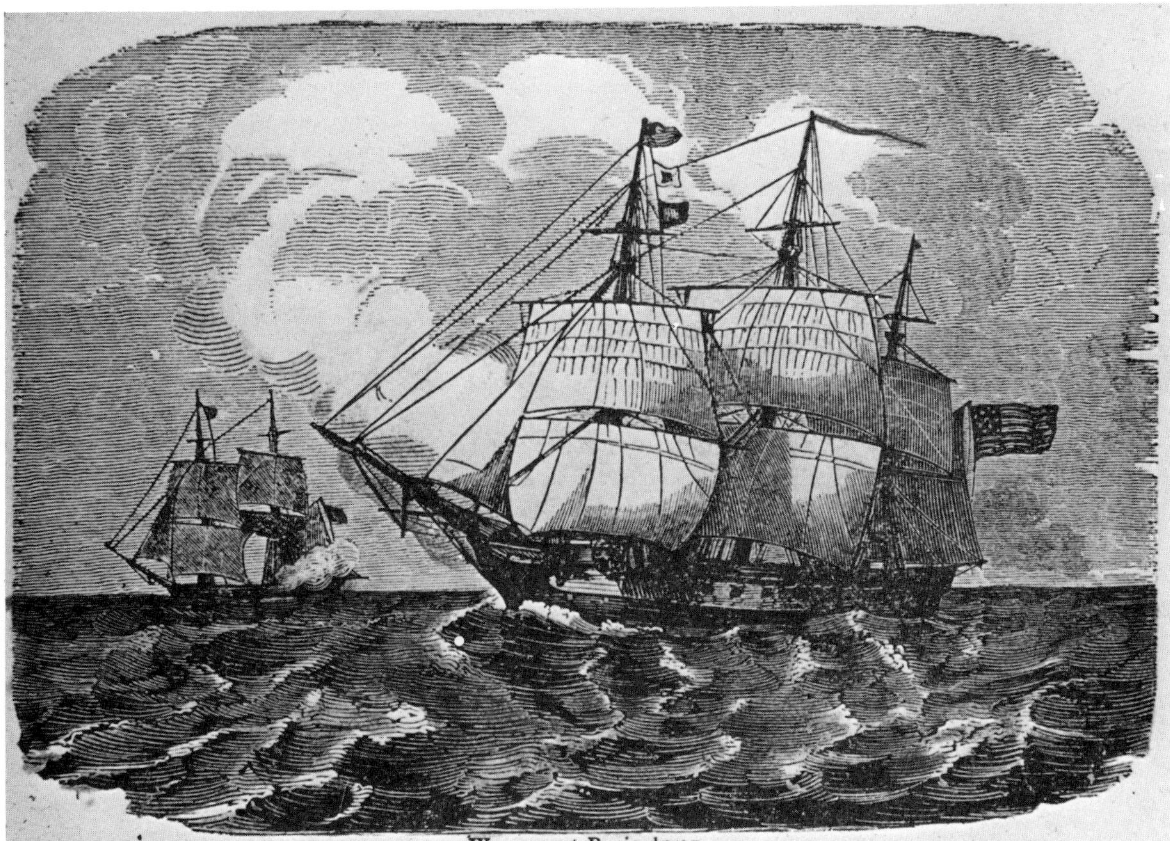

Wasp and Reindeer.

Such evidence of intended nationality was not sufficient to prevent her being transformed into a French frigate, the *Medusa,* which in July 1816 had been lost off the west coast of Africa in one of the most terrible of all recorded shipwrecks; it included well-substantiated incidents of cannibalism among the survivors. Here *Medusa* is shown leaving the port of Rochefort, France, on June 17, with no changes whatever made in the supposed *Constitution*'s American colors. This oddity appeared as the frontispiece to volume 2 of *The Book of the Ocean, and Life on the Sea,* a compilation of nautical goings-on first published at Rochester and Auburn, N.Y., in 1853. Two years of reflection on the manifest absurdity of having pictured a French warship displaying all four of those American flags presumably led the book's publishers to correct the anomaly, so that in their edition of 1855 *Medusa* emerges showing her proper national identity, albeit still as a ship-of-the-line rather than as a frigate as, of course, had been the case with *Constitution* in the first instance.

Now let us consider three views purporting to depict three differing engagements in two different wars of our history. The unquestioned original, by an unidentified engraver after the well-known marine artist Michel Felice Corné (who, incidentally, is widely reputed to have been the first to introduce the tomato as an edible fruit into our domestic diet), is a line engraving of the action between the U.S. schooner *Enterprise* and the Tripolitan corsair *Tripoli* off Malta on August 1, 1801. It was the first encounter at sea since the close of the Revolution with an enemy against whom the young United States was formally at war; the earlier so-called Quasi–War with France had been an undeclared one. Noteworthy also is the astonishing fact that, although *Tripoli* sustained about 60 casualties out of her crew of 80-odd, not one of Lt. Andrew Sterret's men on the *Enterprise* was so much as scratched in the three-hour running fight. The picture is from the first edition of *The Naval Temple,* a popular history of the War of 1812, compiled and published by one Barber Badger of Boston in 1816.

Eighteen years after the view's first appearance, its center section was reengraved on wood to provide readers of a certain R. Thomas' *The Glory of America,* published in New York in 1834, with a totally inaccurate rendering of U.S.S. *Constitution*'s victory over H.M.S. *Java* off the northern coast of Brazil on December 29, 1812. A schooner of 12 guns and a 14-gun polacca, a type of rig all but entirely confined to the Mediterranean, were thus altered (or, more properly, unaltered) into two opposing frigates, one of 44 and the other of 38 guns, meeting each other in the Atlantic, thousands of miles from the site of the *Enterprise* and *Tripoli* confrontation.

Mr. Thomas evidently forgot his prior use of the basic picture as illustrating *Constitution*'s and *Java*'s meeting when in 1847 he brought forth his *History of the American Wars* at Hartford. In it the view, confined to its midsection, was captioned as being of the fight between the American 18-gun sloop-of-war *Wasp* and the British brig *Frolic,* of approximately equal armament, off the Delaware capes on October 18, 1812. The same picture is also known to me to have been employed in showing a piratical foray of one "Misson [a sea-going rogue of whose further identity I am unaware] boarding the English." It is contained in Ezra Strong's lurid *The History of the Lives and Bloody Exploits of the Most Noted Pirates,* issued in 1835 and 1836, also in Hartford.

We might turn now to another specimen of Thomas' guile. In *The Port Folio* magazine, volume 4, number 1, issued in Philadelphia in July 1814, is a handsome, small aquatint of the engagement between the newly built American sloop *Peacock* and the British brig *Epervier,* engraved by William Strickland after Thomas Birch. The action took place off Cape Canaveral, Fla., on April 29, 1814, and ended in the capture of the Royal Navy vessel. As perhaps of some interest, the latter was carrying some $118,000 in private specie, which probably was put to good use by our Treasury Department, which was chronically short of funds in those days. Thomas was inspired to use a wood engraving, obviously based upon the same scene as in the aquatint, as an illustration for his *History of the American Wars,* noted above. It there became a fictitious view captioned, "Capture of the Peacock," a British man-of-war which had been sunk, not captured, by U.S.S. *Hornet* off Demerara, British Guiana, on February 24, 1813, in an entirely different encounter; indeed, the American *Peacock,* triumphant over *Epervier,* had been named in commemoration of *Hornet's* victim.

Thomas' version of The *Port Folio*'s original, without the slightest change made in it, was also employed in showing an action with which I personally am unfamiliar and which appeared in an unidentified history book captioned, "The Victoire engages a Portuguese ship." A versatile performance, surely, for any one picture.

The well-known early American engraver on wood, Abel Bowen, published *The Naval Monument* at Boston in 1816. In it is a view showing the same U.S.S. *Hornet* just mentioned being pursued by the British ship-of-the-line *Cornwallis* in the Indian Ocean, from April 28 through 30, 1815. From an unknown but apparently contemporary source comes the identical view, captioned as being of *Hornet*'s successful fight with H.M. brig *Penguin* off lonely Tristan da Cunha in the South Atlantic some five weeks previously, on March 21. It was happily the last hostile meeting in history between warships of the two English-speaking nations, and involved an encounter at close range, the two vessels being of almost exactly equal force. That circumstance alone leads to the conclusion that the latter is the spurious picture.

From two unidentified books of the mid-19th century come identical wood engravings of two American warships that it would be extremely difficult (if not, indeed, impossible) to imagine as having been more different in every particular except that they were both built in

Above: The U.S.S. Hornet *pursued by the British ship* Cornwallis *in the Indian Ocean, April 28-30, 1815. This print was published in* The Naval Monument *in 1816.*

Below: The same picture is identified as the Hornet's *battle with the* Penguin *off Tristan da Cunha on March 21, 1815.*

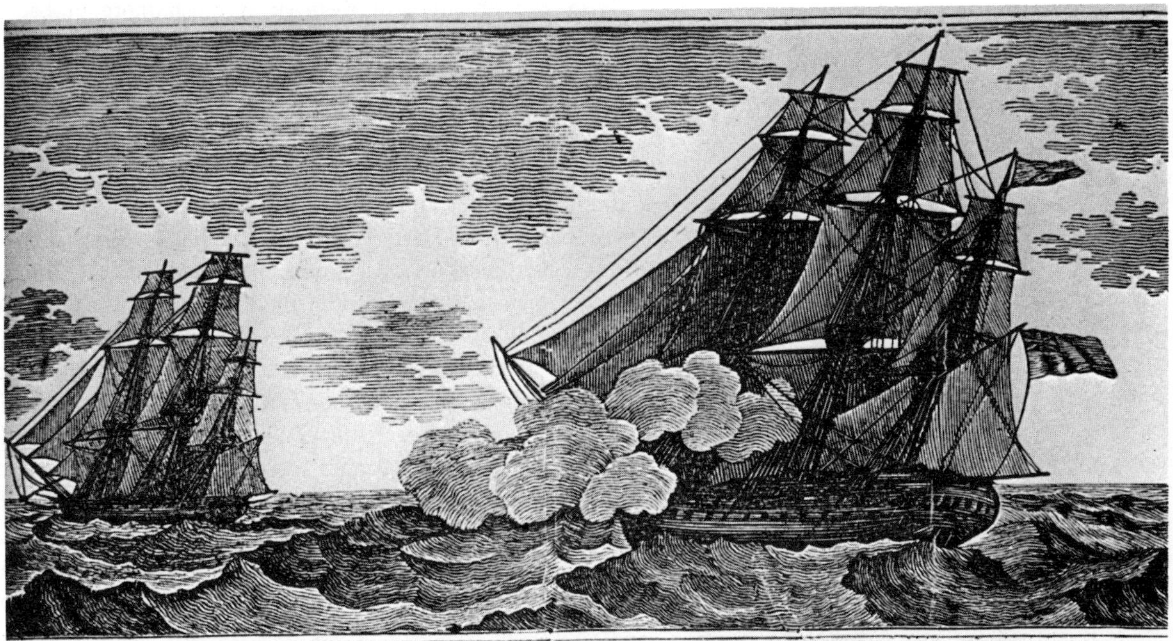

THE HORNET'S ESCAPE FROM A BRITISH 74.

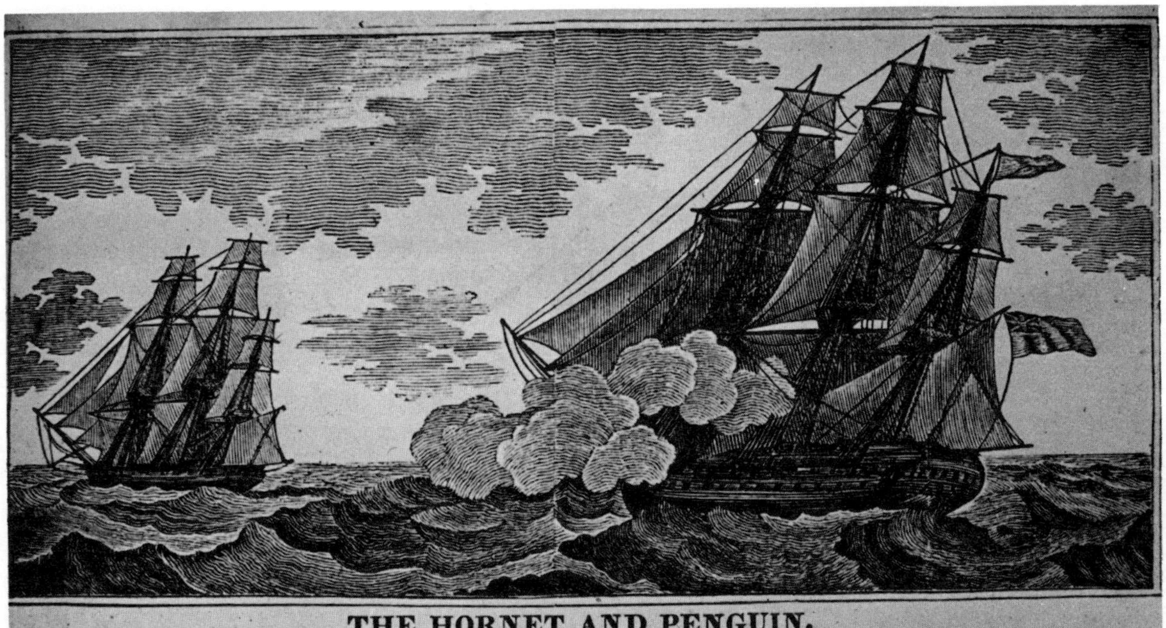

THE HORNET AND PENGUIN.

Above: This engraving is here identified as the Essex, *which was a small, 32-gun ship, launched in 1800.*

Below: The same engraving depicts the Independence, *a much larger vessel of 74 guns.*

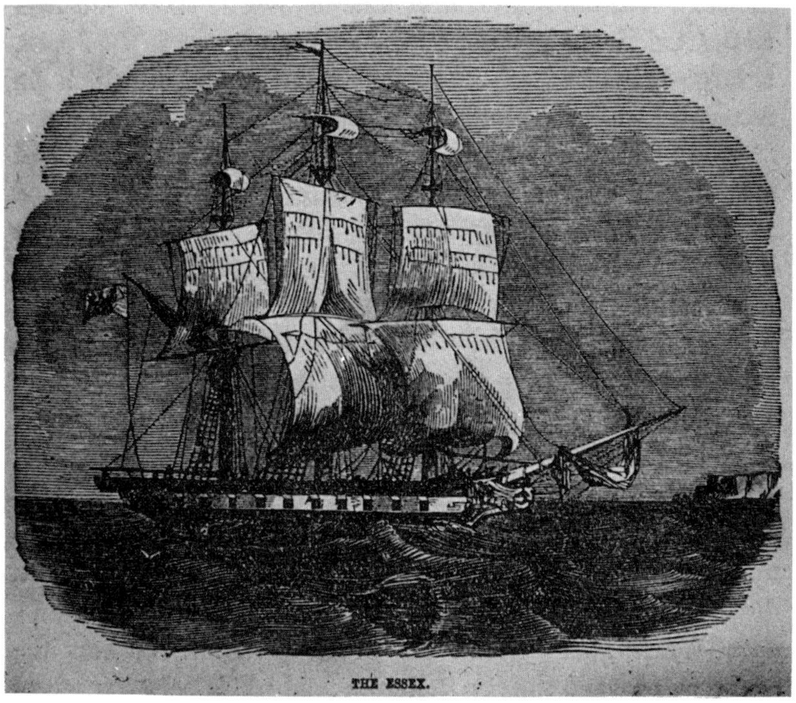

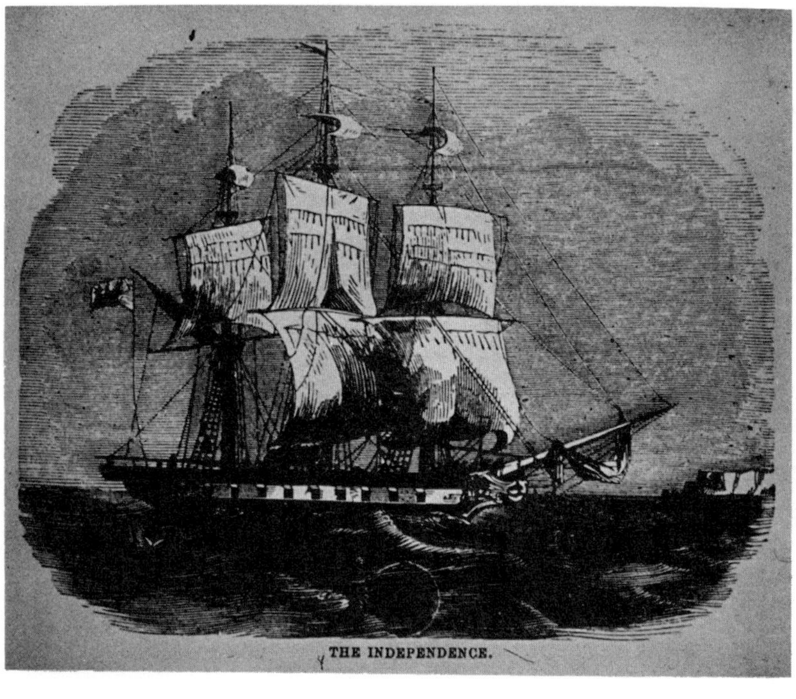

Boston. The 32-gun frigate *Essex,* the cost of whose construction had been raised by private subscription among the citizens of Essex County, Mass., and hence her name, was among the smallest and least powerfully armed of her type in our Navy. Launched in 1800, she was the first American warship ever to enter the Pacific Ocean. *Independence,* on the other hand, was a ship-of-the-line of 74 guns and was completed in 1815, being one of the first of the Navy's very large sailing vessels of war. Her career was not notably distinguished. If the print is in fact of either of them, it is much more probable that it is of *Essex.*

We come now to a wood engraving and to two lithographs completely indistinguishable from each other. The first was an illustration in *Harper's Weekly,* New York, of September 28, 1861. The lithographs were published in the same city and at about the same time by the firm of Shearman & Hart. They supposedly show three different steam gunboats of a group of 24 built for the Union Navy in the autumn of 1861: the *Chippewa,* the *Kanawha,* and the *Winona.* For what my opinion may be worth, I believe that *Harper*'s rendition of *Winona* was the first of the trio to be published and thus is the only true image, the identical lithographs having been copied from it with minor changes in composition.

In closing, let us leave the Navy and go to views of more general early Americana. Among the scenic splendors of the emergent United States which were favored by foreign visitors to our shores 100 and more years ago were Mount Vernon and the lower reaches of the Hudson River. One does not ordinarily associate the surroundings of George Washington's cherished home overlooking the Potomac with the grandeurs of the Hudson, so that the treatment of both as being the same in terms of riverine topography comes, to say the least, as a considerable surprise. Yet identical views, one in line and the other in aquatint, show the two tourist attractions as allegedly possessing exactly the same features. They are illustrations from an English and a German edition of the published travels of an Irishman, Isaac Weld, Jr., who undertook a prolonged trip throughout the United States and Canada from 1795 to 1797. The Hudson is obviously meant as the subject of the engravings, as captioned in the London version of Weld's odyssey. The Berlin editors apparently succumbed to casual inattention as respects their mislabeled offering—or perhaps to sheer whimsy.

Next, three line engravings of New York harbor, all obviously done from the same original plate, are credited to two different artists as well as two differing engravers. What I believe to have been the first scene was engraved by John B. Neagle after John R. Smith; in it, relatively little shipping is shown in the port. Its next reworking, if my hypothesis be correct, was after the original by Smith but engraved by James Archer and presents a few more ships, the rowboat in the lower left-hand foreground having become a two-masted sailboat. In its third appearance, again engraved by Archer but this time after one J. A. Davis, the era of the steamboat is upon us, three paddle-wheelers having been introduced into the composition. Throughout this progression, the distant skyline of lower Manhattan remains completely unaltered, a remarkable occurrence—or lack of one—when it is recalled that New York was the most rapidly growing and changing of American cities during the period, which I estimate to have been from about 1820 to the late 1860's.

Finally, who would or could (or, for that matter, should) believe that a view of the Little Falls on the Mohawk River in upper New York State might ever be considered as in any way appropriate in showing an ancient road built by the Incas near the summit of one of the world's most awesome mountain ranges, the Andes? A travelers' guide to the United States was published in 1839 by Goodrich and Wiley of New York; among its illustrations was a charming, small line engraving of the Mohawk after a drawing by the Irish-American landscapist William Guy Wall (probably chiefly known by you for his part in the production of the "Hudson River Portfolio," containing superb representations of that stream). A horse-drawn barge is depicted, among other things, as passing by on the adjacent Erie Canal. Omitting that quaint touch of local color and with a few other inconsequential changes, such as substituting a Peruvian Indian for an American fisherman, a Neapolitan artist named A. [Antonio?] Parboni subsequently re-engraved the scene as an illustration for an Italian book of travels in North and South America, where it appears in its alleged Andean setting, preposterously enough.

On that lofty note I will take my leave, thanking you for your attention, for your dazzling erudition, and for the opportunity to have taken part in this learned conclave. My particular gratitude goes to Dr. Breitenbach for his kind invitation to participate with you; to my friend of many years, Milton Kaplan, for his patient assistance to me as well as for his encyclopedic knowledge of American historical prints; and, lastly but by no means least, to my long-suffering wife, for her unfailing help and encouragement.

☆ U.S. GOVERNMENT PRINTING OFFICE: 1975 O—508-181